# CHILDREN'S CONSENT
# TO SURGERY

This book is to be returned on or before
the last date stamped below.

# CHILDREN'S CONSENT TO SURGERY

*Priscilla Alderson*

Open University Press
Buckingham · Philadelphia

Open University Press
Celtic Court
22 Ballmoor
Buckingham
MK18 1XW

and
1900 Frost Road, Suite 101
Bristol, PA 19007, USA

First Published 1993

A catalogue record of this book is available from the British Library

ISBN 0 335 157327 (pb)    0 335 15733 5 (hb)

*Library of Congress Cataloging-in-Publication Data*
Alderson, Priscilla.
    Children's consent to surgery/Priscilla Alderson.
        p.   cm.
    Includes bibliographical references and index.
    ISBN 0-335-15733-5.  ISBN 0-335-15732-7 (pbk.)
    1. Children–Surgery–Moral and ethical aspects.  2. Decision-
making in children.  3. Informed consent (Medical law)  I. Title.
RD27.7.A43   1993
617.9'8 – dc20                                                    93-1413
                                                                     CIP

Typeset by Colset Pte Ltd, Singapore
Printed in Great Britain by Biddles Ltd, Guildford and Kings' Lynn

For Patricia Roden, who lived in hospital in the 1920s and has helped to change hospitals for children in the 1990s.

# CONTENTS

# ACKNOWLEDGEMENTS

I am very grateful to the hundreds of people who contributed to this book. Most of them remain unnamed, to respect their privacy. The first to thank are the young people having surgery, their parents, and all the hospital staff who helped with the children's consent research project. They generously gave their time and thoughts in very rewarding interviews. My co-researcher Jill Siddle undertook many of the interviews, Dorothy Clift transcribed interview tapes, and they both contributed very helpful insights and support.

Thanks are due to the Leverhulme Trust and the Royal Liverpool Children's Hospital Trust, Alder Hey, for funding the consent research project 1989–91, and to the Calouste Gulbenkian Foundation for sponsoring the writing of the book 1991–92. Grants from King Edward's Hospital Fund, London, and the Institute of Education for work on consent also partly supported this project.

Others who deserve thanks, although they may not altogether agree with the book, include Naomi Pfeffer, Martin Bax with Maddie Blackburn, Cliff Strehlow and my colleagues at the Community Paediatric Research Unit at Westminster Children's Hospital; Berry Mayall with Ann Oakley and my colleagues at the Social Science Research Unit, Institute of Education, University of London; Anna Coote, Richard Nicholson, Pauline Shelley the librarian of Action for Sick Children; surgeons Anthony Catterall, John Dorgan and Peter Webb; almost 1000 school pupils and their teachers who helped with a survey; countless people who have added their ideas at conferences and seminars or through their publications; and Juliet, William and Anna Alderson for all their practical demonstrations of the theme of this book – the wisdom of youth.

# 1

## SURGERY AT SCHOOL AGE

*Since he was two years old, each year he's been into hospital for something. So if possibly he could get a couple of years off, when he's not in hospital having anything done, well ... We say to him, "There's a chance everything will stay as it is." But it doesn't, and he's continually going in. You think, "That's it for now", and then something else crops up, and so on and on.*

*(Father of Danny aged 10 years)*

Beds were ranged around the large ward, with children sitting or lying on them. Two boys rushed around in wheelchairs, and one, lying on his front and half covered in plaster of Paris, was trying out a large skateboard. Jean, aged 8, lay looking bored and irritated, and beside her sat her mother seeming very tired. I went over to them. 'Hello, we're doing a research project on what children think about having surgery. Might you both be interested in talking to me about your views?' 'Well, er, yes', said Jean's mother. We looked at Jean. 'Yes', she said firmly, nodding dismissively at her mother, 'as long as *she* goes away'.

Before Jean's mother went for a tea break, I explained that our project involved looking at how much young patients were told about their operation and all the planned treatment, and how much they shared and wanted to share in decisions about surgery. Would it be all right if I talked to Jean and her mother before the operation, and to Jean a few days later? I would like to ask about why Jean had come into hospital, and how she hoped the treatment would help her, and also a few questions about her family and school. Of course they could say 'no' if they did not want to take part in the project, and tell me if they wanted to stop talking to me at any time. When I used anything that Jean had said in our reports, I would make sure that no-one would know that she was the one who had made the comment, by changing her name. Jean thought that she would rather be famous than anonymous, so I explained the advantages of confidentiality, and gave them a leaflet about our project to keep.

Later I met Marie, aged 15, and her mother. After the usual explanations, Marie said she would be very interested to take part in our project. 'Oh yes', added her mother, 'and we must call Daddy over'. 'Oh *no* mother', said Marie, but her father and brother were summoned and we all sat in a row along the side of the bed. I avoided issues that Marie might not want to talk about in front of her family, and planned to see her again later on her own. Marie kept giving me expressive looks of amusement or horror at her parents' words, which the others seemed not to notice. The way in which families shared interviews and supported one another, or interrupted, contradicted and quarrelled (as Marie and her father later did), indicated how they might approach decisions about surgery. Before describing more about our interviews, I will explain how the book came to be written and its purpose, but first a note about the terms to be used.

## Terms and attitudes

'Children' and 'patients' can be belittling labels. In some texts, 'children' is replaced by the more respectful 'young people' or 'young men and women'. However, I use 'children' meaning everyone under 18, partly for simplicity, partly because preschool and pre-adolescent children are often included, and partly because all children are worthy of respect. This book examines how the children we met were respected.

Critics of the word 'patients' say that calling them 'clients', 'consumers', 'customers' or 'health service users' is more respectful. Yet here also, the problem lies in the way patients are treated and regarded more than in the actual word, and changing a word does not necessarily change attitudes.[1] It may even obscure the related problems. For instance, 'consumer' ignores the relative ignorance and dependence felt by many patients but, if these are to be attended to respectfully, they first have to be recognized and not hidden inside new words. 'Young patients' is not an ideal term, but is a reminder that these young people were temporarily patients, surrounded by far more complexities than if they were customers in shoe shops, and the book is about how they managed these complexities. Medical terms are listed in a glossary at the back of the book. There is also a list of the names given to children mentioned in the book, with pages listed to help with cross-referral.

## The background on consent

Literature on patients' consent[2] usually assumes that the patient is an adult. It implies that patients can question and talk with doctors on fairly equal terms, and make informed, wise decisions. Lawyers and ethicists tend to write as if, on an invisible seesaw, the doctor and the informed patient can be evenly balanced, their opinions carrying equal weight. Informed consent is the medicolegal mechanism for involving patients who can achieve this intellectual equilibrium, and for excluding those who cannot.

Yet adult patients often do not fit this model. Their relationships with doctors are complicated by anxiety, embarrassment and gratitude. They have an uneasy sense of always being on the receiving end, having nothing to offer except their need. In contrast, the doctor is weighed down by expert knowledge and skill, by the confidence of experience, and the power to offer or withhold many resources. Doctors can choose how much to redress the balance by allowing patients a share in medical information and decision making. Yet patients still risk being left stranded in a vulnerable position if there is no safe and effective treatment to help them to return to health or independence.

If adult patients are relatively light-weight, child patients count for even less. Small, immature bodies are generally believed to contain small, immature minds. Young children are surely unable to absorb, understand and evaluate complex medical information. Even if they have the intelligence to do so, wisdom is another matter. How can they be trusted to assess the likely benefits and harms of proposed treatment in the light of their own best, long-term interests? Children are often thought to be too impulsive and inexperienced to realize that what they want today, they may bitterly regret tomorrow. So young children are dismissed as 'incompetents'[3] and adolescents' consent is somewhat grudgingly considered around the mid-teens, with the proviso that their competence is stringently assessed.[4]

## The purposes of this book

The main purpose of this book is to examine children's ability to arrive at informed, wise decisions about proposed surgery. Are young children inevitably as ignorant and immature as is commonly assumed? To discover the answers, my co-researcher Jill Siddle and I did over 500 interviews. We spoke two or more times with 120 patients aged 8–15 years, and with the adults caring for them while they had surgery, about their views and experiences of children's consent. As a research report, *Children's Consent to Surgery* continues a sociological project on parents' consent to surgery.[5] The two projects contribute practical, personal evidence, to complement the few books concerned with consent to children's treatment[6] which concentrate on abstract theories and impersonal guidance. Our findings are mainly reported as case studies and examples which illustrate aspects of consent; many examples are not necessarily general or typical and are quoted to illustrate the wide range of responses.

Second, the book is a critical review of the care provided in four leading hospitals, set against official recommendations of good practice[7] and our wider experience.[8] Despite our experience, we had not anticipated the amount of suffering which the children were expected to accept – or consent to. Examples are given to show how good practice benefits children. Examples of distress show even more clearly how much children and parents need adequate information and discussion, preparation and support as part of the consent process. Problems are often seen as a one-off failure and blamed on an individual child or parent, doctor or nurse.[9] Yet although personal in their impact, problems are usually general in their origins. They are due to the children's serious defects and diseases, or to the present limitations of medicine, or to hospital organization or staff training. Although the examples show the distress of a few children, they illustrate problems for many others in a similar position. Ways of reducing avoidable distress will be suggested.

The third purpose is to reflect on the child's status in society, and to show that children's consent can only properly be understood within a context of children's rights. This approach includes defining 'knowledge' more broadly, in order to appreciate children's understanding, and to see how their thoughts and feelings and their reflections on their experience are integral to their consent.

The fourth purpose, beyond presenting data, is to consider attitudes. Different adults greet identical evidence of a very young child's maturity with interest, enthusiasm, scepticism or contempt.[10] Later chapters review how adults' attitudes determine children's status. Theories, besides being explicit research hypotheses or questions, are also underlying principles or prejudices, which are the more powerful if they remain unexamined. Discussion of these theories may seem an irritating irrelevance to readers who simply want to read the research results and conclusions. Yet they crucially determine the research findings and the way readers interpret and accept them. This book will be more useful if it helps readers to consider their own attitudes, rather than simply to accept or reject the reported data. Questions to be considered include: What is the difference between a child and an adult? Who do children 'belong' to? Who has authority to intervene in their lives? How beneficial are professional interventions? Who should evaluate the outcome of medical interventions and according to what criteria? How can we study children as sources of data in themselves, and discover their views? Are their views worth examining? What are the relationships between theories about children's (in)abilities and health services policies and practices? Are services planned on the basis that children are passive 'objects of concern'[11] or active partners in their care? Before looking at these questions further, I will explain more about how we set up the project.

### Finding the children

In England and Wales, there are about 10.4 million children.[12] In England, about 1.25 million are admitted each year to hospital as in-patients.[13] Over 70% of them are under 5 years of age, but this figure is misleading. It includes almost 700 000 babies born in hospital, and children aged 15 years and over are omitted. Almost a further 70 000 children aged 0–14 years are treated as hospital day cases. It is estimated that over 3 million children attend accident and emergency (A & E) units each year,[14] accounting for about one-third of all A & E patients.[15] Around 9000 people aged under 19 years are admitted for mental health treatment. Many young women under 19 have an abortion or give birth in hospital; the babies of teenage mothers are at high risk of being born small and early and of needing treatment which their young parents will have to discuss. All these young people, with or without their parents or guardians, may suddenly or gradually face serious decisions about proposed treatment.

Most surgery for children is performed before they are 5 years old. Our first task was to find older children, and since orthopaedics caters for many school-age patients, we approached hospitals with orthopaedic surgeons. At one hospital a consultant, with difficulty, obtained a print-out of the total annual surgery patients by age, which gave little indication of the types of surgery. 'For a hospital seeking trust status we have remarkably poor records, and clearly we have a long way to go', he commented. At another major teaching hospital, after 27 'phone calls attempting to trace the records department (no-one seemed to know where it was), I gave up. A third hospital was being rebuilt. Again no-one seemed to know where the records department was. Eventually I tracked it down to a mobile hut, where a record-keeper helped me to obtain permission to see the annual figures. We applied for access to two smaller hospitals which had such a slow approval procedure that we gave up waiting. Planning the project, raising funds and gaining access to four hospitals took almost two years.

Eventually we gained access to three hospitals in London and one in Liverpool. They are all specialist teaching hospitals,[16] treating patients with the most complex conditions, although one children's hospital provides only a local district orthopaedic service and here children are mainly treated after accidents and for minor problems. We interviewed experienced young patients having non-emergency treatment to see how well, given time, children can become informed and involved. The ages and age spread are given in Tables 1 and 2.

**Table 1**  Age range of patients ($n = 120$)

| Age (years) | 8 | 9 | 10 | 11 | 12 | 13 | 14 | 15 |
|---|---|---|---|---|---|---|---|---|
| Total interviewed | 7 | 8 | 15 | 15 | 19 | 12 | 21 | 23 |

**Table 2**  Age spread of 54 boys and 66 girls ($n = 120$)

| | Age groups | | | Mean age (years) |
|---|---|---|---|---|
| | 8–10 years | 11–13 years | 14–15 years | |
| Percentage of boys in study | 24.6 | 40.0 | 35.4 | 12.4 |
| Percentage of girls in study | 25.9 | 35.2 | 38.9 | 12.1 |

**Table 3**  Reasons for having surgery

| Condition | Patients (n = 120) |
|---|---|
| Scoliosis | 44 |
| Various forms of displaced vertebrae | 7 |
| Spinal tumour | 1 |
| Congenital dislocation of the hip | 10 |
| Perthes disease | 9 |
| Congenital defect or congenital bone disease affecting leg or foot | 22 |
| Malformations of hip, leg or foot due to the effects of muscular dystrophy, cerebral palsy, spina bifida, Friedreich's ataxia or Hurler's syndrome | 18 |
| Post-accident defect | 6 |
| Short stature | 3 |

The mean age of boys and girls in the study was calculated on their individual ages, not on age grouping means. Although this study is not about average patients, a very high proportion of school-age hospital patients have chronic conditions and repeated treatment. Besides their orthopaedic problem, nearly half the children had another serious condition (see Table 3).

The interviews covered a wide range of medical conditions and experiences extending well beyond orthopaedic treatment for 8- to 15-year olds. On average, our interviewees had already had five operations and had stayed in hospital six times. Eight of them said they had been admitted more than twenty times. Only one-sixth had attended less than five out-patient clinics. Thirty-eight fathers and 104 mothers were interviewed.

Gaining access to each hospital involved finding consultants willing to support our application, which they kindly agreed to do. The protocol was then approved by medical committees in two hospitals and research ethics committees in all the hospitals. Nursing managers and ward managers then wanted to vet our research and discuss arrangements. Many hospital professionals generously gave us information and support. Researching in hospitals as an outsider is daunting and lonely work and we were very grateful for their kindness. A few sisters were not pleased to have us around. The mothers' reports on how nurses welcomed or tried to exclude them usually matched our own experiences.

### Listening to children

When we planned to interview young patients, our initial question was: Will they talk to us? In every age group, young patients were keen to talk in detail, a few were shy or became bored. We had planned with the younger ones to include play and drawing sessions, thinking that verbal interviews would be too limited.[17] However, the young people we met were not keen to play or draw, they wanted to talk like the interviewees they saw on television. This was a first indication of how they also wanted to share in medical discussions. Ten-year-old Amy politely indicated that our expectations were unrealistically low. As she said, she was 'only a metre high', and had decided to have months of leg lengthening. When asked, 'So you are having the tops of your legs made longer?', she replied, 'I suffer from achondroplasia and I am having my femurs lengthened'. She raised the conversation to a level suited to her intelligence and dignity.

This chapter ends with describing Danny's unusually complicated case. It illustrates how many of the themes considered throughout this book combine in one example. In some cases, consent is like a maze with the child lost in the middle, surrounded by the obstacles of unpredictable, uncontrollable disease, the uncertainty and half-silence of doctors and parents, and doubts about whether to respect children by giving them information or to protect them by withholding it. These doubts are increased by distress about the information. Children can then be excluded and silenced, perhaps isolated within fears they feel unable to express.

As the opening words to this chapter show, 10-year-old Danny was used to being in hospital. He was due to have leg-lengthening, although the family had not yet been informed about the details. He smiled and joked during his first interview, and told me quickly and almost casually:

Danny: I'm going to have a bone graft in my right leg. Take a little bit from here [touches hip] and put it here [touches ankle] to fix it. And get a pin, just put it in and stitch it, then they wait till they heal it. Then I'll get a wheelchair – be lazy all the time. I like that, better than crutches. And this [thumps his left leg and smiles at the thud resounding from his jeans] is an artificial one, my leg, it's leather, yes, that's my real one [touches right leg].

Int.: And what does your ankle do?

Danny: It keeps going over. I can't walk far without my crutches.

Int.: Has it made your life much different from your friends' life do you think?

Danny: No. It doesn't hurt. Not a lot anyway.

Int.: Is there anything you can't do 'cos of your ankle, that your friends do?

Danny: No, not really.

Int.: Football?

Danny: I can't do football. I can't do any games, I can do hopscotch.

Int.: How will the operation change your life? Will you be able to do anything extra or different?

*Danny*: Don't know. I'll be able to walk without my crutches. I'll take
them to school probably.

*Int.*: Have you had operations before?

*Danny*: I've had loads of operations. The first was when I was two.

*Danny's father*: He's got neurofibromatosis.

*Int.*: What is that?

*Danny*: I've got – like that [shows his elbow] tumours, I get tumours
everywhere – on my arms . . .

*Father*: Fibromas.

*Danny*: Fibromas, all over my head, everywhere.

*Father*: Those are harmless aren't they. But the one that was in your
bone, they had to take that out.

*Danny*: That was when I was four.

*Father*: No, no.

*Danny*: Oh no, I had my leg off when I was four. I had the tumour
taken out here.

*Father*: He had the amputation at another hospital and then we came over
here to get the artificial leg.

During many of our interviews, the family members tended to be matter-of-
fact about serious conditions, to sort out a report they agreed on, and to extend
one another's comments. Like most children, Danny avoided evaluation-
opinion questions which ask overtly or covertly: 'Are you the same as your
friends, i.e. are you normal?' Their impulse was usually to say 'Yes I'm normal'.
He preferred report–description questions, like 'Can you play football?' and
'Why have you come into hospital?', which have fewer evaluative and moral
overtones and refer to practical experience. Children with chronic problems
often seemed to understate or deny them as if they thought of themselves as
'normal' and not having obvious problems. If specifically asked, they openly
said what they could not do. Yet it was as if they often separated activities
they could do with their friends (the possible ones) from those they could not
(the impossible ones) in a practical, unselfpitying way.[18] Possibly Danny did
not want to admit readily that his friends could do things that he could not.
Yet it was as if he took the third question to mean, 'Is there anything you
(want to do which you) can't do because of your ankle which your friends
can do?' So that at optimistic times or because he had trained himself, or been
encouraged to separate off the impossible and not think about it much, he
would reply 'no'.[19] Adapting to disability eases everyday life, but complicates
consent discussions about how much a child wants the hoped-for benefits of
treatment, and will undertake pain and risk in the hope of benefit. Frank discussion can mean breaking through mental defences or 'armour' as a nurse will
describe later.

## Separations

Danny's interviews illustrated several kinds of separation and gaps, apart from the contrast between his chirpy manner and the grim realities. There was the difference between the explanations about treatment and the planned treatment, between expectations and subsequent events. Just before his disease was diagnosed when he was 2 years old, Danny's mother had died of the same disease. (His stepmother will be called his mother.) Parts of his body were treated separately, sometimes at the expense of other parts: 'It was very confusing and sometimes the notes were in the wrong hospital'. Bone was taken from his right fibula in attempts to strengthen his left tibia, but after 15 months in plaster, his lower left leg had to be amputated. His right leg was weakened by the surgery and the extra weight-bearing, especially during long waiting periods for new prostheses and special shoes as well as by fibromas. The surgeon at the hospital treating his left leg stump advised swimming and exercise. The surgeon at another hospital treating his right leg advised avoiding swimming and exercise. Danny's father thought:

> This whole problem's come about because they tried to save the other leg. It's the first time that type of bone graft was carried out in this country for his type of condition, but it was either that or amputate the leg. The surgeon did say he was very dubious because of the state of the bone.

Danny's parents had to cope with past failures, uncertainty and gaps in limited information, while sustaining their own and Danny's confidence in the proposed treatment. His father said:

> He's had an osteotomy to treat a valgus right foot, one that rolls over, but obviously it hasn't worked and it's being done again today. His condition is very rare so there hasn't been a lot that's recorded about what can be done. You feel that everyone is doing what they believe to be in his best interest but they are tending to work a little bit blind. We didn't really know what they were going to do today until Mr X brought us up to date. They was going to do another op that wasn't as lengthy as this one, but it's up to them to judge. It's in their hands isn't it.

Danny's father interpreted last minute uncertainty as a good sign, when asked 'How do you feel about Mr X taking the decision?':

> I'm happy to think someone has taken the time and the trouble to look at it and evaluate the case as they see it. Rather than say, "Oh well, I've said I'm going to do that so I'm going to do it irrespective of __. I can't change my mind now." I'd rather have someone who said, "We're going to look at it, take the whole thing overall", and then come up with what they thought was the best possible solution.

Last year they had to cope with greater uncertainty when a large tumour was removed from Daniel's left leg stump. His father said:

> They didn't know if it was benign, or the total extent of it, or whether they'd possibly do a further amputation until he went to the operating theatre. We couldn't tell Danny exactly what was going to happen. He might possibly have lost the whole of his leg. We had to warn him and he was saying, "I don't mind them taking the tumour but I don't want them taking any more of my leg away". That would have been as bad for him as another amputation. All we could definitely say was there's no way he wants to lose any more of his leg if he can help it, but it may be necessary. They had to take a lot of muscle and that's why it's important he keeps swimming for that leg.

Danny's mother said, 'They treat one leg, but we've got to think about all of Danny'. Danny seemed to find difficulty in reconciling feared past experiences with reassurance about the future.

> *Int.*: Is there anything you're looking forward to about being in hospital?
> *Danny*: Getting over the operation. I hate operations, I've had loads of them. They stick tubes in you, and they're going to stick a pin in my back, ooh!
> *Int.*: What's that for?
> *Danny*: They're going to put some fluid in it if my leg hurts, give me some fluid out the back and it will go into my leg to keep it better.
> *Mother*: To stop it hurting, they explained it all to you, that's the epidural. I'll explain again in a minute.

After he had listened to his voice on the tape-recorder, Danny went off to play snooker, lurching along with a severe limp. His parents explained more about his treatment. They expected the bone graft to take six weeks to heal and then up to four months for lengthening of the fibula. They had prepared Danny for only one operation.

> *Mother*: We didn't realise it was so involved until today. But we said, "once it's done you won't get pain any more and you can throw away your crutches, and you're going to be walking straight". So I think he's geared up, 'cos he's had this treatment in one form or another for so long it doesn't bother him too much. We can say it's not as bad as it was last time, and I don't know about the pain – he's pretty good.
> *Father*: He's not impressed with physiotherapy.
> *Mother*: He doesn't like the pain. But it's not like a child who's never been in hospital who would be terrified. Though he is absolutely terrified of injections.

Perhaps this had prevented Danny from understanding fully that the epidural which seemed like an injection was a means of pain relief. His mother added,

'He's behind at school with all his spells in hospital. And they say with what he's got it's harder for him to learn things, remember and connect things.' Danny and his parents had just joined the Neurofibromatosis (NFT) Society and attended their first annual general meeting (AGM) where they had learnt much about the disease.

*Father*: The fibromas can grow anywhere. I've read it can lead to cystic degeneration of any part of the body, be it soft tissue or bone. It can cause overgrowth in bone and in rare cases it attacks the optic nerve, it can lead to deafness and blindness. [Danny has come back to sit on the bed with them.] That tends to manifest itself around the age of 20 onwards. It's rather like sitting on a genetic time bomb.

[Danny's mother tells him to go and watch television and after persuasion he goes.]

*Int.*: How much has Danny been told?

*Father*: I think he's known exactly what would happen prior to the ops.

*Int.*: What about the blindness and deafness?

*Mother*: There's got to be a point where he knows when he's older.

*Father*: We haven't exactly told him the – worst possibilities.

*Mother*: It depends what the possibilities are.

*Father*: It's a question of coping with things as they arise. I suppose we live in hope that everything will seem to stop.

*Mother*: Yes, it can do just that.

*Father*: And therefore you think, "why bother to say this and that could happen?" No doubt when he's older he'll read about things and find out for himself.

*Mother*: It can cause disfigurement of the face very badly. Of course he didn't come to the lectures. But we found it's called elephant man disease. A man at the AGM looked very much like that. We explained to him some people would look a bit __, but I don't think he sees the connection. Obviously we worry someone's going to turn round and say something to him.

*Int.*: Is there anything difficult you don't want me to talk about with Danny?

*Mother*: Mmm. Only this NFT. But he knows most of it obviously, not all, but you wouldn't tell a child that age. I don't think you could tell anybody, "You have the risk you'll end up blind or deaf", do you? Possibly it might not happen.

*Int.*: Earlier you said he may read it up for himself one day. In some ways would you rather he did that, than the burden was on you of deciding what to say?

*Father*: Well, I think he will ask certain things anyway. If he asks you try your best to explain. Possibly you feel he will find his own level of what he wants to ask you. If we say too much he'll be thinking

> what's going to happen next year? It's a question of trying to find
> a balance between what he can accept and wants to know, as opposed
> to saying about the whole thing.
> *Mother*: We met one girl at the conference in her 20s, who said "My
> parents don't know because I don't want to be responsible for telling
> them what they gave me". The whole thing gets so complicated.

Danny's case illustrates the difficulty of learning what children understand
without asking leading questions that the parents do not want raised. It is not
clear how much Danny heard or understood; the only way to explore this
would seem to be not through research but through a formally agreed part
of treatment. Chapters 7 and 8 look at talking about risk and harm, which
many doctors and parents prefer to avoid with child and also adult patients.
As Danny's mother said, 'You wouldn't want to tell anyone'. Other children
we interviewed lived in the shadow of an uncertain future or an early death
which intensified parents' (and researchers') difficulties in trying to be both
honest and protective.

The history of children's rights, traced in Chapters 3 and 4, records this tension between respecting children's liberties and their need for protection. Beliefs
about children's abilities influence and are influenced by research with children,
which is reviewed in Chapter 5. Later chapters follow children through the
consent process, looking at the knowledge they bring with them into hospital,
how they are informed about proposed treatment, their awareness of choice,
and their wish to have a large or small part in decision making. Children's and
adults' views on the child's competence to make informed decisions will be considered, as well as children's contribution to overall and interim decisions. Danny
was due to have leg lengthening, which is the subject of the next chapter.

## Notes

1  This was shown when, for example, 'idiot' was changed to 'subnormal' to 'mentally
   handicapped' which later changed to 'person with learning difficulties'. Apart from
   changing ideas about causes of a condition and its social significance, the sequence
   expresses unease about continuing discrimination against this group of people,
   rather than about a word. Kevles, D. (1986) *In the Name of Eugenics*. Harmondsworth, Pelican. As suggested later, the word 'patient' should be redefined rather
   than replaced.
2  There are numerous books and papers on consent, many by lawyers and bioethicists.
   The major works include: Beauchamp, T. and Childress, J. (1983) *Principles of
   Biomedical Ethics*. New York, Oxford University Press; Faden, R. and Beauchamp,
   T. (1986) *A History and Theory of Informed Consent*. New York, Oxford University
   Press; Gillon, R. (1986) *Philosophical Medical Ethics*. Chichester, John Wiley.
   McLean, S. (1989) *The Patient's Right to Know*. Aldershot, Dartmouth, takes a more
   liberal view of children's abilities.

3 Buchanan, A. and Brock, D. (1989) *Deciding for Others: The Ethics of Surrogate Decision Making*. New York, Cambridge University Press.

4 National Commission for the Protection of Human Subjects of Biomedical and Behavioral Research (1977) *Research Involving Children*. Washington, DC, DHEW.

5 Alderson, P. (1990) *Choosing for Children: Parents' Consent to Surgery*. Oxford, Oxford University Press.

6 Gaylin, W. and Macklin, R. (eds) (1982) *Who Speaks for the Child?* New York, Plenum Press; Melton, G., Koocher, G. and Saks, M. (eds) (1983) *Children's Competence to Consent*. New York, Plenum Press; Nicholson, R. (1986) *Medical Research with Children: Ethics, Law and Practice*. Oxford, Oxford University Press; Kopelman, L. and Moskop, J. (eds) (1989) *Children and Health Care: Moral and Social Issues*. Dordecht, Kluwer.

7 Department of Health (1991) *Welfare of Children and Young People in Hospital*. London, HMSO, summarizes over 30 years of official recommendations.

8 Between us we had worked for over 25 years with the National Association for the Welfare of Children in Hospital, now Action for Sick Children. We knew some hospitals very well and had visited over 200 hospitals to observe the children's services.

9 This comment is based on the response of many hospital staff when we discussed problems with them.

10 These were among the reactions to my lectures on this research. One person left a meeting in outrage. Children's rights arouse strong reactions. I am grateful to all the people who have helpfully discussed this research at these lectures and seminars.

11 Butler Sloss, E. (1987) *Report of Inquiry into Child Abuse in Cleveland*. London, HMSO, asserts that this should not be the case.

12 Office of Population and Census Surveys (1991) *Mid-1990 Population Estimates for England and Wales*, PP1 91/1. London, OPCS.

13 Department of Health (1991) *Hospital Episode Summary Tables, England, 1987–8*. Government Statistical Service. During the year 1987–88, 1 216 934 children were admitted as in-patients, and 68 423 children aged 0–14 years were treated as day cases.

14 Office of Population and Census Surveys (1987) *Hospital Inpatient Enquiry*, Series MB4, 27. London, OPCS.

15 Caring for Children in the Health Services (1987) *Where are the Children?* London, Action for Sick Children.

16 Three hospitals were for children and one for orthopaedic patients, two were national postgraduate special authority hospitals, admitting children from around the UK and from abroad. One was a supra-regional centre, treating children who live within and beyond the local health region.

17 These methods enrich studies of people's feelings about illness. See, for example, Judd, D. (1990) *Give Sorrow Words: Working with a Dying Child*. London, Free Association Books; or art therapy, such as reported in Isaacs, S. (1991) Images of feeling. *British Medical Journal*, 302, 972–3.

18 Denial as a means of coping for children is discussed in Eiser, C. (1990) *Chronic Childhood Disease: An Introduction to Psychological Theory and Research*, pp. 105–15. Cambridge, Cambridge University Press.

19 One researcher who interviewed parents of disabled children believed that people
   reconstruct their lives into accounts which show them to be coping well as moral
   agents and they avoid discussing failure. Voysey, M. (1975) *A Constant Burden:
   Reconstituting Family Life*. London, Routledge. Other research interviews show that
   it is possible to move from this type of 'public' into 'private' accounts in which
   interviewees discuss anxiety, failure and loss. Cornwell, J. (1984) *Hard-earned Lives:
   Accounts of Health and Illness from East London*. London, Tavistock.

# 2

# LIMB LENGTHENING

*I'm very pleased with the result of my treatment. One leg was six inches shorter than the other, with a little club foot. My [false] leg was made so that my foot hung down in front and people would say, "Why have you got a tennis ball stuck in your sock?" The limb rubbed on it and made it bloody and I thought anything was worth trying. Mr Y said that the options were to chop off my foot, or to make my leg six inches longer. Now my leg is long enough so that my foot fits inside a prosthesis into my shoe. I can wear jeans and wellingtons for the first time. It's brilliant.*

*But it wasn't easy. The pins were in for 11 months. I didn't realize that I should keep moving my leg, and I kept it still, bent at an angle for weeks. They tried to straighten it by forcing it down under anaesthetic and putting it in plaster one Friday. I was in agony through the weekend and when at last they took off the plaster on Monday there was a burn injury where my knee was trying to force through the plaster.*

*The nightmare was having skin releases around the pin sites, which they did five times. One time they did it with local anaesthetic with an injection right into each pin site. That was terribly painful and by the time they'd done the injections and started cutting the skin the anaesthetic had worn off. He said, "We'll cut a centimetre at each pin". I said they didn't need to because I wasn't lengthening any more, and only two sites needed to be done, but they didn't listen. I was scream-ing and my leg was covered in blood. If I could, I would have got off that trolley and run away. I'd like to stab that doctor with a knife. Mr Y always shakes hands and talks to me, but the other doctors don't even look at you or introduce themselves. They jerk you here and there, and never listen to you.*

*(John aged 15)*

Eleven children in our study had surgical limb lengthening, in one case an arm was lengthened. Although they are a small group, their treatment particularly combines difficult clinical and cosmetic, medical and personal decisions, so they will fairly often be referred to. The treatment takes months or years to accomplish, and we came to know some of these children well. As a relatively new treatment, limb lengthening remains partly uncertain and experimental. It is difficult and 'should only be carried out in specialized centres'.[1] The treatment will be described, with the choices it presents. The experience of some children will be considered, followed by a section on evaluating surgical treatments and involving children in making decisions.

The treatment is not pleasant to experience, or to read about. It is so hard

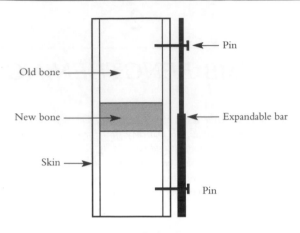

**Figure 1**   Limb lengthening

to explain the experience that informed consent might seem an impossible ideal. A nurse commented, 'We show them the apparatus, and get them to handle it, and see it on other children. But they can't have any real idea until they wake up with it on. That is always a tremendous shock.' Limb lengthening raises questions about the cost of 'normality'. Social pressures and unhappiness about being unusually short lead children to undergo months of pain and immobility, to add a few inches to their height which in medieval times would have been well within the average range. Although the lengthening technique has been known for many years,[2] it began to be used with British children at Sheffield Children's Hospital in 1985. Six years later, over 100 children had been treated at Sheffield and the technique was being offered at a few other British hospitals. The technique is used for two purposes: to increase the height of children who are very short for their age, or to even up the lengths of one short and one longer limb.

The usual method is that, in the operating theatre, the surgeon breaks the bone and fixes a steel apparatus to each end of it (see Fig. 1). As new bone grows to heal the break, the two parts of the bone are very slowly pulled apart, if all goes well at a rate of one millimetre each day. It is possible to gain several inches of new soft bone, which will gradually become dense and hard. Another method is to fix the apparatus so that it pulls on the growth plates at each end of the bone to promote extra growth. The procedure is likely to be more painful since the bone is not first broken under general anaesthetic, but the plate is slowly fractured 'by 33 days' through the lengthening.[3] In 50 per cent of these cases, the growth plate is damaged, and so this treatment is usually attempted with adolescents who have finished most of their natural growth.[4] Various types of apparatus have been developed around Europe, the most common being a single expandable bar with one or more pins at each end. The Russian circular frame with four bars and many pins is becoming popular with surgeons; it can correct structure as well as length if bones are bent or malformed.

## Choices

The treatment presents choices, usually made by the surgeons. Although there are wide variations in practice, each surgeon we observed appeared to follow his own methods,[5] and not discuss alternatives with patients. With short children having treatment for both legs, Italian surgeons prefer to do one leg, often the femur and the tibia, at a time.[6] The children are fairly mobile and able to lead a more nearly normal life. Spanish surgeons favour doing both legs at once, both the femurs at one stage and both tibias usually at another stage. This method is more likely to result in equally long legs, because if a complication prevents further growth in one leg, treatment on the other can be stopped. The risk with the Italian method is that if the first leg treated grows very well but the second does not, the child is left with a severe limp and imbalance, and all the discomfort, embarrassment, potential damage to the hips and spine, and other problems which leg equalizing is designed to treat. However, with the Spanish method, children are far less mobile; some remain in wheelchairs, sometimes with their legs always extended in attempts to prevent knee and ankle problems. Whereas certain doctors try to prevent complications through plasters and immobility, others believe in regular vigorous physiotherapy. A recent idea is to have a machine which ensures continuous automatic leg bending starting shortly after surgery, working throughout the night. Weight-bearing is encouraged by some surgeons to promote bone growth; others discourage it as a risk to the fragile new bone.

Between 5 and 14 days after the first operation, lengthening begins. The screws on the frames are turned two or four times a day by nurses, parents or the child. To help to control pain and prevent damage to the nerves, muscles and blood vessels, the number of turns each day may be reduced or stopped. At one centre, children stay in hospital through the months of lengthening; at other centres, the children live at home and are treated at frequent out-patient clinics – some surgeons encourage their early return to school, others support the use of home tutors. The same amount of time that is spent on lengthening will probably be needed for strengthening the new bone. To prevent fractures, the child may wear an external splint, calliper, strut or plaster, or else have an internal metal rod or plate fitted, and removed in a later operation.

The number of operations during the process varies between surgeons, and also depends on whether there are complications, internal or external strengthening, and skin cutting. At one hospital, the skin is massaged to help it to stretch as the leg grows. Massage before physiotherapy also loosens the skin, and removes the crust which, when it sticks to the pin sites, makes movement very painful. At other hospitals where massage is not practised, the skin is 'nicked' where it 'heaps up' against the pins as they are wound apart. This may be done on the child's bed or in theatre with a full general anaesthetic and all the procedures as for major surgery.


## Complications

The process is fraught with physical complications;[7] the social complications will be considered later. One surgeon we interviewed remarked, 'There are so many complications that are sure to happen that now we call them "incidents" which I think is the right approach'. The physical complications include prolonged pain, muscle spasms, infections in the pin sites which have to remain as open wounds throughout the growing period, swelling and discolouration, muscle weakness, stiff joints and tight tendons, deformities of the hips, knee or ankle which may require corrective surgery, damage to the nerves and circulation which in extreme cases could necessitate amputation, fracture and bending of the leg bones, bone that will not grow or harden, broken apparatus, and back pain. Some surgeons report an 'acceptably low complication rate', without stating whether this is the surgeons' or the patients' assessment.[8] Whereas some surgeons believe that, for short stature, the 'benefits may not justify the expense, morbidity, and risk of the procedure',[9] others assert that 'this method is based on sound principles and is free of major risks'.[10] Some authors cautiously advise that leg lengthening 'is recommended when amputation is the only other surgical alternative and a full, complete informed consent is given to [sic] the parents and patient'.[11] This strange but fairly common understanding of patients' consent sees the active doctor 'giving' consent 'to' the passive patient, a reversal of the reality when consent is given by patients to doctors.

Responses to the complications again involve questions and choices. What is the best way to prevent and treat bone, muscle and skin complications? How much can and should long-term pain be endured or relieved? How are infections best prevented and treated? Yet the primary questions within these kinds of evaluative questions which involve 'best' and 'should' are: Who is qualified to give the answers – doctors, parents or children – and according to what criteria? Answers to these questions will be considered later.


## 'Clinical' and 'cosmetic' treatment

Surgeons usually require rigorous psychological assessments of very short children before they will accept them for treatment. It may have been a sign of effective screening that the short stature children in our study were very keen to have the treatment and, on the whole, to tolerate the difficulties. Increasing height is seen as 'cosmetic', but to these children it was also functional.

However, far less attention was paid to psychological screening and discussion with the unequal leg length cases, than to the short stature ones. This treatment was judged to be 'clinical' (to prevent future injury to the hips and spine) and some surgeons assumed that the need was either so obvious, or else so important, that it did not need much explanation. Yet some patients took the opposite view. To very short children who wanted treatment, their need was obvious, indeed urgent. Some of the unequal limb length children, however, did not think they needed or wanted treatment. They were the ones who needed very careful discussion, to ascertain their hopes and fears, their knowledge and misunderstandings. If treatment was still believed to be medically essential, they were the ones who needed detailed explanations and possibly persuasion.

Efua, aged 9 years, was vague during her interviews about why her arm was being lengthened. She talked about the very heavy apparatus, the pain of lengthening, and of being pushed against doors by children at school. She did not express any worry about having a shorter arm. For a while she had been turning to contract, instead of expand, the fixator because it was less painful, until this was discovered. Andy, another 9-year-old, was hazy the day before his operation about why he was in hospital. 'We know very little about the body, we have to listen to the experts', his father told me. 'He's very easygoing, he doesn't really think about it. He trusts us'. 'I knew they were going to stretch the bone, but I hadn't thought how they'd do it', said Andy. He had no complaints about his life, and was a junior motorbike racing champion. After much treatment for congenital scoliosis, Sharon did not want to have leg lengthening. Her mother, a clerical officer, said:

> Sharon had three months of leg lengthening and six months in plaster. Neither of us was prepared for the amount of pain; it really was pain from start to finish. That's what they didn't warn us about. They say a 6-year-old wouldn't understand, but even a 6-year-old does understand that excruciating pain. The leg gained five centimetres but she lost it again when her leg broke twice, so we're back to the four centimetre difference.
>
> They need to treat people as individuals and listen to them. She's never been able to move her ankle anyway, but the physios were quite aggressive. Each new physio would shout at her to move her ankle, and I'd say, "She can't, read your damn notes". If your knee's swollen and agony, you *can't* move any more.

Sharon added:

> Even if you try your hardest, they don't seem to notice or believe you. One made me cry all the time. I fell over with the fixator on. At first they put it in too close to the top of my leg. I was screaming all the first three weeks because it was embedding. Then I had to have another

operation and they had to make the hole bigger to move it. They kept changing the treatment, trying different kinds of cleansing, and deciding whether I had to walk or not.

During the out-patient clinics of Andy's and Efua's consultant, much time was carefully spent measuring the limbs. If there was a leg length difference of four centimetres or more, parents were advised that the child's name would be added to the waiting list, and the lengthening technique was mentioned. For example, 'It may take months for the bone to grow longer and then to harden. It's a long painful business, but they don't seem to mind it. One girl was even turning the screws the wrong way, to make it shorter instead of longer. It's quite fun really'. Our observations and interviews indicated that little tended to be said to children.

### Information and support

Once treatment began, nurses were the main informers. They emphasized either a paediatric or an orthopaedic approach. The paediatric approach concerned teaching and helping children and parents; it was considered essential to enable children and parents to cleanse the pin sites, which in every hospital was done without pain relief. A paediatric-orientated nurse told us:

> We'd like to see far more preparation and support for families, with photographs, written materials and handling the equipment, building up for nine months before the treatment. One consultant talks very much with the child. He sits back and says, "What do you want?" Children often say they are all right and the parents get very tense at first. But it is important that the child wants the treatment, and is not being pressured by other people.
>
> Even if they are very well prepared, and even if the child wants it badly, there is a stage of distress, maybe hysteria and rejection, shortly after the operation. Inevitably there's a lot of panic, covering up the fixator and not wanting to see it. We do a lot of work sitting down and chit chatting about it, listening and comforting and supporting. They all go home after about two weeks, as soon as they and their parents can clean the pin sites and do the physio. They are treated as out-patients after that.
>
> The children massage their pin sites. Occasionally the skin needs a small snick, this is done on the child's bed with a local anaesthetic. They clean their own sites as much as possible, from five years upwards. A nurse does the first two days. She sits on the bed and talks about how much it will hurt at first, but each day will be easier. Next day the mother does one site, and the next day the child does one. They shout at the nurse, but then can have a cuddle afterwards. The first dressing is by far the most difficult. It is vital to build up their confidence. It is easier

if they are contributing and don't have a fear of "this thing" on their leg, even if all they do at first is hold something while the nurse does it. We use just boiled water and cotton wool buds, no antiseptic or creams which are soggy and encourage bacteria. The simpler it is, the more easily the families can do it well.

Another nurse said, 'We'd never use surgical spirit on pin sites. If you did that, you wouldn't be able to get near the child a second time.'

In marked contrast, in the traditional orthopaedic approach, the nurses take charge. Jenni's case illustrated the mainly orthopaedic approach. Jenni, aged 11, had one leg nine centimetres longer than the other. She said, 'I don't mind the limping, it's the built-up shoes. They're red and everyone stares at them. I get lots of back problems. I'm very good at games. I'm the only girl at school to get two golds, for hurdles and high jump'. Her mother was a shop assistant and her father mended machines. Jenni's home was two to three hours journey from the hospital. She was referred from another hospital, and came in for surgery before she met the consultant and before the lengthening was explained.

The other hospital said I'd have an operation and be in for three or four weeks, not six or seven months. I came in on Wednesday and had the operation on Thursday. They showed me the pictures when I came in and I thought they were disgusting. When I had it on, I wouldn't look at it at first; the nurses do my dressings, and my mum does them at weekends when I go home.

Jenni and her mother were afraid of hospitals. Her mother said:

Jenni very, very much wanted the problem corrected but she's terrified of operations and didn't realize what the treatment would be. It's essential for her to stay in during the week so she gets proper care. We didn't realize until we'd arrived with no suitcase, and after driving along all those strange roads, that I would be allowed to stay. I felt torn between Jenni and my husband, so I visit twice a week.

Jenni and her mother both spoke more freely when the other one was not present. During her months in the ward, Jenni often looked upset or angry. Once she jarred her leg against the bed and wept with pain. A nurse said, 'No, no, don't cry, take deep breaths'. The pin sites were covered with large brown stained pads. Jenni liked some of the nurses who often talked with her, plaiting her hair and helping her to put on make-up. When asked 'Who do you chat to if you feel upset?', Jenni replied curtly, 'Mum'. Her mother looked pleased and surprised, but it was not clear whether this was a compliment or an accusation that her mother was not present enough.

Jenni's parents talked of being informed about a second operation.

*Mother*: I think it's very disappointing, that there's no decision. We didn't get a chance to talk to Mr X on the ward round. We've got to

wait two or three more weeks for him to decide. We'd got all geared
up in case he was going to put in a plate today. Her knee has twisted
round a lot.

*Int.*: Were you warned this might happen?

*Father*: No. Well it might have been mentioned. I suppose it's obvious
it could happen if you think about it.

*Mother*: Just before the first operation, I think they said her knee might
go out. They're deciding whether to put in a strut or a plate for about
two years. I don't think they told us about that before. We're learning
as we go along. It's still a fraction short and the other leg is growing.
If it gets worse [the difference in length] they'll slow the other leg
down.

*Jenni*: They won't!

*Mother*: We don't know what it involves. It's rather confusing. They say
it's grown eight and a half centimetres, that's nearly four and a half
inches isn't it? And it has to stop now. Mr X has been reviewing the
growth. He says in leg lengthening it stops and starts, it's unpredictable, so he's not sure whether he'll have to stop the other leg.

*Jenni*: He better not!

*Mother*: We'll have to see.

*Int.*: What do you think about the amount of information you were
given? Was it enough, or too much or too little?

*Mother*: Enough I'd say.

*Jenni*: I reckon they should have told me about the pin site release.

*Mother*: You'd only be more nervous.

*Jenni*: I specially don't like the skin nicking, in the treatment room where
they clean the pin sites, and I have four skin nicks. The worst bit is
when they put the needle [for local anaesthetic] right in. That hurts
and stings so much I'm screaming.

In Jenni's ward, a controlled trial of pin site cleansing was being conducted,
comparing saline, surgical spirit and doing nothing. The cleansing was done
by nurses in the treatment room to ensure that conditions were 'controlled'.
Jenni was in the surgical spirit group. Her mother believed that Jenni had to
stay in hospital to ensure that the sites were properly cleansed by nurses,
'because we couldn't do it properly. She's screaming each time before she even
gets into the treatment room'.

## Ambiguity

When we discussed informed choice, Jenni and her mother described ambiguous responses. Her mother thought that 'now, at 11 she can understand the
relevant medical information as well as I can. As we're not often here, Jenni

explains it all to us, she probably understands better than I could'. Her mother also thought that at 16 years, Jenni would be able to make a wise choice about proposed surgery: 'She's sensible and can give the right answer now – for someone else – but not for herself. She'd pull off that lengthener if she could decide. I wouldn't trust her over cleaning the pins. She wouldn't!'

When her mother said that Jenni had 'shared the choice with her parents and doctors', Jenni looked amazed and argued that a choice between boots and treatment was not a choice but something she was forced into.

> *Mother*: But it was your choice. So many others need this treatment, and have to wait because of you.
> *Jenni*: Yes, I thought I was on my own.
> *Mother*: You don't realise.
> *Int.*: Jenni, who do you think decided that you should have the treatment?
> *Jenni*: My parents.
> *Mother*: Well, they wouldn't have done it if you didn't want it.
> [Jenni still looked surprised as if she had not thought of this.]
> *Int.*: Who do you think should decide?
> [Jenni hesitated for some time but eventually said "the doctors".]
> *Int.*: When do you think you'll be old enough to decide for yourself about whether to have an operation?
> *Jenni*: When I'm 15.
> *Int.*: Would you sign the consent form then?
> *Jenni*: [Looking worried] Oh no, not until I'm 16 or later.

It was as if Jenni and her mother separated making a choice from the risks of responsibility and blame which neither wanted to carry. Later when Jenni had gone to do school lessons her mother said, 'Well, I suppose it was the doctors who decided. Jenni and I disagree a lot. She can have her way in some things, but when it's her leg, something so important, well it's *got* to be done, so she'd have to have it', as if Jenni had no choice. After her plate operation, Jenni was asked again who she thought should be the main decider; this time she said she didn't know, and her mother later said, 'We're guided by the doctors'.

### Outcome

Months after Jenni had gone home, when telephoned to arrange a follow-up visit, her mother agreed at once, but she was asked to check with Jenni. Her mother agreed to do this and then said that after they left the hospital:

> At first she was very pleased, thrilled to wear ordinary shoes for the first time in her life. At the clinic the registrar said she was fine, but the physio saw her, and said at once she'd have to go back into boots. Jenni broke

her heart. We waited three months then went back to the clinic. They said there was a seven centimetre difference, but Mr X wasn't there so nothing could be decided. By that time her legs were very uneven. She still has her knee bent and the tendons are too tight. We're supposed to do exercises but we're not sure what to do, and the physios are too busy to see us to explain. I don't know if the plate in her shorter leg has stopped it from growing, but the difference has happened so suddenly.

The registrar said leave it until the next clinic in another three months. But what will the difference be then? Might she need even more treatment? There wasn't time to ask all the questions I had, and I do want to talk to Mr X, just to get some answers. Jenni hates going all that way to the hospital, and hearing bad news, getting upset, and then I have to get her home again. She uses crutches again now, and she's frightened to go out she's so wobbly. We don't know how much weight she should put on her leg. I don't think Mr X knew quite what to expect. He said to us, "In theory it should grow the same as the longer one, but in practice we're not certain what it will do". I think he only tells you what he thinks you can cope with at the time. It's taken so much longer than we expected. I don't know what to do for the best. They may stop the good leg growing, or wait until she's older and shorten it. The registrar said, "What do you want?" But I don't want to decide, and maybe make the wrong decision. I'd rather be guided by them.

Jenni definitely doesn't want any more ops. Unluckily she went to the dentist and she's got to see the orthodontist. She was screaming before they even started, she was so frightened. It's good in the hospital but we do need back-up at home. Just half an hour a month to talk to a physio for reassurance and support.

As limb lengthening is a new process, few physiotherapists in local hospitals know how to treat it. A few hours later, having checked with Jenni, her mother said, 'She doesn't want to talk about it. It's too upsetting. She'd feel differently if everything was going well'.


## Evaluation

For years, some doctors have argued that every medical intervention – new or established – should be assessed through well-conducted trials. One large review assessed numerous perinatal practices for whether they reduce poor outcomes, seem promising but are of unproven benefit, are used but the outcome is not known, or should be abandoned in the light of available evidence.[12] Only a few practices fell into the first group. Perinatal care is mainly for healthy mothers and babies who can thrive on non-interference. Orthopaedics is much concerned with people longing for relief from pain, disability or deformity, who may be prepared to endure painful treatment for the hope of slight relief. Yet it could be argued that their vulnerability and distress make stringent evaluation of their treatment even more important.

Limb lengthening is very costly in its demands on health service resources and on patients and their relatives. John's mother (see beginning of this chapter) said, 'It was very hard on John's father. John was horrible to him for months, but luckily his father could take it, and we are still married – we just made it'. John was delighted with the outcome of his treatment. Sharon showed that certain surgery does more harm than good, whereas Amy thought it worthwhile to embark on the second stage of lengthening to gain more height when she was 12. Both their mothers spoke of the great strain on the whole family. For some, the treatment itself changes their ambitions. Jane, aged 15, was 'breaking her heart' over her short stature, her mother said. She found the treatment extremely distressing, but eventually decided that she was pleased with her longer femurs and content with her new height. Although shorter than she had originally hoped, she refused offers of further treatment. She still walked with difficulty and used a wheelchair, which she had not needed before treatment, 18 months after leg lengthening began.

How can the costs and benefits be assessed in order to decide the final gain or loss?[13] When one surgeon was asked how he would measure outcome, he replied, 'I would assess function and structure and check that the mechanics are correct, that kind of thing'. When asked in what proportion of cases the function was satisfactory, he said, 'It varies enormously, I couldn't possibly talk in terms of percentage of cases'. Yet this is a crucial matter for patients to know before they can give reasonably informed consent. If the success rate in these two limited criteria, function and structure, is high, they may well think that the risks and pain are worth undertaking. If the success rate is low, and they are likely to be left with weak, uneven or twisted legs, even less able to walk and run after treatment, they may be wary of accepting proposed treatment.

The surgeon's evaluation was limited as well as vague. He did not appear to take account of psychological or social gains and losses, such as how the child's education, job opportunities, relationships, self-esteem, enjoyment of life or happiness might be affected. Such factors can only partly be evaluated by the surgeon. The child's and the parents' personal assessments are also extremely important. After staying in the ward for four months, Danny (Chapter 1) had lost his chirpy manner. He looked listless and sad and had dark rings under his eyes. However, months later during his follow-up interview at home, everyone was pleased that his leg had grown so well and was 'lovely and straight'.

> *Mother*: Mr X is amazed his right leg is so good. He wants to lengthen the little stump below the left knee.
> *Int.*: Why?
> *Father*: To give greater leverage for the prosthesis. Danny said, "I don't

want them doing that!" And Mr Z who looks after him for amputation said there was no point. A lot of trauma and no great benefit.
Mr X gave us three months to think about it. Danny was adamant
he didn't want it. We said no.

*Mother*: Mr X said, "It would be interesting to see how the left leg
responds", but is it for the benefit of the patient?

*Father*: He genuinely felt there was some advantage to Danny, but it is
a technical challenge. There's a problem in his left leg bone anyway.

*Mother*: He's going to senior school soon, he doesn't want another six
months in a wheelchair.

This was the kind of medical and personal balance which so many parents came
into the wards and clinics hoping to discuss, but little time was allowed for
this.

Research on measuring the outcome of surgery illustrates how varied and
uncertain many present assessments are. It is not generally agreed who should
make assessments (surgeons, other professionals, patients), what they should
assess (function, general health, psycho-social factors), how they can assess these
(questionnaires, interviews, follow-up clinics), when to make assessments
(weeks, months, years after surgery), how to interpret the data collected (such
as exactly what 'good' or 'poor' function means) and who the results are for
(surgeons, other professionals, managers, patients).[14] Should patients know,
for example, that one surgeon is very successful and another is less so?

Some of the questions leg lengthening raises are: How worthwhile is the
physiotherapy? What problems does it prevent and how effectively? Do months
in a wheelchair create more complications than they prevent? Is the stress of
staying in hospital for months justifiable? What is the likely success rate of
each treatment and how is 'success' defined and measured? Different methods
can be evaluated in randomized controlled trials, in which patients agree to
be randomly allocated to one treatment or another so that the comparative
merits can be tested. A review of the medical journals up to December 1991
showed no randomized controlled trials of leg-lengthening methods. Orthopaedic surgeons are urged rigorously to research their 'strongly held opinions
which are unsupported by scientific evidence'.[15] The difficulty with trials is
that relatively few children have this treatment. If the different methods were
explained to them, they are likely to have strong preferences and not wish to
be randomized. Many surgeons prefer to use their favoured methods, and dislike
impersonally randomizing their patients. Failing trials, at least surgeons could
systematically collect data, and publish their success and complications rates so
that some comparison could be made and gross benefits or problems
clarified.[16]

The editor of the *British Medical Journal* argues that 'the scientific base of
medicine is weak'.[17] He cites medicine's history of fashions for useless and
harmful treatments, wide variations in practice between countries and between

consultants, the lack of proper scientific evaluation, and the poor or non-existent evidence on the outcome of treatment. 'Only about 15 per cent of medical interventions are supported by solid scientific evidence, 85 per cent are not', partly because health care is so immensely variable and unpredictable. Doctors are urged to be more critical and analytical, and to admit their ignorance: 'everyone involved in health care and research should insist on evidence for statements and should focus on outcomes'.

Patients benefit when doctors are willing to reassess and revise their opinions in the light of new questions and evidence, and to admit mistakes or shortcomings. Some clinical specialties take this very seriously.[18] One cardiac surgeon now videos his operations, and reviews videos with parents, if they wish, to explain his work. The heart doctors have the advantage of working in teams based in their own units with regular review meetings, supported by far more generous research and evaluation resources than the orthopaedic consultants have. The latter also tend to be more isolated, and to have less time for vital discussion and critical reflection. If benefits are not measured, how will harms be recorded and in future avoided? How will doctors and patients make informed decisions partly based on essential information that can only be gained from patients?[19]

Pressures of time in the health services lead many surgeons confidently to encourage an incessant stream of patients to accept proposed treatment. One surgeon described his working compromise:

> Leg lengthening is a major procedure with surgical complications and I do stress this. I assure you that it can be very devastating to see these major complications. Nevertheless one can achieve quality in leg lengthening, and although I spend a lot of time trying to put them off, I also point out the benefits and advantages. You no longer see those high raised boots on people around the city, and that is due to leg lengthening. But yes, it's a very difficult technique, surgically, socially and psychologically. The counselling is the most important. One must get it right at the very beginning.

## Standards of care for children

After we had visited a hospital which organized a detailed preparation programme on leg lengthening,[20] we gave a written report of our visit to sisters in every ward in our study. Some were very pleased to receive the report, some were affronted at the suggestion they had anything to learn from another centre. Medicine is changing rapidly, and as one doctor said, 'The only way you can remain a centre of excellence is by growing and changing all the time, being willing to examine your own work very critically, and to learn from your patients, and from your colleagues, and other centres'.

Children are at risk of their distress being underestimated. Although orthopaedics literally means 'correcting children', most surgeons work mainly with adult patients and so may be less aware of children's interests than paediatricians are. Even in paediatrics, high levels of distress from neonatal care onwards are accepted and even enforced.[21] One professor of child health defined the aim of child health services as ensuring that children 'reach adulthood with their potential uncompromised'[22] rather than that they enjoy childhood, implying that childhood is just a prelude to the worthwhile adult years. Although the *Court Report*[23] advocated children's interests so eloquently, it opened with the definition: 'By health, I mean the power to live a full, *adult*, living, breathing life in close contact with what I love – I want to be all that I am capable of *becoming*' [my emphasis]. The report's title, *Fit for the Future*, partly implies that child health services attend to future adults rather than to present children.

Adult-centric thinking is common. 'We can do limb lengthening up to about 30 years of age', remarked one consultant, 'but we prefer to do it much earlier because adults seem to have more psychological problems than young children do'. Children experience severe problems with this treatment. Adults' distress is not more serious, but is likely to be taken more seriously by other adults. When children do not understand the need for treatment, it is humane to inform and prepare them. If they still do not accept the need for treatment which is not urgent, it is preferable to wait until they are ready, rather than to force interventions on bewildered, unwilling patients. The metal apparatus is being used with babies as an alternative to plasters. The clinical outcome may be improved, but the extra problems for the child and relatives need to be taken into account if the treatment is to be assessed adequately. Such assessment includes some understanding of the history and law about children's rights, which are reviewed in the next two chapters.

### Notes

1 Faber, F. *et al.* (1991) Complications of leg lengthening. *Acta Orthopedics Scandinavcia*, 62(4), 327–32.

2 Peterson, D. (1990) Leg lengthening procedures: A historical review. *Clinical Orthopedics*, 250, 27–33; Moseley, C. (1989) Leg lengthening: A review of 30 years. *Clinical Orthopaedics*, 247, 38–43.

3 Jones, C. *et al.* (1989) Epiphyseal distraction monitored by strain gauges: Results in 7 children. *Journal of Bone and Joint Surgery*, 71(4), 651–6, reports that attempts to expand the growth plate 'at the lower femur produced many complications' but at the upper tibia there was 'excellent bone production and few complications'.

4 Aichroth, P. (1991) Lecture at Multi-Disciplinary Conference on Limb Lengthening at Westminster Children's Hospital, London, December; Fjeld, T. and Steen, H. (1990) Growth retardation after experimental limb lengthening by epiphyseal distraction. *Journal of Pediatric Orthopedics*, 10(4), 463–6.

5 All the consultants and senior registrars observed during the project were men.

6 The smaller lower leg bone, the fibula, does not need to be treated and adjusts as the major lower bone, the tibia, lengthens.

7 Paley, D. (1990) Problems, obstacles and complications of limb lengthening by the Ilizarov technique. *Clinical Orthopedics*, 250, 81–104; Hrutkay, J. and Eilert, R. (1990) Operative lengthening of the lower extremity and associated psychological aspects. *Journal of Pediatric Orthopedics*, 10(3), 373–7; Galardi, B. *et al.* (1990) Peripheral nerve damage during limb lengthening. *Journal of Bone and Joint Surgery*, 72(1), 121–4.

8 Paterson, J., Waller, C. and Catterall, A. (1989) Lower limb lengthening by a modified Wagner technique. *Journal of Pediatric Orthopedics*, 9(2), 129–33.

9 Price, C. (1989) Limb lengthening for achondroplasia. *Journal of Pediatric Orthopedics*, 9(5), 512–15.

10 Catteneo, R. *et al.* (1988) Limb lengthening in achondroplasia by Ilizarov's method. *International Orthopaedics*, 12(3), 173–9.

11 Chandler, D. *et al.* (1988) Results of 21 Wagner limb lengthenings in 20 patients. *Clinical Orthopaedics*, 230, 214–22.

12 Chalmers, I., Enkin, M. and Keirse, M. (eds) (1989) *Effective Care in Pregnancy and Childbirth*. Oxford, Oxford University Press.

13 Bowling, A. (1991) *Measuring Health: A Review of Quality of Life Measurement Scales*. Buckingham, Open University Press, reviews a range of outcome evaluation measures but notes lack of attention to patients' assessments.

14 Kelley, M. (1991) Measuring outcome in common surgical procedures. Paper presented to the Annual Medical Sociology Meeting of the British Sociological Association, York, September.

15 Chalmers, I., Collins, R. and Dickersin, K. (1992) Controlled trials and meta-analyses can help resolve disagreements among orthopaedic surgeons. *Journal of Bone and Joint Surgery*, 74B(5), 641–3.

16 A detailed instance of the lack of scientific evidence is reported by Cooter, R. (1987) The meaning of fractures. *Medical History*, 31, 306–32. Orthopaedic surgeons took over the treatment of fractures from general surgeons, between the world wars, through claiming higher success rates; the claims were entirely unsubstantiated.

17 Smith, R. (1992) The ethics of ignorance. *Journal of Medical Ethics*, 18, 117–18, 134.

18 Alderson, P. (1990) *Choosing for Children: Parents' Consent to Surgery*. Oxford, Oxford University Press, ch. 4. However, much of the measurement was of mortality rather than morbidity, the main concern in orthopaedics.

19 Doctors are urged to involve patients, e.g. in Frater, A. and Costain, D. (1992) Any better? Outcome measures in medical audit. *British Medical Journal*, 304, 519–20.

20 I thank the nurses who gave us so much time and information during our visit to Sheffield.

21 Guillemin, J. and Holmstrom, L. (1986) *Mixed Blessings: Intensive Care for Newborns*. New York, Oxford University Press. It appears to be easier to withhold and withdraw unhelpful treatment in the UK than in the USA.

22 Hull, D., Preface to Wyke, S. and Hewison, J. (1991) *Child Health Matters*. Milton Keynes, Open University Press.

23 Report of the Committee on Child Health Services (1976) *Fit for the Future*. London, HMSO.

# 3

# CHILDREN'S HUMAN RIGHTS

*It's my leg. I do what I like with my leg. But I'd just say, if you've got to do an operation, get it over and done with.*

*(Danny aged 10)*

*With leg lengthening, only the person who is going to have it can decide whether to have it. I decided when I was eight.*

*(Amy aged 10)*

*It's my life, I should be the one who decides whether to have the operation.*

*(Jane aged 15)*

*I don't care who decides about the operation, as long as I get better.*

*(Louise aged 8)*

*When you are eight, I think you tell your parents when you need an operation. We all decided about my heart operation together, we knew we had to because I was so breathless.*

*(Heidi aged 12)*

*My doctor and my mummy decided about my operation. They knew what I wanted. After all she is my mum and I do trust her.*

*(Linda aged 8)*

Adults' consent involves the right to make personal decisions which are respected. This chapter reviews how rights tend to be understood in ways which exclude children, and undermine respect for their consent.[1]

## Autonomy and protection

The modern idea of the rights of man is only about 400 years old, and the first rights were to autonomy, as self-determination, non-interference and the right to make personal decisions. Women and children had no rights because they were seen as man's property.[2] In the nineteenth century, for example, Charles Dickens tired of his wife and sent her to live in another part of London when their youngest son was 6 years old. She never spoke again to her six younger children until after Dickens's death years later. Even today, charters which declare the right of 'everyone' to vote or to work imply that children are not anyone.

A view of the child's mind and body as temporary, and relatively worthless, pervades the history of childhood.[3] Reformers have usually treated children 'as things, as problems, but rarely as human beings with personality and integrity'.[4] The view of children as not fully human has continued well into this century, such as when they are seen as 'unrestrained, greedy and cruel little savages', and not yet 'civilised beings'.[5] In many childcare manuals, the future adult is implicitly seen as a butterfly imprisoned in a chrysalis (the child) and needing protection from any harm the careless child might do to it before the date of magical release (the age of consent). Ironically, during this century, the first to recognize the child's autonomy, there has been unprecedented insistence that children conform to a 'well-adjusted, clockwork' norm. 'Bad habits', such as thumb-sucking, were not written about in previous centuries; they probably existed but were accepted. 'It suddenly became important that they be stopped . . . As in almost all aspects of baby-care, intrusion and interference, tinkering about with the works, were getting more marked'.[6]

Rights were expanded from the early rights to *autonomy* to include rights to *resources*, such as education, and recently to include rights to *protection from harm*.[7] This stretched the meaning of 'rights' from the original idea of non-interference into active interference on the child's behalf, from regarding children as property into rescuing them from parental assault. The Cleveland Report in 1987 was praised for recognizing that 'the child is a person – not an object of concern'.[8] Yet it did not recognize that children's ambiguous status in society relates to their mistreatment and urgently needs to be addressed.[9] Child abuse is endemic, rather than a series of aberrant actions by pathological individuals. It is encouraged by beliefs about adults' rights over children,[10] 'original sin' and not 'sparing the rod',[11] seeing the child as not quite human but 'a mixture of expensive nuisance, slave and super-pet',[12] and parents' expectations of a 'perfect baby' which are inevitably disappointed.[13] There is growing concern about the rights of children in care, but this stems from scandals about severe mistreatment.[14] As shown later, children in hospital have certain autonomy rights, but schools deny basic rights to their pupils,[15] and are imposing unprecedented amounts of compulsory tests and curriculum subjects on them. Parents, not children, are perceived as the consumers of education.[16]

When far more respect is accorded to adults than to children, childhood is seen as a prelude to adulthood rather than a worthwhile time in itself. Medical treatment may then be advised 'as early as possible', in the belief that distress and disruption matter less in early childhood. The future adult's putative interests may also be set in conflict with the child's present needs. (Tina will debate this issue later.) Adults' belief in their superior wisdom is used to justify enforcing a child's obedience. Adults' wisdom greatly benefits children, but not always, and enforcement itself can be harmful. The alternative to force is reason, but adults frequently believe that children cannot reason. Chapter 9 considers force and reason and children's rationality.

## Rights and rationality

The tradition mentioned earlier of respect for rational man's autonomy was founded on the belief that, as man is capable of pure reason and of correctly answering moral questions, his decisions must be respected.[17] Later, philosophers acknowledged that not all moral questions have 'correct' solutions; instead, they advocated liberty itself as the greatest good. 'In the part which merely concerns himself [man's] independence is, of right, absolute. Over himself, his own body and mind, the individual is sovereign',[18] whether he makes wise or foolish decisions. However, children must be protected until they reach adulthood when they are then free to make foolish decisions. The two meanings of competence, wisdom to know the correct decision, or else courage to make a best guess and to take responsibility for mistakes, contradict one another. Yet both are integral to modern meanings of competence. Asking adults when they think a child becomes competent is a kind of trick question which usually ends in contradictions. For example:

> *Int.*: When do you think your daughter was or will be able to decide for herself about the proposed operation?
> *Mother*: Well, now at twelve she is very sensible. I think she could decide now.
> *Int.*: What would you do if you disagreed with her decision?
> *Mother*: I don't think we would disagree, she's very sensible. But then, I suppose if it's life-threatening, I'd want to have the last say – just in case.

The tradition of children's supposed irrationality restricts their opportunities to make major and minor choices, and can result in serious problems. For example, children in care who 'run away' can be locked up without any trial or discussion. Yet punishment does not solve the original problem, whereas assuming that the child has motives, and calmly discussing them, can lead to helpful solutions.[19] Denying children's rationality can trap them into a lethal silence if their protests about violence and sexual abuse pass unheard.[20] One example is 8-year-old Lester, who died after running away from home for the fourth time because of daily beatings. After Lester's earlier attempts to escape, a police surgeon found lesions on him which would have amounted to grievous bodily harm to an adult. Parents are entitled to hit their children, so the surgeon described the lesions as 'trivial' and the police took him back home. Lester's repeated statements that he would rather die than return home were ignored.[21] In 1958, the Lord Chief Justice said that to hear a 5-year-old witness would be 'ridiculous';[22] his opinion was reasserted during an English case in 1987, although witnesses aged 3 and 4 have long been respected in Scotland. Police and social workers criticize the English attitude for leading 'to the abandonment of prosecution for a large number of serious violent and sexual offences against children'.[23]

Children's rights to resources and protection are promoted far more than their autonomy rights, although some conventions enshrine children's rights to freedom of expression, of thought, conscience and religion, and of association.[24] Resources and protection tend to be justified in terms of children's best *interests* usually as defined by adults, in contrast to *rights* as chosen and claimed by the right-holders. Young people are often more concerned about their right as they see it to stay out late with their friends, than about their best interests as perceived by their parents to be safe at home. Experts' advice about child care which used to be framed in terms of 'what is right for children' is being rewritten as 'your child's right to', for instance, music lessons. If the child does not need or want these, such advice plays on fashionable rights language and distorts its meaning. Rights can be claimed in the wrong context. When adults define children's rights, rights language can be more oppressive than other terminology if it suggests freedom and choice when these are actually missing.

A distinction between adults and very young dependent children is obviously needed. Yet distinctions which are too rigid and sweeping, which attribute all wisdom, knowledge and prudence to adults and all folly, ignorance and self-destructiveness to children, do not fit reality. Already handicapped by inexperience, children are further disadvantaged by unfair prejudice. One way to justify rights for children is to question whether right-holders must be so highly rational. As one philosopher remarked: 'if rational is what nineteenth century gentlemen are, then children no less than women will come to grief in the rationality stakes'.[25]

Another philosopher has criticized the idea of rational autonomy, which splits apart the world of reason where we think we can be in control, from the world of feeling where we are driven and constrained by our needs and desires.[26] This split assumes that we can only be rational when we rise above feeling and need. And yet rights take their meaning and are understood through such needs as relief from disease and pain. When rights to medical care are derived from needs, very sick children who would traditionally be excluded from being right-holders as too emotional, can be included *because* of their feelings, and the knowledge they have gained through suffering. This new approach is being widely adopted; just one instance is a recent expert report on pain which stresses that only the patient can know how severe the pain is, and how much pain relief is needed.[27] Needs and rights which arise through the feeling world are often understood through distress and failure, not through reason alone. Yet in this society, professional knowledge is highly valued and 'lay' knowledge is not, academic theory takes precedence over physical and emotional experience. The different sources of insight are too often used divisively, leaving children who try to argue their rights on the grounds of their experience of need at a distinct disadvantage.

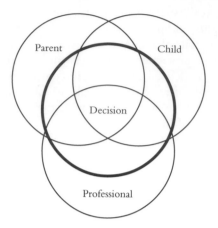

**Figure 2**  Decision making for children as an arena in which rights converge
and conflict

### Rights and power

Three approaches to rights affecting children have been described as parentalist,
interventionist or libertarian.[28] Parentalists believe that parents must decide
for children until they are of age.[29] However, during the past hundred years,
teachers, doctors, health visitors, social workers and psychologists have
gradually encroached on the parents' domain. The second group, interventionists, believe that at times, professionals should take over parents' rights to decide
the child's best interests.[30] Decision making for children can be seen as an
arena in which power shifts back and forth, as it is contested or shared between
parents and professionals and, more recently, children (see Fig. 2). Professionals
also often have to decide when to treat parents as joint or rival or proxy clients
with or for the child, and how to balance the sometimes conflicting needs of
the child-as-an-individual and the child-in-the-family.

Child libertarians consider that children should have the same rights that
adults have as soon as they are old enough to exercise them.[31] One example
is driving a car. If the driving test and penalties for bad driving were made
much tougher, we could allow sensible and skilful children to drive, and clear
the roads of dangerous drivers of any age. Many people disagree and some
become angry at the suggestion. They assume that children may have the skill
but certainly cannot have the sense and maturity to drive on public roads. Yet
we accept cycling, which raises questions about how we value children's safety.
The irritation provoked by the driving example reveals widespread resistance
to children's rights. Even liberal, indulgent adults realize the limits of their
tolerance and respect for children.

## Rights and consent

This brief review is intended to show how children's consent is respected if children's rationality and rights are respected. The right to consent has an impact on all other rights. Consent is about selecting options, negotiating them, and accepting or rejecting them. Beyond making a decision, consent is about making an informed choice and becoming emotionally committed to it. Consent can only happen when there is no force or coercion. It is about deciding one's own best interests and preferences; it determines whether children can decide which rights they prefer to have, or whether adults choose for them. Children may choose different rights from those which adults choose for them, as shown by an assembly of 500 children. The 6- to 8-year-olds voted for the right to choose their own leisure activities and to help weaker people. The 9- to 12-year-olds voted for the right to have a good environment and to help the less well-off. Those aged 13 and over voted to be listened to, to give opinions and to take their place in society.[32] Children's ability to consent depends partly on whether they can speak for themselves, or at least as partners *with* their advocates, or whether adults speak entirely *for* them.

Many adults sincerely believe that: children and adolescents are incapable of adult maturity; adults' decisions should take precedence over children's wishes; if necessary for the child's good, adults' decisions must be enforced; logically, enforcement includes resorting to violence. Yet the concept of children's consent assumes that: at least sometimes, children are capable of adult maturity; children can be right and adults may be wrong; serious disputes can be addressed through discussion rather than enforcement; violence against children is rarely if ever justified.

Rights theories have disadvantages.[33] They are only models which change over time, and are partial tools to help us to understand some aspects of conflicts. They are useful at a political level, such as generally regulating contracts and relations between patients and doctors. But rights theories are too impersonal and confrontational to explain all the varied, complex relationships between children and parents or caring professionals. Rights tend to be based on selfish individualism, and a take-it-or-leave-it pattern of relating, which resolves conflict by ending contact.[34] This does not allow, for example, for the trust which Linda spoke of at the beginning of this chapter. Respect for children's rights is often complicated by loving concern, by parents identifying closely with their child, and by uncertainty about the best choice. Although rights theories are useful for clarifying children's growing independence, they need to be complemented by other theories which appreciate the child–adult interdependence shown in the following two examples.

### Amy and Tina

Efforts to increase the stature of very short children illustrate tensions between their rights and interests, as this section considers in relation to Amy aged 10 and Tina aged 12, both about a metre high. Amy said:

> When I was eight I asked my parents if the doctors could do anything to make me taller. Is there a tablet or anything that would just make me sprout in the night? But no there isn't – yet . . . I visited several hospitals and learnt about surgical limb lengthening. The surgeon explained about the treatment, which would take 15 to 18 months. He talked about the complications such as infection and how they could treat it, and I saw the apparatus they use.

Amy's mother commented: 'This was a decision that only Amy could take. No-one else could do that for her, only she knows how very much she needs it. The treatment is so long and painful, you couldn't enforce it on anyone'.

Later, when she experienced setbacks, such as the soft new bone breaking, and treatment and immobility continuing for far longer than they had expected, Amy and her parents thought that these should have been explained more fully. Yet Amy was convinced that knowing these risks would not have changed her decision, and at 12 years she willingly began the second stage of lengthening. Amy knew what having no treatment would involve: being treated as very much younger than her age, being unable to keep up physically with her friends, or reach items on shop shelves, and countless other daily frustrations. She weighed up the personal and medical factors, her hopes, fears and values, as she described during detailed interviews. Whether she could 'really' understand will be discussed in later chapters, but Amy and her mother, a physiotherapist, believed that she could.

Amy's decision is contentious. Some surgeons refuse leg lengthening to achondroplastic children 'because they really want to look normal but they never can be'. Some think that short people do not have the right to costly treatment, that 'beds should not be used for purely cosmetic lengthening, but for clinical lengthening, to prevent arthritis and future back and hip problems arising from leg inequality'. A paediatrician with achondroplasia argued that leg lengthening is not in children's best interests. He discussed their right, instead of adapting themselves so painfully to fit society, to be respected by society which should adapt to accommodate short people (by altering the design of shops, public transport, housing, and so on). This is the policy of the organization for thousands of dwarfs, the Little People of America[35] and of the American government.[36] Yet despite the access for disabled people movement, British society takes little interest in adapting to non-standard people. Amy found that the play specialist in her ward, who also has achondroplasia, supported her decision, favouring the right to have help in adapting to fit society. The opposite responses of two professionals who shared Amy's condition illustrate uncertainties about how to make a 'wise' choice in Amy's case.

Like Amy, Tina held strong views and expressed them fluently. 'Most of the doctors I go to talk over my shoulder to my Mum and I don't like that. I'd rather they talk to me, 'cos I think, "Cor, well, I'm having the operation, why are you talking to Mummy?" ' Besides being achondroplastic she has dysplasia, or soft, flabby joints, and pseudoarthrosis, congenital bone problems which would make surgical leg lengthening far more complicated. Tina had surgery when 'they'd found that three of the bones at the top of my spine was squashed'. Six months after her operation, Tina discussed height treatment at home with her mother and aunt. She had just been shopping in Oxford Street in her wheelchair with her metal halo fixed to a body plaster, which set her neck at an awkward angle.

*Tina*: I'm happy as I am really.

*Aunt*: In a lot of senses you're not.

*Mother*: She's not happy to be the way she is.

*Aunt*: But she accepts the way she is.

*Int.*: Lots of people say, "Children can't decide for themselves because they'll regret it later".

*Tina*: That's exactly what mum said. But if I make the wrong decision it's my own fault, not my mum's.

*Int.*: What if they say one day, "We could have done something but now it's too late". Do you think you might feel awful?

*Tina*: Well you never know. There might be something, but you can't cure it [short stature] with having that operation.

*Int.*: If there was a helpful treatment, would you say, "Yes I'll have that"? You wouldn't be too scared? [Tina's mother laughs]

*Tina*: Now I know what she's talking about. Injections!

*Mother*: The whole point is that they are trying a new booster of hormone injections. They want to try it out on her for a year. It helps their bones to become stronger and grow. They're doing trials on children who are achondroplastic to see if it helps. They don't really know. When they get the results from trials they suggest Tina has this done, but it means an injection every day. Now I know for a fact, if they was to give her a hormone tablet every day she'd be quite happy to take that. She doesn't want it because it's an injection. But injections are not that painful, it's not going to damage her for the rest of her life. For a year it's not going to hurt to try, especially if it gives her four inches or so. She'll be grateful when she grows up.

*Tina*: You see!

*Aunt*: Which is true, Tina.

*Tina*: Don't you start.

*Mother*: I won't listen to that argument. If it was the leg extensions I could see her point. That has to be her choice, putting up with that thing on your leg and being in a wheelchair for two years, and that long hard painful haul. I wouldn't say, "You've got to have it done". But one injection a day, and her being totally unreasonable about it, just fear of injections. And I've said, "No, you have it done". Until she's 16. But she wants to be able to make the decision herself.

*Tina*: If it was 5 years ago, when I couldn't accept the way I was, then I'd have them, wouldn't I.

*Mother*: Well there's no reason why not now. It won't hurt you.

*Tina*: It would.

*Mother*: That's what worries you. You're not against the odd four inches are you?

*Tina*: Yes. I'd rather stay like me. I don't want false bones and all that stuff.[37]

*Mother*: It's not false. I have to be guided by the doctors, and if they think it's fair enough, it might help.

*Tina*: Yes but they're not sure. My bones are different, they're soft. If anything happens to me it's going to be your fault.

Later her mother returned to Tina's comment, 'I'd rather stay like me'.

I can see her point and to a large extent I agree with her. Society should change to be more open-minded and accept people in all shapes and sizes. But Tina's growth is slowing down and it needs a boost. In adult life she'll suffer from all sorts of problems. You've got the added thing of not having any grip, nothing can improve that, so if we can improve other areas . . . She really is adamant about this hormone, but when I get the results of the study they're doing, then I'll decide. What she doesn't like is that it'll be my decision and not hers until she's 16. And I'll be giving her the injections every day, at first.

Tina insisted that she wanted to adapt her setting rather than herself. She emphasized the difference which adaptations in the house made, with stools so that she could use the kitchen like everyone else.

I was scared of ever being on my own when there weren't no adaptations in the house. I couldn't reach no doors or light switches. I was afraid they'd go out and leave me. I feel much safer now it's adapted.

Amy and Tina both showed impressive confidence, charm and dignity. They liked going out to see their friends in their electric chairs, not seeming to be embarrassed by their ungainly medical apparatus. Although heightening treatment is called 'cosmetic', their main concern seemed to be a complex sense of identity in which appearance was most important for the effect it had on other people's estimation of their ability. Amy was angry to be treated as so much younger than her years; she identified her rights and interests in having treatment. Tina wanted the right to be accepted as herself. They were both ambitious and conscious of their future interests; Tina wanted to be a lawyer and did not see why height should be an obstacle. Tina might seem inconsistent in saying that she would not blame her mother if treatment was withheld, but that she would blame her for enforcing treatment. However, she was consistent in allotting, in each case, the risk of blame to the person who made the decision and in stating her willingness to accept blame for her own mistakes.

Amy's mother reluctantly gave up paid work and coped with much family upheaval during Amy's long treatment. Yet in some ways she had the easier position, because she and Amy agreed, and identified her rights with her interests. Tina and her mother were split in several ways. Tina wanted the right to choose and to safeguard her present identity. Tina's mother felt that she must exercise, in Lord Scarman's words, 'parental right or power of control of the person and property of the child [which] exists primarily to enable the parents to discharge the duty of maintenance, protection and education until he reaches such an age as to be able to look after himself and make his own decisions'.[38] She wanted to safeguard the rights of the adult Tina, and Tina's interests as she might perceive them then, in preference to her present perceptions. A further pressure was that the innovative treatment might not work. Her mother would then have to try to undo any damage done to Tina's self-esteem by persuading her that she would be better if she were taller, and show that she was loved and accepted for herself.

Less than one per cent of children with short stature have hypopituitary problems or are 'midgets' (people under 4' 10" of average proportions).[39] Most have average size head and body but very short limbs resulting from bone anomalies. Yet almost all the medical papers are about the first group who have been treated with hormones for many years. Treatment is increasing for both groups, as medical concepts of desirable height rise, so that in the near future many more children and parents will be faced with dilemmas about whether to accept treatment. Parents try to support children who discontinue treatment which fails, or which they find too distressing. The mother of one 10-year-old who could not tolerate the treatment said:

> He is an exceptional and unique person. He likes to maintain his integrity as a human being, and he felt violated by the way they treated him, dirty. I found that he had put the clothes that he had worn at the clinic and even his teddy in the rubbish bin. I felt his refusal was right. He may have a small body, but he has a *great* personality.

As medicine brings more children inside the range of accepted 'normality', it is harder for those who cannot or will not fit in to have their rights and interests respected as children and as adults. 'Best interests' and rights in such dilemmas as 'cosmetic' treatment and risky medical trials are hotly disputed in every age group. There is no clear evidence that adults' answers to these dilemmas are wiser than children's answers.

The main reason for denying rights to children is the assumption that children are foolish, and that respecting their autonomy will sabotage their rights to necessary resources and protection. 'Give them a choice and of course they won't have their operation or go to school' are typical arguments. Women were similarly regarded not too long ago. Sensible women ensured their rights to resources and protection by sacrificing autonomy and by obeying their father or husband. Yet in effect they had privileges but no rights, and depended on men's whim or goodwill. Women acquired legal rights to resources, such as equal pay, and to protection, such as from rape within marriage, only after they had gained civil autonomy, such as through the right to vote. The key to respect for all women's rights is respect for their rationality and autonomy, recognition that women are no less rational than men. The key to respect for children's rights is respect for their rationality. Chapter 5 reviews the evidence on children's reasoning. Human rights can be empty slogans unless they are enshrined in law. The next chapter considers how far the law enforces children's rights.

## Notes

1 For debates about children's rights, needs and interests, relative and absolute rights, subjective and objective ones, see Alderson, P. (1992) Rights of children and young people. In Coote, A. (ed.), *The Welfare of Citizens: Developing New Social Rights*, pp. 153–80. London, Rivers Oram and IPPR.
2 Locke, J. (1924) *Two Treatises of Civil Government*. London, Dent; Jordanova, L. (1989) Children in history: Concepts of nature and society. In Scarre, G. (ed.), *Children, Parents and Politics*, pp. 3–24. Cambridge, Cambridge University Press; Grimshaw, J. (1986) *Feminist Philosophers*. Brighton, Wheatsheaf, analyses sexism in rights philosophy.
3 Hendrick, H. (1990) Constructions and reconstructions of British childhood: An interpretative survey, 1800 to the present. In James, A. and Prout, A. (eds), *Constructing and Reconstructing Childhood: New Directions in the Sociological Study of Childhood*. Basingstoke, Falmer Press.
4 Freeman, M. (1983) *The Rights and Wrongs of Children*. London, Frances Pinter.
5 Freud, A., Introduction to Buxbaum, E. (1951) *Your Child Makes Sense: A Guide for Parents*. London, Allen Unwin.
6 Hardyment, C. (1984) *Dream Babies: Childcare from Locke to Spock*. Oxford, Oxford University Press.
7 Plant, R., op. cit., note 1, pp. 15–30, argues that protection is included in the early rights to autonomy. The recent difference is legal recognition of women's and children's rights to protection from assault by men who live with them.
8 Butler Sloss, E. (1988) *Report of Inquiry into Child Abuse in Cleveland, 1987*. London, HMSO.
9 Kessel, R. (1989) (Mis)understanding Cleveland: Foundational issues and the sexual abuse of children. *Paediatric and Perinatal Epidemiology*, 3, 347–52.
10 Violence Against Children Study Group (1990) *Taking Child Abuse Seriously*.

London, Unwin Hyman. The vast majority of cases of violent abuse are by men against women and children.

11 Miller, A. (1985) *Thou Shalt Not Be Aware: Society's Betrayal of the Child*. London, Pluto Press.

12 Holt, J. (1975) *Escape from Childhood*, p. 15. Harmondsworth, Penguin.

13 Sheper Hughes, N. (1987) *Child Survival: Anthropological Perspectives of Treatment and Maltreatment of Children*. Dordrecht, Kluwer.

14 Levy, A. and Kahan, B. (1991) *The Pindown Experience and the Protection of Children*. Stafford, Staffordshire County Council, is one of several reports.

15 Such as what to wear, when to speak, whether to stay inside during winter play hours and many more general rights. Newell, P. (1991) *The UN Convention and Children's Rights in the UK*. London, National Children's Bureau.

16 Department of Education (1991) *Parents' Charter*. London, HMSO.

17 Kant, I. (1984) Groundwork of the metaphysic of morals. In Paton, H. (ed.), *The Moral Law*. London, Hutchinson.

18 Mill, J. (1982) *On Liberty* (1859). Harmondsworth, Penguin.

19 Lindsey, M. (1990) Getting it right for children in care. *Children First*, Autumn, p. 19. London, UNICEF.

20 Kitzinger, J. (1990) Who are you kidding? Children, power and the struggle against sexual abuse. In James, A. and Prout, A. (eds), *Constructing and Reconstructing Childhood: New Directions in the Sociological Study of Childhood*, pp. 157–83. Basingstoke, Falmer Press.

21 Newell, P. (1989) *Children are People Too: The Case Against Physical Punishment*, p. 25. London, Bedford Square Press.

22 The Wallwork Ruling [42 Cr, App. R. 153, 1958].

23 Report of the Advisory Group on Video Evidence (1989) Chapter 5. London, Home Office.

24 United Nations (1989) *Convention on the Rights of the Child*. New York, United Nations.

25 Hughes, J. (1989) Thinking about children. In Scarre, G. (ed.), *Children, Parents and Politics*. Cambridge, Cambridge University Press.

26 Seidler, V. (1986) *Kant, Respect and Injustice: The Limits of Liberal Moral Theory*. London, Routledge.

27 Royal College of Surgeons of England, College of Anaesthetists (1990) *Pain After Surgery*. London, RCS.

28 Franklin, R. (ed.) (1986) *The Rights of Children*. Oxford, Blackwell.

29 Goldstein, J., Freud, A. and Solnit, A. (1979) *Before the Best Interests of the Child*. New York, Burnett Books.

30 Rose, N. (1990) *Governing the Soul: The Shaping of the Private Self*. London, Routledge, critically examines interventionism.

31 Holt, J., op. cit., note 12; Farson, R. (1978) *Birthrights*. Harmondsworth, Penguin.

32 *L'Observatore Romano*, 28 November 1989, p. 12.

33 This section owes much to Mary Midgley's (1989) *Wisdom, Information and Wonder: What is Knowledge For?* London, Routledge; and (1981) *Heart and Mind: The Varieties of Moral Experience*. Brighton, Harvester; and to her lecture at the Institute of Philosophy, London, 10 January 1992.

34 Pfeffer, N. and Coote, A. (1991) *Is Quality Good for You?* London, IPPR, illustrates the limitations of commercial concepts of rights when applied to welfare services.
35 Ablon, A. (1984) *Little People in America: The Social Dimensions of Dwarfism*. New York, Praeger; and (1988) *Living with Difference: Families with Dwarf Children*. New York, Praeger. These two books never mention surgical limb lengthening, but only surgical correction to straighten bent limbs and to alleviate back and hip problems which severely affect Little People. The British orthopaedic surgeons who are so anxious to correct asymptomatic deformities in children in order to prevent arthritis in mid-life do not appear to discuss with families possible long-term problems associated with leg lengthening. This further complicates Amy's decision. The paediatrician's view was likely to have been influenced by this knowledge. However, he had succeeded in public life, whereas the play specialist may have felt more handicapped by her height.
36 The Americans with Disabilities Act (1990) and the merits of importing such regulations in to the UK are argued in Bynoe, I., Oliver, M. and Barnes, C. (1991) *Equal Rights for Disabled People: The Case for a New Law*. London, IPPR.
37 Part of the uncertainty is due to unknown long-term risks which are seldom discussed with patients. From 1959 to 1985, about 1700 children were given growth hormone extracted from the pituitary glands of cadavers. The hormone is now linked to cases of the fatal Creutzfeldt-Jakob disease. Dyer, C. (1992) New cases feared after six die from disease linked to growth treatment. *Guardian*, 3 April.
38 Scarman, L.J. [1985] *Gillick* v. *West Norfolk and Wisbech HA* 3 All ER 421.
39 See Ablon, A., op. cit., note 35. This is an American definition which is disputed by short people who disagree with being labelled as abnormal.

# 4

# CHILDREN'S LEGAL RIGHTS

*At 13 no-one wants to be treated as a child any more. You get tired of people talking as if you're a tot. You want to be involved. If it was left up to me I'd probably have my spine operation, but it wouldn't be left to me. You don't make decisions like that, on your own, until you leave home when you're 18 or 19.*

*(Bridget aged 15)*

*If I didn't want the operation, my parents wouldn't make me have it. If I was going to die they'd make me. It would be the only sensible thing to do, but I'd agree.*

*(Gemma aged 11)*

*I would like to see the age limits completely scrapped, and maturity brought in. As you grow up, your age has a stereotype. I'm trying to escape from that stereotype.*

*(Robin aged 13)*

Laws on children's consent will now be reviewed, to see how they interpret children's rights. 'Nor has our law ever treated the child as other than a person with capacities and rights recognised by law'.[1] Lord Scarman's optimistic view of children's legal rights is challenged by the history of their human rights just reviewed. Until fairly recently, minors under 21 or 18 years of age were legal 'infants' meaning 'without speech' and officially were not heard. The law respected a father's rights to determine his child's fate. If there was no father, until this century English law had thought 'almost exclusively of infant heirs, and had left other infants to shift for themselves and to get guardians as best they might'.[2] The law was mainly concerned to protect property and inheritance, not children.

Anglo-American law's respect for adults' rights to physical and mental autonomy forms the legal basis of adult patients' consent as a defence against assault. 'Every human being of adult years and sound mind has the right to determine what shall be done with his own body'.[3] The Department of Health stated that a competent 'patient has a fundamental right to grant or withhold consent prior to examination or treatment' and 'refusal must be respected'.[4] Children whose minds are judged to be sound have certain autonomy rights, and this chapter summarizes legal debates about children's competence.

## From age to ability

Legal views of children's competence to consent are changing in many countries from an emphasis on a stated *age* of consent to interest in individual *ability or competence*. Laws based on a stated age illustrate the injustice of defining an age of competence. During this century, the age when women could begin to vote has fallen from never, to 30, to 21 and now 18 years. Since 1962, Canada has allowed minors from 14 years upwards rights of consent to medical treatment. Scottish law allows quite extensive common law rights to girls at 12 and to boys at 14, in contrast to the English ages of 14 for boys and variously 12, 14 or 16 for girls,[5] who until 1929 could marry at 12. Many laws state ages from nought to 21 years when children become entitled to certain adult rights. For instance, at 12 years of age, you can buy a pet in England.[6]

By 1991, three US states had a legal age of consent of 19 years, and the others had one of 18 years,[7] but many states allow certain minors the right to consent to treatment without their parents' knowledge. These exceptions depend on the required treatment, not the child's maturity; they include treatment for contraception and abortion, for alcohol and drug dependence and psychiatric disorders. The exceptions may even be said to be defined by immaturity, in that they tend to concern deviant or risk-taking behaviour. The legal exceptions are pragmatic, to enable young people to seek help and treatment which their parents might veto. Yet the questions remain: If 'deviant' minors can consent to abortion, why cannot their possibly more mature and prudent peers consent to appendectomy? An arbitrary 'age of consent' raises the anomaly of the magic birthday. How can someone be an incompetent infant one day, but a mature adult the next?

## The *Gillick* case

Legally effective consent based on competence rather than age would resolve some of these unjust inconsistencies. Yet questions then arise about defining competence. Such questions were discussed in England in the mid-1980s when Mrs Gillick, a Roman Catholic mother of ten children, took her health authority to court. An Act in 1969 had stated:

> The consent of a minor who has attained the age of 16 to any surgical, medical or dental treatment, which, in the absence of consent would constitute a trespass to his person, shall be as effective as it would be if he were of full age; and where a minor has by virtue of this section given an effective consent to any treatment it shall not be necessary to obtain any consent for it from his parent or guardians.[8]

Mrs Gillick wanted to ensure that children under 16 *could not* give consent, something which the Act omitted to state. She was mainly concerned to ensure that children could not have access to advice or treatment for contraception without their parents' consent.

The case went through three hearings. In the first, Justice Woolf was surprised that the law was so vague on children's consent to medical treatment. He ruled that a child under 16 can give a 'true consent' depending on her 'maturity and understanding and the nature of the consent which is required. The child must be capable of making a reasonable assessment of the advantages and disadvantages of the treatment proposed'.[9] Mrs Gillick went to the Court of Appeal and the leading judgment of Lord Justice Parker agreed with her. A girl cannot give valid consent on her own behalf, at least until she is 16. A doctor who treats her without her parents' consent violates the parents' rights and is actually assaulting her.

*Gillick* was complicated by the issue of contraception, and whether doctors were guilty accomplices if girls under 16 used prescribed contraception when having illegal sexual intercourse. Concerned that doctors would refuse to help girls under 16 with contraception for fear of litigious parents, and that teenage abortion and birth rates would rise, the Department of Health (then the DHSS) appealed to the House of Lords. By a three to two majority the Lords ruled that children under 16 can give legally effective consent to medical treatment. Parental power is transferred to competent children, not shared with them. In 1970, Lord Denning spoke of parents' 'dwindling right which the courts will hesitate to enforce against the wishes of the child. It starts with a right of control and ends with little more than advice'.[10] Lord Scarman echoed this view:

> . . . as a matter of law the parental right to determine whether or not their minor child below the age of 16 will have medical treatment terminates if and when the child achieves a sufficient understanding and intelligence to understand fully what is proposed.[11]

It is the doctor's duty to decide when a child patient is competent[12] and, if a competent child wishes to exclude the parents, always to advise that the parents should be involved, but not to enforce this.[13] The Law Lords' rulings in *Gillick* included that: a competent child is one who 'achieves a sufficient understanding and intelligence to enable him or her to understand fully what is proposed'; the child also has 'sufficient discretion to enable him or her to make a wise choice in his or her own interests'. Later chapters will consider children's understanding of medical information and their capacity to make wise choices. The complexity of the *Gillick* rulings is indicated by the length of one legal chapter which discusses this single case in 66 pages.[14] Lawyers have debated the way *Gillick* has redistributed power in the family, away from parents but possibly, regarding medical decisions, towards doctors rather than towards children.[15] However, the law does stress that a decision made under any kind of pressure is not consent.[16]

## The Children Act

The *Gillick* ruling has opened the way for children to have the right to be consulted seriously about all decisions which affect them: medical treatment, residence and contact with their parents, their education, religion and welfare.[17] The ruling was echoed by Parliament in the 1989 Children Act for England and Wales, which has one reference to consent, or rather to refusal. The Act is mainly about children in need of local authority services, and states that when a court orders an assessment, 'if the child is of sufficient understanding to make an informed decision he may refuse to submit to a medical or psychiatric examination or other assessment'.[18] Although publicity for the Children Act included some talk of 'children's rights', the Act does not include the phrase. Instead, there is more concern to emphasize parental responsibilities and economically to curb professional interventions. The Act was influenced by bitter reactions to the Cleveland cases when, on medical advice, social workers removed many children from their homes believing them to be at risk of sexual abuse. Guardians *ad litem*, who now advise courts on whether a child is competent, are concerned that sexually abused children whom they judge to be competent will refuse to be examined from fear or embarrassment, or because of pressure from possibly abusing parents. Crucial evidence which could assist in rescuing the child from an abusive parent may then not be obtained. Others argue that a case seldom rests solely on evidence from one medical examination.[19]

When adults make decisions for and with children, the Children Act repeatedly reminds them to 'have regard in particular to the ascertainable wishes and feelings of the child concerned'. They should also give due consideration 'to the child's religious preferences, racial origins and cultural and linguistic background'. Initially, this looks respectful, but the concepts behind 'wishes and feelings' are rather woolly and emotional compared with lawyers' rational opinions and judgments, and continue traditional prejudices about children's irrational nature. To 'have particular regard' may be nothing more than a gesture; it does not mean 'act upon'. The Act begins by stating that 'the child's welfare shall be the court's paramount consideration'.[20] As discussed earlier, 'welfare' – like 'interests' – when defined by adults, can disregard children's stated preferences and rights. Yet the Act and its numerous training programmes have a growing impact on local authorities, many agencies working with children, and magistrates courts.

## Retracting children's legal rights

Before October 1991, when the 1989 Children Act came into force, the case of *in re* R was heard in July 1991 by the Court of Appeal (which had ruled in favour of Mrs Gillick). R, aged 15 years and 10 months, was thought to be severely disturbed and suicidal.[21] She told her social worker that she had consented to sedation 'because she felt she had no choice, since if she refused they would have injected her with drugs anyway'. When R became a ward of court, the social services department gave permission for doctors 'to administer anti-psychotic medication to her'. Later, on the advice of an experienced social worker, who 'decided that R sounded lucid and rational' at a time when the staff were insisting that she needed anti-psychotic treatment, the local authority withdrew permission for R to have drugs administered against her will.

Her child psychiatrist considered that R 'is of sufficient maturity and understanding to comprehend the treatment being recommended and is currently rational'. Yet he was concerned that she did not realize how much she still needed treatment, to ensure continuing recovery and to control a cyclical illness with violent mood swings. He advised that it was essential that R stay in a psychiatric unit, and only on condition that the unit staff should have 'an entirely free hand in regard to administration of medication to her, whether she was willing or not'. This would be an 'absolutely necessary' last resort at times when she would be unable to give informed consent. The local authority disagreed, but the Court of Appeal ruled that R should be moved from her children's home to the psychiatric unit with authority given to the staff to treat her without her consent if this seemed to them essential.

The leading judgment by Lord Donaldson stated that 'it was far from certain' that R could understand adequately, and therefore she was not 'Gillick competent'. He introduced new concepts into the debate about children's consent.[22] One was the idea of consent as a key which could be turned by the child and by either parent, so that even if one or two refused, a doctor could still proceed safely with the consent of the third. Another new concept was the phrase 'Gillick competent child', by which he meant an intelligent child who could be listened to but overruled like any other child. The actual Gillick ruling treated a competent child on the same level as a competent adult, not on the inferior level proposed by Lord Donaldson, who said:

> If Lord Scarman intended . . . to say that in the case of a "Gillick competent" child, a parent has no right either to consent or to refuse consent, his remarks were obiter[23] . . . Furthermore I consider that they would have been wrong.
>
> One glance at the consequences suffices to show that Lord Scarman cannot have been intending to say that the parental right to consent terminates with the achievement by the child of "Gillick competence" . . . Doctors would be faced with an intolerable dilemma, particularly when the child was nearing the age of 16, if the parents consented, but the child did not. On pain, if they got it wrong, of being sued for trespass to the person or possibly being charged with criminal assault, they would have to determine as a matter of law in whom the right of consent resided at the particular time in relation to the particular treatment. I do not believe that this is the law.

A further view of Lord Donaldson's was that consent is about saying 'yes' but not about saying 'no':

> [Other judges have] decided that a "*Gillick* competent" child has a right to refuse treatment. In this I consider that they were in error. Such a child can consent, but if he or she declines to do so or refuses, consent can be given by someone else who has parental rights or responsibilities. The failure or refusal of the *Gillick* competent child is a very important factor in the doctor's decision whether or not to treat, but does not prevent the necessary consent being obtained from another competent source.

Lord Donaldson asserted the court's right and, in appropriate cases, 'duty to override the decisions of the parents or other guardians, . . . or children who are its wards or in respect of whom applications are made for, for example, section 8 orders under the *Children Act*, 1989'.[24]

Lord Donaldson's arguments about consent as a key, and parents being able to overrule competent children have been criticized as 'wrong'[25] and 'frankly unconvincing'.[26] Just as *Gillick* was complicated by contraception, *in re* R was complicated by mental illness and fluctuating competence, where patients may be in greatest need of treatment when they are least able to have the capacity to consent. Lord Donaldson's statement that R's understanding was 'far from certain' has been criticized as 'too flimsy' a basis for the judgment:

> Given the importance of capacity to consent in protecting a child's, or indeed an adult's, autonomy, there should be a presumption of capacity. This would be the normal principle; where incapacity is alleged it is for the person asserting the allegation to prove it.

R's case could have been discussed within provisions made by the Mental Health Act 1983 (Sections 2,3,5,131) for children and adults, without needing to refer to *Gillick*.[27] Psychiatrists are reluctant to invoke the Act because of adverse effects on patients. Yet patients have greater rights under the Act than when admitted 'voluntarily', which with minors often means with their parents' agreement, and taking children to court can have even worse consequences for them, including stress, stigma and publicity.[28] Critics of the court ruling also assert that it is already a daily responsibility 'to assess the capacity of people of whatever age to make decisions, and [doctors] are trusted to do so . . . (Compare if you will the assumption that the judge is quite competent when it comes to assessing a young person's capacity to take the oath!)'.[29] Lord Donaldson here appeared to be reintroducing a problem which other judges had settled.

Back in 1962, medical guidelines took the notion of assent (at least not saying 'no') as an immature form of consent.[30] Laws based on preventing assault would seem to regard enforcing unwanted treatment as a worse offence than withholding desired treatment. Consent is not just saying 'yes'; it is a considered judgement, an informed choice and a voluntary commitment.[31] These terms lose all meaning and consent is a farce if patients are forced to agree with their doctor.

At present, doctors may proceed if one person with parental responsibility consents and the other refuses to give proxy consent.[32] However, a competent patient's own decision not only carries more weight than proxy decisions but also makes them redundant. One lawyer commented: 'It would certainly be dangerous for a doctor to rely on a parent's consent in the face of opposition by the child'.[33] A QC agreed, concluding her critique of the *in re* R ruling:

> Lord Donaldson's views bring an undesirable uncertainty into this area of law, it remains to be seen whether they are followed, or whether the classic *Gillick* analysis prevails . . . Any doctor would be unwise at the very least to treat a minor who gives an "informed refusal" to the treatment against his or her wishes . . . There will always be cases at the edges where difficult, finely balanced decisions have to be taken . . . It seems to me that the substantive decision in *Gillick*, now incorporated into statute and Government guidance, that doctors must apply their minds to the question of the child's capacity to consent, as opposed to simply relying upon parental consent, stands.[34]

In June 1992, Lord Donaldson made a similar ruling *in re* W. W's parents and more recently her grandfather had died, and foster care had not been satisfactory. W refused to eat, saying that she wanted to live with a family and not in a children's home. Her arms had been encased in plaster to prevent her from removing a feeding tube and damaging herself. As soon as she was 16, she applied to the courts to support her adult right to refuse enforced treatment, under the 1969 Act.[35] As with *in re* R, the evidence and the judges' commentaries show discrepancies. W, her psychiatrist and her barrister Allan Levy QC[36] argued that her condition was not life-threatening, and given time, respect and the care she requested, W would begin to eat again. The judges, and the 'objective legal evidence', dismissed the possibility of time by reconstructing her serious condition as not only a threat to health, but also a threat to life, an emergency.

Again the judges avoided treating W as a mentally disturbed adult who needed enforced care under the Mental Health Act 1983, and treated her as an incompetent child. They ruled that people aged under 18 have no absolute right to make their own decisions on medical treatment. The judges reasserted the medieval powers of the courts,[37] of parents, and local authorities over minors, and stated that W's views 'were of no weight' in the court's decision. The ruling repudiated the Children Act's statement that children could refuse court-recommended medical and psychiatric examination, and that courts should take account of children's views. Commentators deplored the ruling, which set back the rights of all young people more than 20 years, could result in enforced abortions on young women, and is 'entirely out of line with national and international thinking about the place of adolescents in our society'.[38] W preferred not to appeal to the Law Lords who might have given a different judgment, given the uncertainty and change in the law.

### Liberty or protection

Children's rights continue to be an arena for contests between professionals, parents and children. Liberal lawyers interpret the Children Act phrase, 'if the child is of sufficient understanding', with the final *Gillick* ruling, and the UN Convention on the Rights of the Child now ratified by the government, to mean that competent minors can make all kinds of personal decisions. Commenting on *Gillick*, the lawyer John Eekelaar wrote gloomily about conflict between children's right to autonomous choice and to protection: 'there is no room for parents to impose a contrary view, *even if this is more in accord with the child's best interests*' [his emphasis].[39] He wonders whether 'inhibition up to a defined age' such as 16 might not be better, 'in case the failure to exercise restraint unduly prejudices a person's basic or developmental interests'. Yet he stresses that 'capacity' includes maturity in making wise choices, as Lord Scarman ruled, and he concludes that 'children will now have, in wider measure than ever before, that most dangerous but precious of rights: the right to make their own mistakes'.

Others take a more robust view: the only way to develop autonomy is to risk making mistakes; few decisions are so major or irrevocable that they will seriously and permanently harm a child; and age is no safeguard since adults make plenty of errors too. Child and adult patients' autonomy is limited in three important ways. First, in law, no-one, for example, can consent to being maimed without justification.[40] Second, in medicine, patients can only respond to medical proposals, they cannot insist on having interventions which doctors do not wish to provide.[41] Third, philosophically, though autonomy is sometimes defined as freedom from all constraint, the maturity to want to choose is gained through countless cultural influences and values which contribute towards, as well as constraining, each personality. Adults' and children's autonomy is partial and relative.[42]

The *in re* W ruling in July 1992 received very varied responses. Some legal experts attacked the ruling for creating a 'situation which is bound to cause confusion and misery for no good reason' by denying young people rights to consent and refuse.[43] In contrast, the leading paediatric journal published a quick response from a conservative lawyer, stressing that 'the parents' wishes have to be taken into account' without giving this point any legal reference, and concluding that 'the courts would probably override the child's refusal on the grounds . . . that consent and refusal involve different degrees of capacity'.[44] The main effect of the present state of the law on children's treatment is likely to make doctors and parents err on the side of caution, and to override children's refusal, partly for fear of having to be answerable, ultimately, to conservative judges.[45]

## Children as witnesses

The law has contributed to the understanding of children's consent by commissioning research into children as witnesses in court. Their ability to recall and recount events under stress, and to distinguish reality from fantasy, has been investigated. Researchers have also examined egocentricity as a moral and cognitive weakness in child witnesses. Some researchers conclude that the real danger of egocentrism may be that of the interviewing adult who is unable to appreciate the child's view.[46] Even preschool children can be reliable witnesses and can recall and reconstruct central events accurately, when they are carefully questioned, treated considerately, and have a 'support person' present throughout the proceedings,[47] although the legal system at present tends to work against respectful treatment of children at many levels.[48] 'A child should be presumed to be a competent witness, unless there is good reason to reach a different conclusion'.[49] This suggests that as anxious patients they are also likely to be able to understand and remember more information than used to be thought possible.

## Children and bioethics guidelines

Over the past five decades, bioethics guidelines, which have quasi-legal status, have helped to raise standards of consent to medical research and treatment. Treatment and research frequently overlap when medical interventions are being assessed. The place of children as research subjects has changed considerably through the decades. From ignoring or forbidding research on children, guidance moved to permitting it as long as research was first conducted on adults, and then on older children, except for conditions affecting only infants or babies.[50] In a U-turn, a recent report stated that the first experiments are likely to be conducted 'in early childhood and even before birth'.[51]

Research with children is among the most contentious issues in medical research.[52] This is partly due to confusion between research and therapy, the individual and collective needs of children, and the interests of children and of researchers. Guidelines have shifted from primarily protecting research subjects[53] towards advocating research as of direct benefit in itself. To sort out the contradictions in research guidelines, it is necessary to see why they were written and by whom (lawyers, doctors, civil servants); the relative values expressed about research; and the authors' beliefs about children's integrity, ability to consent,[54] interests, and need for protection.[55]

## Interpreting children's medicolegal rights

These qualified rights could more accurately be termed responsibilities:

> No one can *dictate* the treatment to be given to any child, neither court,
> parents nor doctors . . . The doctors can recommend . . . and also refuse
> to adopt treatment . . . The inevitable and desirable result is that the
> choice of treatment is in some measure a joint decision of the doctors
> and the court or parent[56]

and presumably of older child patients – (the ruling concerned a baby). All are
constrained by consideration of the child's best interests. The courts preserve
their wardship powers. They generally support medical powers to administer
only that treatment which doctors choose to offer. *Gillick* recognizes that the
child's right to autonomy is important but balances this with attention to the
child's welfare as defined by the court.[57] Many legal judgments are based on
unusual, complex and contentious cases, so although future law is inevitably
affected by them, generalizations can be invidious. In the present state of flux
concerning children's legal status, the clearest conclusion is perhaps that the
trend towards growing respect for children's rights and abilities will, with setbacks, continue. In time, judges will realize how liberally young children's
rights and choices are respected by growing numbers of health professionals,
as shown in later chapters. However, doctors have more choice than parents
have.[58] Parents must provide health care and seek medical help as much as a
'reasonable parent' would do.[59] They can refuse medical treatment if their
objection is reasonable.[60] Yet they cannot obtain treatment without the agreement of professionals, or insist that it is provided.[61] Intentionally ending a
child's life is outlawed as murder; professionals must provide reasonable *care*,
but their duty to provide medical *procedures* extends only to what a 'reasonable
doctor' would do.[62] Reasonable doctors can recommend or withhold treatment. They may only override the parents' refusal if giving emergency, lifesaving treatment,[63] unless authorized by the court.

The difficulty here is that there is no agreed 'reasonable' standard, and in
disputed cases medical opinions differ. So far, the courts have always respected
clinical over parental judgment, allowing doctors and not parents to be the final
arbiters in treatment decisions.[64] English courts uphold any clinical decision,
as long as a few doctors support it, even if most doctors would disagree. In
contrast, if parents want to prove negligence, they have the virtually impossible
task of showing that no responsible paediatric team would agree with a decision
that has been made for their child.[65] Judges have never ordered doctors to
provide treatment against their clinical judgment.[66]

The courts have been asked to set a standard ruling, either that the court
should always choose life over death (sanctity of life)[67] or that treatment should
always be provided unless the child's life would be 'demonstrably so awful' and
too full of pain and suffering (quality of life).[68] The courts rejected such

general rulings, concluding that each case must be decided on its merits and on the child's best interests as determined by lawyers and advised by doctors. Whereas some believe that clearer general rulings would be fairer, others believe that these would be too impersonal to address the complexities of each case.

The legal bias against parents is still more heavily weighted against children, especially since the 1992 W case.[69] It seems that the door has closed (probably temporarily) on seven years of respect for under-16-year-olds[70] and on 23 years of respect for 16- and 17-year-olds.[71] The judgment treats children as a different species from adults; that the identical action, which would be battery on unconsenting adults, can be legally desirable on unconsenting children. This conclusion implies that children's unilateral refusal cannot possibly be wise, and that enforced treatment either does not harm children or that such harm does not matter (a question discussed in later chapters). Yet in relation to adults, the harm of battery is among the most serious offences against the cornerstone of Anglo-American law, respect for autonomy. The rising levels of reported cruelty and neglect by parents is cited by child advocates as a major reason for respecting children's decisions in preference to their parents'.[72]

Chapters 3 and 4 have reviewed historical and legal views on children's right to choose. Evidence of children's abilities is perceived differently through each person's experience and prejudices. What you find partly depends on what you are looking for. Researchers are prejudiced by their own attitudes towards children's rights as the next chapter on research shows. The chapter considers how research on childhood challenges or supports Lord Donaldson's view that children differ fundamentally from adults, and Lord Scarman's view that certain children are mature and competent.

## Notes

1 Lord Justice Scarman, *Gillick* v. *West Norfolk and Wisbech AHA* [1985] 2 WLR 480.
2 Pollock, F. and Maitland, F. (1968) *The History of English Law*, ii, 444, quoted in Eekelaar, J. (1986) The emergence of children's rights. 6 *Oxford Journal of Legal Studies* 161.
3 Judge Cardozo (1914) In *Schloendorff* v. *Society of New York Hospitals* 211 NY 125.
4 Department of Health (1990) *Patient Consent to Examination or Treatment* HC (90) 22, pp. 1, 5.
5 Kennedy, I. (1988) *Treat Me Right*, p. 82. Oxford, Clarendon Press.
6 Children's Legal Centre (1991) At what age can I . . . ? *Childright*, 73, 11–14.
7 Robinson, R. (1991) Consent and confidentiality for adolescents in the US. *British Medical Journal*, 303, 539.
8 Family Law Reform Act (1969) Section 8.
9 *Gillick* v. *West Norfolk and Wisbech AHA* [1984] 1 All ER 373.
10 Lord Justice Denning, *Hewer* v. *Bryant* [1970] 1 QB 357, 369.
11 *Gillick* v. *West Norfolk and Wisbech AHA* [1985] 3 All ER 423. Children's

independence is recognized in later statute law; when children are capable of consenting to an application to see their health records, parents may only apply with the consent of the child. Access to Health Records Act 1990, Section 4(2).

12 Later specifically stated in Age of Legal Capacity (Scotland) Act 1991, Section 2(4). The validity of a child's consent turns on personal capacity as judged by the 'opinion of a qualified medical practitioner attending him'.

13 The duty is again emphasized in DHSS (1986) HC(86)1. *Family Planning Services for Young People*; Department of Health (1990) *Consent to Treatment*. London, HMSO.

14 Kennedy, I., op. cit., note 5.

15 Bainham, A. (1988) *Children, Parents and the State*, p. 147. London, Sweet and Maxwell.

16 Adults having mental health treatment, like minors, may be assessed for their competence. A clear definition of capacity (I have used competence, the US term) is given in the *Code of Practice Pursuant to Section 118(4) of the Mental Health Act 1983* (1990) London, HMSO. Chapter 15 sets out the basic principles of consent to 'medical treatment', which covers all nursing and other physical interventions (15.3): possessing the capacity to make a choice in relation to a particular proposed treatment (knowing the risks, benefits, alternatives, etc.), understanding that consent is 'voluntary and continuing permission' (15.9), each patient must be informed 'fully, frankly, and truthfully' (15.11), with 'reasonable care and skill' (15.13) and the patient should be told that consent 'can be withdrawn at any time and that fresh consent is required before further treatment can be given or reinstated' (15.12).

17 See Children's Legal Centre, op. cit., note 6.

18 Children Act 1989, Part V, Section 43(8).

19 Robinson, R. (1991) Physical signs of sexual abuse in children. *British Medical Journal*, 302, 863–4.

20 Children Act 1989, Section 1(1)(b).

21 *In re* R. (A Minor) (Wardship: consent to treatment) [1991] 3 WLR 592.

22 These are critically discussed by several lawyers, as summarized, for example, in Montgomery, J. (1992) Parents and children in dispute: Who has the final word? *Journal of Child Law*, April, 85–9. This review includes discussion of respecting children's ability to consent to certain decisions at certain times, disagreeing with Donaldson's view that only complete and permanent capacity can be respected.

23 Extra to the case and therefore not binding on future cases.

24 Donaldson appeared through case law to be trying to rewrite Parliamentary law, by saying that the one mention in the Children Act of allowing a child to decide could be overruled by the courts. The courts preserve their wardship powers which, as shown by cases of consent to the sterilization of incompetent adults, are greater than parental powers; courts can allow treatment which parents cannot.

25 Lawson, E. (1991) Are Gillick rights under threat? *Childright*, 80, 17–21.

26 Douglas, G. (1992) Limiting Gillick. *Bulletin of Medical Ethics*, 75, 34–5.

27 Health Advisory Service (1986) *Bridges Over Troubled Waters*. London, HAS.

28 Anon. (1992) Sectioning is not stigma. *Childright*, 90, 2, puts the arguments against every point made in favour of avoiding sectioning.

29 Kennedy, I. (1988) The doctor, the pill, and the 15-year-old girl. In *Treat Me Right*, pp. 52–118. Oxford, Clarendon Press.

30 Medical Research Council (1962–63) *Responsibility in Investigations on Human Subjects.* London, HMSO.
31 Meanings of consent are discussed in Alderson, P. (1990) *Choosing for Children.* Oxford, Oxford University Press. 'Voluntary' consent is emphasized in the *Nuremberg Code* 1948, and 'informed' consent in the *Declaration of Helsinki* 1964, revised 1989.
32 Children Act 1989, Section 2(7)(8).
33 Douglas, G., op. cit., note 26.
34 Lawson, E., op. cit., note 25.
35 See note 8.
36 Co-author of the *Pindown Report*, Levy, A. and Kahan, B. (1991) *The Pindown Experience and the Protection of Children.* Stafford, Staffordshire County Council, which castigates cruelty by social workers.
37 Bynoe, I. (1993) Legal issues. In Alderson, P. (ed.), *Young People, Pyschiatric Treatment and Consent.* London, Institute of Education.
38 *In re W.* [1992] Weekly Law Report 3: 758–82; (1992) Law Report in *The Times*, 15 July, *Independent*, 14 July; Dyer, C. (1992) Judges reject medical right of under-18s. *Guardian*, 11 July; Braid, M. (1992) Anorexic teenager can be treated against her will. *Independent*, 1 July.
39 Eekelaar, J., op. cit., note 2.
40 Dworkin, G. (1987) Law and medical experimentation: Of embryos, children and others with limited legal capacity. *Monash University Law Review*, 13, 189–208, quotes [1981] All ER 1057.
41 *In re J.* [1991] 3 All ER 930, 934.
42 O'Neill, O. (1984) Paternalism and partial autonomy. *Journal of Medical Ethics*, 10, 173–8.
43 Anon. (1992) Anorexic case will create chaos. *Childright*, 89, 2.
44 MaCall Smith, I. (1992) Consent to treatment in childhood. *Archives of Disease in Childhood*, 67(10), 1247–8.
45 Although so far the courts have always granted power to doctors to treat or to withhold treatment against parents' and children's preferences as *in re R.* (1991) and *in re W.* (1992). In the case of baby J. (June 1992), doctors were allowed to withhold intensive treatment against the mother's requests; a caesarean was authorized by the High Court against the wish of the woman concerned, Mrs S, October 1992. The power of the courts to uphold patients' wishes against medical advice has been described as symbolic rather than actual. Montgomery, J. (1992) The contribution of the law towards raising standards of consent. In Alderson, P. (ed.), *Consent to Health Treatment and Research: Differing Perspectives.* London, Institute of Education.
46 King, M. and Yuille, J. (1987) quoted in Spencer, J. and Flin, R. (1990) *The Evidence of Children: The Law and Psychology.* London, Blackstone Press. For the importance of egocentricity, see Chapter 5.
47 Murray, K. (1988) *Evidence from Children.* Edinburgh, Scottish Law Commission.
48 King, M. and Trowell, J. (1992) *Children's Welfare and the Law.* London, Sage.
49 Scottish Law Commission (1988) *The Evidence of Children and Other Potentially Vulnerable Witnesses*, p. 82. Edinburgh, Scottish Law Commission.
50 British Paediatric Association (1980, revised 1992) *Guidelines for the Ethical Conduct of Research Affecting Children.* London, BPA.

51 Report of the Committee on the Ethics of Gene Therapy (1992) London, HMSO.

52 Neuberger, J. (1992) *Ethics and Health Care*. London, King's Fund, reports that this was the most commonly debated issue in research ethics committees which she observed.

53 Nuremberg Code (1947).

54 Which is still disputed for all under-18s by some lawyers; see Royal College of Physicians (1990) *Research Involving Patients*, pp. 19–20. London, RCP.

55 These questions are considered in Alderson, P. (1992) Did children change or the guidelines? *Bulletin of Medical Ethics*, 80, 21–8.

56 Lord Justice Donaldson, *in re* J. [1991] 3 All ER 930, 934; confirmed *in re* W. (1992) *The Times*, 12 June.

57 As discussed with examples in Montgomery, J. (1992) *Journal of Child Law*, April, 85–9.

58 This summary is influenced by Montgomery, J. (1992) Parents and children in dispute: who has the final word? *Selective Treatment of the Newborn* (unpublished paper).

59 Children and Young Persons Act 1933, Section 1(2).

60 *Oakley* v. *Jackson* [1914] 1 KB 216.

61 The cases on this point concerned limited health resources and postponed operation, not the issue of withholding life-giving, urgent surgery. *R* v. *Central Birmingham HA* (1988) 24–25 November, unreported.

62 *Bolam* v. *Friern HMC* [1957] 2 All ER 118.

63 *Gillick* v. *West Norfolk and Wisbech AHA* [1985] 3 All ER 402, 432.

64 *R* v. *Arthur* (1981) 78 LSG 1341.

65 *Maynard* v. *W. Midlands RHA* [1985] 1 All ER 635.

66 Even if the court believes that treatment should be given, *in re* W. (1992) *The Times*, 12 June.

67 *In re* J. [1990] 3 All ER 930, request made by the Official Solicitor acting for the child.

68 *In re* B. (1981) [1990] 3 All ER 927.

69 *In re* W. (1992) *The Times*, 12 June.

70 *Gillick*; see note 1, op. cit.

71 Family Law Reform Act 1969, Section 8.

72 Lee, C. (1988) *Friday's Child: The Threat to Moral Education*. Northampton, Thorsons, shows how some parents enforce decisions about contraception and abortion on their child which are guided by their own interests and are against the child's.

# 5

# REVIEWING RESEARCH ABOUT CHILDREN

*There was no objective definition of "scientific" and "non-scientific" research. The tendency was for any research involving the use of questionnaires, and submitted by whatever discipline, to be regarded as "non-scientific". Those research ethics committees [RECs] which were largely medically dominated thus tended to class as "non-scientific" a great deal of [psychosocial] research. Discussion often focused on the delivery of "soft data" and on the poor design of questionnaires. [Some doctors] thought the research methods used by other disciplines were inadequate and that the data were not to be trusted. It was therefore remarkable to see other RECs welcome non-medical research, and, in two cases, discuss ways of encouraging more qualitative research on the effects of certain treatments on patients.*[1]

This chapter reviews research about children and ways of hearing or silencing them. Does research provide clear empirical evidence about children's ability to consent? Varying types of research will be considered: 'scientific' or 'hard' and 'non-scientific' or 'soft' research, research which fits children into adult perspectives, or which attempts to understand children's perspectives. There is very little direct research on children's consent but much medical, natural science and social science work indirectly relates to this topic. Rather than reviewing all this research (investigation, measurement, observation, interviews, evaluation, experiment), the chapter mainly discusses its influence on current understandings of children and their consent.

## 'Hard' and 'soft' science

To define science narrowly as investigating 'hard' physical data has several effects on the scientific and public understanding of children and their consent. Vast areas of life, such as personal feelings, experiences, perceptions, motives and relationships tend to be excluded as 'soft'. Yet these areas are integral to consent, so that children's consent has been almost entirely neglected as a research topic. As a part of research method, requesting the consent of child research subjects has only recently begun to be considered. Ethics guidelines reflect the troubling conflict between respecting and using research subjects.[2] At best, requests for consent tend to be inconvenient, at worst they make, for example, covert research impossible. In many schools, experiments in learning methods are conducted without any kind of consent. The convenience to researchers of dismissing children's capacity to consent is an important factor in their neglect of this topic. There is little evidence of children being involved in research as informed and willing partners, to the extent that they influence research methods, theories and conclusions. Such involvement tends to be seen as risking 'contamination', and threatening the objectivity[3] and efficiency of the research enterprise.

'Hard' science follows models of animal research and concentrates on investigating children's physical development and behaviour.[4] When children's personal thoughts and feelings in the context of each individual life are ignored, medical scientists become the sole assessors of treatment. As discussion on evaluating leg lengthening (Chapter 2) shows, medical–physical evaluation alone is far from sufficient. Each child's personal assessment is also important.[5] Like the law which is built on past precedent, natural science tends to be conservative,[6] concentrating on present evidence, the *status quo*, and assuming that one 'correct' scientific analysis is realizable. This approach tends to avoid considering possibilities and alternatives. Scientists are as deeply affected as everyone else by fashionable beliefs, such as that children are incompetent to give consent. By accepting and not questioning common prejudices, partly by default researchers reinforce prejudice against children.

A major aim in research is to discover general laws. Examples such as Harvey's discovery of the circulation of the blood are clearly valuable in understanding and treating children's bodies. General laws are less useful when applied to children's minds; they tend to underestimate children's abilities, motives and informed choices, all important aspects of consent. Instead of being acknowledged as moral agents, children can appear to be blindly driven by their biology, such as when a small boy's love for his mother is seen as an Oedipus complex. Researchers' pursuit of general laws could be termed the Icarus syndrome, after the myth of the boy Icarus, escaping from a labyrinth on wings attached by wax, who flew too near the sun. The wax melted, he lost his wings, and fell into the sea. After assessing data, scientists take flight towards heights of general theories which may have a tenuous link to the evidence. Two such theories from countless examples are that children feel less pain than adults because their nervous system is not fully myelinated, or that babies feel no pain because they have no memory.[7] The theories have been refuted by research[8] and by everyday evidence, yet they still powerfully influence hospital practice (see Chapter 10). Icarus myths on the egocentric and morally immature child and the isolated adolescent will be reviewed later.

People who criticize 'soft' research,[9] which investigates intangible issues such as children's opinions, raise questions which they should have to answer. Do they mean that children's opinions are not worth examining? If so, why not? Or do they mean that the research methods are unsatisfactory? If so, what alternative, effective methods would they propose? Methods suitable for examining microscopic tissue are unsuitable for examining children's hopes and fears. Meanwhile, researchers are developing theories and methods for investigating patients' views, which can result in far richer evidence than assessment of biological reactions alone can provide.

One contribution of 'soft' research is reflexivity, examining the researcher's own motives and reactions. The study of babies and children, for example, is:

> . . . a venture in self-reflection . . . Scientists studying babies do not simply measure and calculate, they take part in a debate about the moral status of human life which stretches back through countless centuries of poetry and religious teaching . . . Scientific observations about babies are more like mirrors which reflect back the preoccupations and visions of those who study them like windows opening directly on to the foundations of the mind.[10]

So the psychologist John Bowlby studying maternal deprivation assumed that the ideal mother–baby relationship mirrors an ideal of the ever-attendant-wife-and-gratified-husband relationship. Psychologist Jean Piaget envisaged the young child as a lonely scientist struggling to solve intellectual problems, isolated from social and emotional ties. Scientists project onto research their own dreams, as when they perceive the human body in terms of clocks, pumps, computers or malleable genes.[11] Earlier chapters on rights and the law have shown how context-bound, partial and disputed adults' perceptions of children inevitably are; scientists are influenced by their time and place.

## Measuring children, normality and abnormality

Data gathered to classify children into predetermined categories, such as those plotted on percentile development charts, provide research-based knowledge which can help to alleviate and prevent disease and disability. Yet they contribute to narrowing notions of 'normality' and acceptable physique, with an accompanying increase in practical and emotional problems for children deemed to be 'abnormal'.[12] If research takes the individual as the unit of analysis, the social context disappears and the person tends to be seen as the problem. An example of such victim-blaming is given by a government survey of disabled adults which asks: 'Does your health problem/disability make it difficult for you to travel by bus?' Rewritten by a disabled professor, the revised survey enquires, 'Do poorly designed buses make it difficult for someone with your health problem/disability to use them?'[13] The look-after-yourself health ethic and growing attention to subcellular medicine are both expressions of individualism,[14] which can limit choice for disadvantaged people.

Discriminating notions of normality, pathology and dysfunction governing physical assessments are also applied to children's cognitive and emotional development. Young children are the most intensely examined, controlled and professionally treated social group.[15] Children's services shape and discipline the 'crude raw material' of childhood to produce adults fit for society.[16] When average development is defined as 'normal', children who do not conform to the average – and very few do – can easily be perceived as 'abnormal'. When the descriptive term 'average' changes to the prescriptive term 'normal', professional discourse becomes morally loaded with such injunctions as 'your child "should" be taller/speak more clearly/be more confident', and so on. Parents and children are then liable to become depressed about the child's progress, or to have unduly high expectations which are later disappointed. Either course can threaten children's well-being and freedom of choice.

Ideals of normality fan the flames of parents' potent anxieties from pregnancy onwards.[17] Many children urgently want medical help and are very grateful for it. Yet not everyone shares the same vision of normality, as regards using limbs conventionally, and *looking* like other children. Some disabled children prefer using wheelchairs to callipers (see Sally and Moira later), because this enables them to *behave* more like their friends. 'She's always out in her chair with her friends', said Sally's mother, 'She's not disabled to us, she's normal'. Adults who insisted that Moira use callipers increased her loneliness and frustration, adding social handicap to disability. There are physical benefits when children delay using wheelchairs, but there are also social costs which should be evaluated with the person most directly affected.

Attempts to impose normality were made 30 years ago on children with tiny arms and legs whose mothers had taken the drug thalidomide during pregnancy. In some cases, their feet were amputated in order to fit on long false legs and they were forced to walk on these, although terrified of falling because their short arms could not protect them. A psychologist researching with these children found that they hated the prostheses but that no-one was listening to them. 'At first I felt very lonely. I began to say that we should not be doing this. I was the only adult saying so, and I was very unpopular'.[18] Today, adults affected by thalidomide seldom use prostheses, many use their feet as hands and have devised their own normality. As children, their attempts to use their feet (which adults discouraged) developed into valuable skills. Back pain now appears to be less severe in those who were the first to give up walking on false legs. Beside the millions of pounds spent on 'hard' medical and technical research, almost nothing has been spent on social research and support for people affected by thalidomide. Yet disability is a social and emotional experience rather than a medical one; it can be made worse by medical interventions, including doctors' advice to parents to leave their child in hospital. The history of surgery raises questions about how doctors could have persisted with certain treatments and patients or parents have accepted them.

## Research on consent

Psychological studies of consent tend to measure adult patients' ability to recall and recount the medical explanations they have been given.[19] Little attention has been paid to other elements of consent: how patients evaluate information, draw on their personal experience and values, and arrive at decisions. These activities tend to be vague and immensely varied, slipping through the grid of 'hard' research methods. The activities also elude assumptions underlying most research on consent, such as that doctors are active and patients are passive, that professionals are expert and patients are ignorant, that informed consent is about reasoning which is only obstructed by emotions such as anxiety.[20]

Yet to understand consent, it is first necessary to accept that at least some patients can be active and knowledgeable, decisive and responsible, and that their feelings and experiences can be valuable sources of understanding. To do so involves questioning the current very high regard for professional expertise and the dismissal of lay knowledge. Some doctors dismiss as nonsense the idea that any lay person can give informed consent. To which non-medical people, such as lawyers, reply that informed consent does not require highly specialized medical knowledge. It requires a grasp of the salient issues which a reasonable doctor would tell, a prudent patient would want to know[21] and the individual patient wants to know.[22] However, lawyers also argue that disputed cases should be settled by lawyers or that disputes concerning children should be left to the common sense of judges.[23] Psychoanalytic commentators have stated that parents should always decide for children, provided a psychiatrist ascertains who is the 'psychological parent' or the adult closest to the child.[24] Psychiatrists argue that they should assess cases of uncertain competence to consent. Medical researchers discuss how consent threatens research by lowering recruitment rates, and how consent upsets some patients,[25] and so on. Almost all publications on consent are written partly to stake claims for the author's profession and its unique expertise. Patients cannot claim a professional expertise, and their views are seldom heard, so that by default they seem ignorant and passive when all the professional literature is reviewed. This book aims to redress the balance a little, by reporting young patients' active expertise.

Young patients suffer double discrimination as patients and also as children. The qualities attributed to adult patients – ignorance, inexperience, too much emotion, too little rationality, helpless dependence – are also attributed to childhood. Indeed, the major criticism of doctors by advocates of patient consent is that they are paternalist, treating patients as if they are children.[26] Paternalism is now widely believed to be inappropriate towards adults, but is still accepted for children. Yet paternalism differs from fatherliness, as the gospel story of the prodigal son shows; the good father allows his son to make terrible mistakes but still loves him, combining trust and freedom with support. Paternalism combines mistrustful denial of information and choice with, often covert, compulsion. Researchers' beliefs about children's cognitive and moral development, which promote paternalism and thereby increase doubts about children's abilities to consent, will now be considered.

## Cognitive and moral development

As an institution, childhood (not individual children) is a set of beliefs and practices determining how children are treated and how they respond. In most times and places in the world, after infancy children have not been markedly distinguished from adults.[27] People aged 12 years are treated like adults in one society and as helpless dependants in another, or in the same society. Ann Solberg's research with Norwegian 12-year-olds shows how the ones whose parents expect them to take on adult responsibilities can do so, but the ones who are treated as immature and irresponsible tend to remain so.[28] The view that all children need special care and protection has only taken hold on the public imagination during the past few centuries, mainly in the western world. A huge change occurred in British society during the nineteenth century when all children were confined to school. Formerly streetwise Victorian children were denied 'socially significant activity',[29] and this probably reduced their 'sense of their own value . . . Whatever the compensation, the school put these children into the servitude of a repressive innocence and ignorance'.[30] The rigid age-banding, and schoolteachers' claims that children do not learn unless they are formally taught by experts, are seldom questioned today.

The segregation of children into age and stage groups was further encouraged by Piaget, who believed that children develop through inexorably unfolding cognitive stages, like the physical stages of development which are scarcely affected by external forces. He thought that children can rarely grasp certain concepts before the ages of 7 or 11. For example, in repeated experiments, he asked children to point out a spot on a model of three mountains which could not be seen from certain other sites. Children under 7 years did not solve the puzzle. Piaget then inferred that these children could not appreciate another person's viewpoint and did not have 'role-taking skills'. He labelled them as egocentric,[31] which he had originally set out to prove following Freud's theory that the child is narcissistic.[32] Piaget aimed to examine what children can(not) do, rather than what they might achieve with a little help. He concluded that many children think illogically, instead of looking for their own sense and meaning. He also assumed that limitations resided in the child and not in his own research methods. His findings reinforced children's particularly dependant and infantile status at that time in Europe, and their apparent need for very protective adult control.

Piaget's concepts of morality still influence assessments of children's capacity to make moral decisions. He assumed that social awareness originates in competition, and that morality begins through observing and later formulating rules, which are 'accepted by all'.[33] While he praised 'the splendid codification and complicated jurisprudence' of boys' marble games, Piaget had little time for girls' 'polymorphous and tolerant' games in which older girls flexibly allow younger ones to break the rules, and he dismissed their morality of inclusion. Building on Piaget's theories, the psychologist Kohlberg proposed six stages of moral development from trying to please other people to using abstract universal principles. Many adults never reach the highest stage.[34] If these masters were right, there would be little point in trying to involve children in thinking about consent to surgery, because they would be unable to grasp the basic intellectual and moral concepts. Bioethicists who value respect for autonomy most highly envisage consent as an independent decision, made by the patient without any interference.[35] As shown later, most children and parents we interviewed did not hold this isolationist position. They saw consent as a joint decision, and also held opposite views to Piaget's about girls' relative maturity. However, in the traditions of Piaget and Kohlberg following Kant these interviewees would be classed as immature and therefore incompetent.

Piaget's work, developed in the 1920s and 1930s, has been refuted. Psychologists find that 3-year-olds can solve the abstract mountain puzzle and harder puzzles, too, when they are translated into personal terms of naughty boys hiding from policemen.[36] Experiments with babies have shown that they appear to reason and to link cause and effect in ways which were once thought to be impossible in small children.[37] Detailed observations of 1- and 2-year-olds have found their intense empathy with other people, and their moral appreciation of others' approval or distress.[38] It seems that Piaget could not appreciate the child's viewpoint when designing dull, repetitive tests; he then projected his own egocentrism onto his research subjects. Piaget was so convinced of the young child's egocentricity 'shut up in his own ego [and] following his own fantasy'[39] that he interpreted all his data to support his theories.

Kohlberg's scheme of moral development has been similarly reassessed by the psychologist Carol Gilligan. She agrees that many people, mainly women, seldom progress beyond Kohlberg's third stage of helping and pleasing others. At stage four relationships are subordinated to rules, and at stages five and six morality involves reflective understanding of impersonal universal principles and individual rights.[40] Yet Gilligan questions the hierarchy, saying that level three, a personal caring morality, is not inferior but complementary to Kohlberg's level six of abstract principles. Gilligan's insights have been welcomed for recognizing the mature morality of many women, thus granting them a new moral status. In so doing, her work also recognizes the mature moral understanding of many children.

The psychologist Erik Erikson shared Piaget's and Kohlberg's assumption that increasingly isolated autonomy was essential for adolescents' moral development: 'In order to become conscious of one's ego, it is necessary to liberate oneself from the thought and will of others'.[41] Maturity was therefore seen as a process of growing away from the parents.[42] However, when Terri Apter interviewed mothers and adolescent daughters, many said to her: 'We must be very unusual but we are not growing apart, we're becoming closer'.[43] Apter concluded that the autonomy trajectory does not fit many girls, and possibly many boys. As well as growing in independence, adolescents mature through deepening relationships, fitting Gilligan's concept of a morality based on relationships rather than on rules.

Piaget described his stage theories as real, and directly reflecting 'actual psychological activities' in the child's mind.[44] Yet theories are only patterns describing experience, whether in their narrow sense as hypotheses tested by research, or in their broad sense of working assumptions. Despite recent understanding of children's early intellectual and moral maturing, outdated theories continue to dominate professional and public beliefs about childhood. Developmental theories possibly remain popular because they support psychologists' claim to unique and powerful expertise in testing and classifying children, and interpreting between 'the child's world' and 'the adult world'. For example, the paper 'There's a demon in your belly'[45] ('demon' as a misunderstanding of oedema or swelling) purports to show how children grow through the unrelated Piagetian stages, from early 'magical belief' in the causes of illness, to 'multiple factors' in adolescence. There is no acknowledgement that children tend to believe what adults tell them, that people of all ages have magical beliefs (such as guilt) about illness, and that knowledge dramatically changes through personal experience. The paper reports healthy children's views.[46] It would be more logical to attribute children's misunderstandings not to biological immaturity but to inexperience; young children are like adults handling a foreign language or a new experience with quick-witted inference. Many adults are also confused by medical terms.

Piaget's theories have been used almost as facts on which to found bioethics guidance.[47] In 1989, an example on 'incompetents', referring to Piaget's mountain test, stated:

> Role-taking skills are also thought to be necessary to enable a child to consider as potentially valid both a position presented to him or her by the physician and his or her own, different position, so that the alternatives can be weighed against each other. These skills are undergoing substantial development in the 8 to 11 age period, and are often quite well developed by 12 to 14.[48]

These authors continue with an elaborate analysis of competent thinking. It is perceived as a set of mechanistic skills, isolated from experience, feeling and the social context. The skills include the ability to concentrate,

> to weigh more than one treatment alternative and set of risks simultaneously (i.e. cognitive complexity), ability to abstract or hypothesise as yet non-existent risks and alternatives, and ability to employ inductive and deductive reasoning . . . and abstract concepts in problem solving.

It is questionable how expert in the listed skills people need be to qualify as competent, and whether they actually think in this way. The philosophers label young children as 'incompetents' because they are supposed to be incapable of 'cognitive complexity', to have unstable, transient values, no real concept of 'the good', of death, of their future, or their likely future values.

The children in our study clearly did not realize how incompetent they were supposed to be, because they insisted that research interviews should not be conducted during soap opera viewing times. Almost everyone was enthralled by *Neighbours* and *EastEnders*. Each series shows a large cast connected by confusing inter-marriage and inter-generational networks, and long-standing friendships and feuds, grappling with a constant onslaught of ethical dilemmas. One example is a black headmistress deciding whether to agree to an abortion after her fetus has been diagnosed as having sickle cell disease. Her husband, a church elder, threatens to leave her because he cannot accept abortion. Her children anxiously await her decision. A further complication is that each scenario lasts only a few seconds. A police raid fades into a scene of a teacher reprimanding pupils, followed by an argument about rainforests, then back to the police. Each series demands acute observation, rapid interpretation of numerous understated details, sophisticated knowledge of wide-ranging social issues, and formidable powers of concentration, association and memory. Otherwise, each episode is a bewildering, boring kaleidoscope. Yet children can discuss the characters' biography and motives.

Children's cognitive and moral development is not as inexorably slow as Piaget believed, and their thinking does not fit the abstracted list quoted earlier. Risk and benefit concern actual or potential experiences, and are understood through the imagination, a potent skill in children, but not mentioned in the list of competence skills. Children's well-developed sense of morality and justice is shown, for instance, in their response to *Blue Peter* television charity appeals, and their concern about ecology. Many children adopt lasting moral values, and little is known about how rare or common are precocious examples like Dante's life-long passion for Beatrice, which began when he was 9 years old.

Yet children's abilities and adults' perceptions are partly structured by such beliefs, so that Piaget still leaves a strong practical as well as theoretical legacy. For example, thousands of American adolescents are thought not to have access to necessary health treatment because until they are 18 or 19 they must first obtain their parents' consent. Many young people do not want their parents to be informed about, for example, their alcoholism or HIV status, so they avoid requesting treatment. A Congressional report found that the slight psychological evidence about adolescents' competence to consent to treatment was too varied and inconclusive, and too unrelated to real life situations. Although the report called for young people to be more involved in making decisions about their health care,[49] it recognized that parents' rights would be threatened. The popularity of Piaget's theories has outlasted their credibility perhaps because they are convenient to the most powerful group of all, adults.

Traditional beliefs have to be re-examined if children's abilities are to be appreciated.

### Observing and interviewing children

Gradually researchers are becoming more interested in observing and listening to children. Yet children's views and how they make sense of the world are seldom researched, perhaps because adults have little interest in what children think, children's views are not facts, and rigidly controlled research methods are seldom helpful for eliciting personal views.[50] You might as well use a paper shredder to catch fish. However, children's views have to be understood if their decisions are to be respected.

Ways of recording and appreciating children's views include the following. John Holt studied children learning for themselves, and created a child-centred critique of adults' teaching theories.[51] James Robertson captured on film the child's-eye-view of being in hospital through the scenes and his commentary, in order to shock adults with infants' bewildered distress, and so to stimulate political change.[52] Through psychoanalytical interpretations of history, Alice Miller examined why societies are so cruel towards children and mistrustful of them, and why adults suppress awareness of children's suffering and memories of their own childhood.[53] Virginia Axline explored through therapeutic play the nature of autism,[54] and Dorothy Judd used similar methods to explore with 7-year-old Robert his experience of dying of leukaemia.[55] Although not technically research reports, these books describe detailed and innovative ways of understanding children.

The anthropologist Myra Bluebond-Langner partly shared the private worlds of dying children in an American oncology unit, finding that 3- to 9-year-olds had far more understanding than the adults caring for them realized.[56] Ann Hill Beuf observed children in American hospitals. She notes that the sociologist Erving Goffman criticized mortification rituals in institutions which treated adults 'like children', but asserts that neither should children be treated in this way.[57] Maureen Oswin recorded the subtle, complex emotions and behaviour of children in subnormality hospitals, including some who were inaccurately dismissed as 'vegetables'.[58] Eva Noble, headmistress of a long-stay hospital school, recorded long observations of individual children, showing the boredom, misery and emptiness of the lonely hours in their cots,[59] and compiled a book of expressive poems and drawings by the children.[60]

The psychologist David Bearison felt that, when using only impersonal, statistical data from his 'scientific' research with children with cancer, he was discarding the heart of the work. His book on in-depth interviews with eight children aged 3–19 years vividly conveys their deep need to share their feelings and to be properly informed. 'They didn't want to tell me and that's one thing I hate. I don't care how bad it is, I wanna know what's going on'.[61]

Jill Krementz spent weeks talking with 14 children aged 7–16 years, each with a different chronic illness or disability. Eight-year-old Lauren illustrates how mature and eloquent the children are. She has juvenile rheumatoid arthritis and believes, 'My responsibility is to take care of myself'. She explains her drugs and exercises and their good and bad effects, her differences from other children and how she copes with these, and her family life and ambitions.[62] Research with children in local authority care illustrates wide differences between adults' and children's beliefs, the importance of taking time to listen to children and of encouraging them to share in making personal decisions.[63] In one psychology project, 60 girls aged 4 years in turn wore a dress holding a tape-recorder while they were at nursery school in the morning and at home in the afternoon.[64] The girls constantly questioned their mothers about a vast range of topics: Does the Queen always wear a crown? How do ships float? They learned in a far richer way from their mothers than from their teachers, and were active learners instead of depending on being professionally taught. The findings have implications for health treatment, research and education. Mothers and children are the main providers of child health care,[65] and they become knowledgeable through experience. The girls' curiosity suggests that patients tend to be full of questions but, as in the girls' relationship with their teachers, patients say little to doctors, giving professionals the impression that they are uninterested or ignorant.

The above examples illustrate how acutely aware many young children are, how potently they express themselves through their words and behaviour, and how much they need to be listened to and respected. Many of the examples also show how adults who listen to distressed children often have to cope with their own pain and difficulty, and examine their own responses in order to understand more clearly what the children are telling them. They also often have to overcome taboos and prejudices. Bluebond-Langner resisted the hospital staff's insistence that she should wear a nurse's uniform, and identify with the adults which would have made her work impossible.

Interpretive research methods are more likely than 'hard' methods to elicit children's views. Adults' views are not seen as necessarily more valid than children's views. Uncertainty, emotion, unpredictable change and conflicting opinions are accepted as worth examining, although they cannot be precisely measured or replicated. The researcher–subject relationship is regarded not as irrelevant or potentially contaminating, but as an integral part of the research which encourages or inhibits responses. Observation and informal open-response interviews are partly attempts to soften the 'expert' researcher–relatively 'ignorant' subject relationship into one of some equality and shared discovery, partnership rather than control. Replies are considered in the light of how the very varied respondents understand and make sense of the world, as active subjects rather than passive objects.[66]

## Research on or with children

Although Paulo Bagellardo published his *Little Boke on Diseases of Children* in 1472, interest in childhood disease developed in the nineteenth century when children's hospitals were opened. Research *on* children only began seriously in the twentieth century. Despite the examples just described, it seems that research *with* children has hardly begun, and has not yet influenced mainstream research. Open any paediatric or developmental textbook and you are unlikely to find an individual child named or quoted or whose views are considered. Even progressive multidisciplinary books are much the same. *Listen, My Child has a Lot of Living to Do* is about parents' perceptions of services for their dying children, and professionals' work.[67] *Child Health Matters*[68] assumes that the client of child health services is the mother, although one chapter contrasts mothers' and health visitors' views of 21-month-old children. Health visitors tended to see the child as a project, a passive, pre-social work object to be controlled, disciplined and stimulated. The mothers tended to see their children as active, stimulating and determined, they 'commandeered dustpans, stirred the cake-mix' and did not fit the textbook models. Whereas health visitors valued professional opinions as factual and superior to lay knowledge, the mothers valued their own personal experience and what they learned from their children. The chapter represents a shift towards respecting lay knowledge and experience, opening the way to respect children's as well as parents' views.

One purpose of the above research review is to justify our chosen methods, a mixture of observing, in-depth interviews and quantitative analysis of certain interview replies. In-depth interviews rely on 'grounded theory'; the interest is in generating rather than testing theories during the interviews, and developing and refining these in later interviews:

> Grounded theories can emerge which, instead of forcing data into preconceived "objective" reality, seek to mobilise as a research tool the categories which the participants themselves use to order their experience.[69]

Collecting, analysing and interpreting data are integrated rather than distinct activities, and may be shared with interviewees, such as by discussing meanings in their replies with them. This method is time-consuming in tape-recording, transcribing, collating and analysing masses of informal and varied data. The advantages of the mixed method are that it can examine conflicting meanings, such as of 'competence', and can follow very varied individuals through time.

## Research methods used in the children's consent study

### Interviewing

Interviewing includes observing the context and the people concerned, asking formal questions, encouraging free-response replies, listening to the tone of the replies and noting things that are left unsaid, such as the emotional texture of the talk. Young people's response to us – friendly, suspicious or independent – is likely to reflect their initial responses to doctors and nurses who discuss their treatment with them. Around the interviews in our research, we spent weeks observing in the hospitals. Everyone we met who was affected by the project was given a leaflet, explaining how and why the project was being done.

The 20 pilot interviews covered all the details we needed, and were included in the full study of 120 children. The interview with parents included 47 variables on the family background, and parents' views of their child's experiences, needs and abilities. Each child's first interview included 30 questions about their views of their experiences and interests. The post-surgery interview with the children covered 30 variables about perioperative experiences and preferences, and further views about consent. Follow-up questioning was conducted on average 31 weeks after surgery, with 55 questions about recovery, any help needed and received, and children's views about the outcome. We also asked how families negotiated everyday and medical decisions. Interviews with 70 health professionals covered ten questions, mainly about when they thought children were able to be informed and involved in consenting to surgery, and how they defined and assessed competence to consent.

The interviews lasted between 10 and 120 minutes, on average half an hour. All the interviewees were sent a brief report of the project findings. We used open questions such as 'Why have you come into hospital?' and 'How have you been getting on since I last saw you?', and filled in the 'missing' answers later. Some children preferred more structured interviews, working through the list of questions giving fairly brief answers except when a topic was of extra interest to them. We made copious notes, and one-third of the interviews were tape-recorded – with consent. Tape-recording was useful with younger children, who seemed to rely more than older ones on eye contact and our encouraging nods; these were easier to give if we were not writing. Research suggests that general questions, with minimal prompting, elicit 'the best blend of completeness and accuracy' from adult and child interviewees, including those with learning difficulties. Specific interview questions increase completeness but at the expense of accuracy, particularly with children. 'Children aged 8–12 years, of a wide range of abilities, can be just as reliable witnesses as adults', in free-recall interviews.[70]

### Other questioning methods

Follow-up enquiries were completed with 62 children on average six months later. Some young people lived hundreds of miles from the hospitals, so we interviewed 38 of them at home, five in hospital when they were in for months and three by telephone, besides making many other calls, such as to arrange visits. The children tended to talk very easily, as if they were well used to spending hours on the 'phone. The mother of one 10-year-old commented: 'She likes telephoning. I think you'll get more out of her that way. If you'd come to visit us I think she'd have been more shy talking face to face'.

We also tried postal follow-up enquiries with a small booklet of 55 questions with tick-a-box lay-out and space to add comments. These were sent to 22 children, 16 of whom completed and returned them, with varying amounts of help from their parents. We did not send reminders. When we requested a follow-up interview, there were two refusals who did not want to talk about failed treatment. One other visit which could not be arranged was to Kerry, who died six months after her operation. She helped with the pilot study report, hoping that it would help to improve some aspects of care for future patients. The original research budget was for interviews with a total of 40 children and for 20 follow-up visits. The Liverpool hospital granted extra funds and interviewees responded so helpfully that we were able to complete three times the interviews originally planned. Telephone and postal questionnaire approaches were mainly attempted as experiments. They turned out to be more effective than we had hoped and could usefully be developed in further research projects, at least after contact has been established in face-to-face interviews.

## Talking and drawing

Interviews consist of more than words, and discussion of children's art can illuminate other aspects of their conversation. Jacqueline Goodnow[71] describes the time and effort children put into observing and recording the world, and refining their skill. She shows the form, economy and order in children's drawings, as well as the unity, balance and rhythm which young children quickly learn how to manage. Children create order, solve problems and make sense of the world through their drawing as through their language. Violent drawings can be a harmless way of coping with rage, and so can violent language be, as when John said that he wanted 'to stab' the doctor who would not listen and who was stabbing him. One 10-year-old went through many operations. When asked, 'What would you do if you disagreed with your mum and dad?' (about consenting to surgery), he replied, 'I ought to be the one to decide. I would kill them'. He showed some of his grief and rage that his growing autonomy was frustrated by his condition and frequent surgery. In drawing and talking, children are fresh and inventive, using common symbols to create original work. Phrases such as 'I have a headache in my tummy', instead of being seen as a sign of immaturity, can be seen as an example of the ingenious use of a limited vocabulary.

Judith Rubin sees art[72] as holding a tension between opposites: between rigidity and chaos, discipline and flexibility, free association and critical scrutiny, between passively allowing the subconscious to emerge and actively expressing it. The interview involves similar tensions, and the children indicated awareness of working within them. Some looked uncertain or surprised at certain questions, as if these were too obvious or else were irrelevant.

Eight-year-old Linda asked, 'Why do you want to know?' when I enquired about her school. Elizabeth asked to have extra interviews, but would then wait for me to choose a topic and ask opening questions, setting a framework for her to talk within. When asked, 'How have you been getting on since you came home from hospital?', 10-year-old David folded his hands, took a deep breath and then began a long, detailed and (for our purposes) highly relevant and well-selected account of his recovery. Some people used the interview as a forum to develop or argue over their views. John turned his home interview into an exhibition of all his false legs, acquired over 13 years.

The few drawings we collected were, like the interviews, expressive and structured. A 6-year-old boy, who was too young to be in the study, gave me a picture. His parents were not able to see him during his weeks in London, moving between two hospitals to have spinal surgery. On a hot summer day, he drew himself wearing gloves in a snowstorm, as if to express his sense of helplessness during adversity. Philip, aged 14, began his post-surgery interview with interest, but after a while he found the pain of sitting in a chair was too much, and asked to be helped back to bed. A heavy boy with muscular dystrophy, he needed to be lifted in a hoist. After 30 minutes, the nurses had time to move him, and it took almost another half hour slowly to do so. Philip was patient and dignified in his extreme helplessness. He drew a neat diagram-drawing to explain his spinal fusion; the drawing and his measured speech suggested his efforts to invest order and meaning in his stressful and uncontrollable experiences.

## How do child interviewees differ from adults?

During our project this question became harder to answer. Whereas some researchers treat children almost as a different species, others believe that children do not differ significantly from adults.[73] Any difference lies mainly in the interviewer if she protectively forces children into an adult–child relationship, instead of treating them as mature, competent people. Some children are shy or hesitant, like some adults, but we also met confident, fluent 8-year-olds. Adults tend to make more connections, and to reply in more detail at greater length than very young children.[74] This difference is a matter of degree rather than of kind, and is perhaps less due to immaturity than to children's inexperience. When they are experienced, many give mature replies. The theory that social skills develop through set stages has been criticized by sociologists,[75] psychiatrists[76] and psychologists,[77] who report sophisticated young children negotiating and making sense of the world. Four-year-olds have been found to sustain hour-long, detailed accounts in response to a series of related questions, starting with 'Tell me what you did yesterday'.[78] Two-year-olds can discuss their depression following a disaster.[79] Our requests for accounts of recent experiences elicited fuller responses than directly asking for opinions or personal evaluations, with children and adults. In working as far as possible with children's informed and willing cooperation, we tried to talk on the child's terms, to chat about their lives and interests if they seemed to want to, to gain their confidence and appreciate their viewpoint. Sympathetic and respectful interviewing is obviously important with all age groups. We sat at an equal eye-level, except when a child sitting on a bed looked down on us. Occasionally, we had to reword phrases for younger children, or their parents did this.

### Children and parents

Researchers usually prefer to interview children away from their parents, to 'standardize' interviews. We left children and parents to decide whether to be interviewed separately or together. Asking parents to leave would have implied that we had the right, like some hospital staff, to direct the family, which would have begun an entirely wrong, inhibiting relationship. The more interviewees are left in charge, the more revealing they can choose to be. Also, anxious people in hospital have to observe enough rules, without researchers telling parents whether they should leave or stay. However, some parents and children did constrain one another, and they indicated who tended to be the dominant, subordinate or supportive members of the family, and how they were likely to approach decisions about surgery.

Usually, the parents were interviewed first, alone or jointly with the child, partly to explain the project and ask their consent. A few children who readily agreed to take part in the project, and whose parents were then interviewed in their absence, seemed to become suspicious that we had entered an adult conspiracy against them. It was important to see whether children wanted to be interviewed first. Some parents offered to leave, 'otherwise she'll only look at me for the answers'; some stayed until their child had relaxed and was talking happily. Others stayed nearby. Some interviews developed into conversations with the child and parents working out their answers together, a very few parents took over. One mother dominated her daughter, poking her to answer more promptly or answering for her. Later I tried to get the 10-year-old girl to talk for herself, but she preferred having her mother to answer for her. Home visits showed the range of backgrounds; one day the visit was to an inner-city home with large holes in the floor, and the next day to a mansion with horses in the stable yard.

### Selection and bias

Nurses advised us when they preferred us to avoid certain vulnerable patients. Otherwise, we went round the wards looking for young patients who fitted the age and experience criteria. We did not attempt to obtain a representative or matched sample. Samples carefully selected for class, sex, ethnicity or intelligence are obviously important in research intended to obtain predictable, repeatable results. In order to show that a certain diet benefits boys with cystic fibrosis but not girls, the more carefully selected and matched the groups of patients, the more valid the results. However, we did not do this kind of research. We are not claiming that our study is representative or replicable. In any group of 120 young patients having elective orthopaedic surgery, or of 70 health professionals, we would expect a different spread of replies, although possibly across a similarly wide range. Replicable findings emphasize similarities between people and their common factors. Our research mainly concerns differences among young people in their abilities and interests, the advantages of respecting these differences, and the difficulty of attempting to classify people. Replicable findings tend to measure static, standard responses, but many social processes are dynamic and unpredictable; children may mature or regress.

Our report says little about class, ethnicity and sex for three reasons. First, they are vague concepts. Class no longer necessarily relates to employment, income, housing, intelligence, education, social networks or lifestyle. Ethnicity in Britain is complicated rather than defined by colour, language, religion, place of birth, diet and customs. Sex might seem an obvious variable, yet as gender it becomes ambiguous; do differences between boys and girls relate to nature or nurture? Second, our main concerns are age, ageism and the differences, if any, *between child and adult patients*, before considering class and other ways of explaining differences *between children*. Third, class, poverty, ethnicity and disadvantage are so important that each needs detailed separate studies on how they affect child patients. We have added details, such as some parents' employment, to some examples so that readers can draw their own conclusions about their influence.

Some researchers admit their lack of neutrality, such as:

> My intention is to raise important issues – not to put them to rest. As one involved in children's liberation, as an opponent of the routinization and emotional sterility of American medicine, and as one who has been the mother of ill children, I have been influenced by ideas and events that give this essay the critical and outraged tone that it has at times. I want readers to be aware of this. But I do not want you to think for a moment that I would want it to be otherwise.[80]

Research which takes children's views seriously can seem biased, but it is no more biased than traditional research which ignores their views. All research is biased in that it is undertaken within a certain discipline which concentrates on certain issues and ignores others. Our concerns included the individual child's abilities, views, and past and future life outside the hospital. Having spent time in hospital with our own children, we identified with many of the mothers' views, just as surgeons adopt their profession's viewpoint and language. Reporting people's changing opinions is not a clear factual process. We have tried to be impartial and to acknowledge the problems of trying to pour shifting realities into the concrete mould of a table of figures. Besides declaring unavoidable bias, ways to deal with it are, as far as possible from hundreds of examples, to report those which reflect the range of replies, to set some replies in a numerical framework and to show which replies are unusual.

Consent is understood by seeing how individuals perceive and experience it, as case studies or anecdotes[81] can convey. Although there is a risk of drawing misleading conclusions from individual cases, the risk equally applies to thousands of figures. The anecdote has been called 'the very quintessence of science – and of medical science most particularly'; respect for the anecdote is a means of keeping critical medical analysis alive, as well as of attending carefully to each patient.[82] Anecdotes have been derided as gossip, but they can consider details which many children find extremely important, and which are essential to any comprehensive report of children's views on consent.[83] Case studies prevent knowledge from becoming harmfully and misleadingly impersonal; they also enable research subjects to speak for themselves. However, the 120 life stories we collected spread across the topics of each chapter; the task of selecting and editing the personal accounts to fit into the book has often felt like performing surgery on them.

In conclusion, the history of research shows how perceptions of children are coloured by the researchers' time and place. Traditional methods tend to use children as silent objects. If children are to be heard and understood as competent actors, and followed through the consent process, research methods must be developed further. As shown in later chapters, the evidence that older children differ from adults and that they need different protections and consent procedures is not clear. Since children are so complex, findings from many kinds of research can complement one another. Reviewing various theories of childhood, two authors conclude that there are many conflicting, partial accounts, and that no single account is sufficient.[84] They warn against the dangers of reducing a child to any one model (such as the surgical patient, the research subject, the school pupil, the son or daughter). It is important to respect many aspects of each child's life. The following chapters report the findings of our study, starting with children's expectations before surgery.

## Notes

1 Neuberger, J. (1992) *Ethics and Health Care: The Role of Research Ethics Committees in the United Kingdom*, p. 28. London, King's Fund Institute.

2 This is considered in Alderson, P. (1990) *Choosing for Children: Parents' Consent to Surgery*, Chs 6, 7, 9. Oxford, Oxford University Press.

3 The concept of SOAP – Subjective patients' comments, Objective staff observations, Analysis of causes, Plan of management – is based on the common assumption that scientists' and professionals' views are objective, and that patients' and research subjects' are subjective. Wilce, G. (1988) *A Place Like Home*. London, Bedford Square Press. Yet every viewpoint is partially subjective. If a view is assumed to be objective

because it is held by professionals, children's differing views are liable to be dismissed.

4   Many leading researchers and 'experts' on children, from Darwin onwards, originally worked with animals: Freud with conger eels; Truby King with calves; Piaget with shellfish; Watson, also a biologist, studied children's behaviour but not their minds; Bowlby began with ethology.

5   Eiser, C. (1990) *Chronic Childhood Disease: An Introduction to Psychological Theory and Research*. Cambridge, Cambridge University Press, regrets that 'evaluations sadly lack methodological rigour. It is almost impossible to make even gross generalisations about the relative efficacies of different procedures' (p. 10).

6   Benton, T. (1977) *Philosophical Foundations of the Three Sociologies*. London, Routledge.

7   Eiser, C., op. cit., note 5, reviews research refuting these and other theories.

8   Some scientists still assert that it is impossible to prove that babies feel pain, despite clear behavioural responses, and biochemical and 'massive shock' reactions in babies having surgery with inadequate analgesia. Anand, K., Sippel, W. and Aynsley-Green, A. (1987) Randomized trial of Fentanyl anaesthesia in pre-term babies undergoing surgery. *Lancet*, i, 243–8.

9   Like the REC members in note 1, op.cit. Accusations that research is 'unscientific' tend to confuse 'soft', invisible data, with 'soft' working methods, which are sloppy and biased. It is important to criticize poorly designed research, but it is illogical to confuse the supposed quality of the working methods with that of the data. High and low working standards occur in all kinds of research.

10  Bradley, B. (1989) *Visions of Infancy: A Critical Introduction to Child Psychology*, pp. 9–10. Cambridge, Polity Press.

11  Merchant, C. (1982) *The Death of Nature*. London, Wildwood House.

12  The US National Institutes of Health have stopped enrolment for short but not hormone-deficient children in hormone growth trials, because of protests that short stature was being created as a disease resulting in discrimination and 'gross violation' of ethical principles. *British Medical Journal*, 305, 492–3 (1992).

13  Oliver, M. (1990) *The Politics of Disablement*. Basingstoke, Macmillan.

14  Crawshaw, M. (1992) Clothier: The missing parts. *Bulletin of Medical Ethics*, 79, 15–19, a critique of the Report of the Committee on the Ethics of Gene Therapy (1992). London, HMSO, points out the Report's social context of political individualism, and the consistently anti-disability language.

15  Rose, N. (1990) *Governing the Soul: The Shaping of the Private Self*. London, Routledge.

16  Armstrong, D. (1983) *Political Anatomy of the Body: Medical Knowledge in Britain in the Twentieth Century*. Cambridge, Cambridge University Press. Armstrong shows how medical surveillance, concentrating on child health, was directed towards reinforcing social control of the population. Stacey, M. and Davies, C. (1983) *Division of Labour in Child Health Care*. Coventry, University of Warwick Report, documents the public–private and gender divisions in child health which reinforce men's power over mothers and children. Child health surveillance does not entirely serve children's interests; it began in the early 1900s to improve the nation's stock and ensure a healthy army.

17  Katz Rothman, B. (1986) *The Tentative Pregnancy*. New York, Viking, shows how antenatal screening raises anxiety so that women view their pregnancy as 'tentative',

uncertain of a happy outcome. The medicalized ideal of the perfect child is criticized in Goodey, C. (ed.) (1991) *Living in the Real World: Families Speak about Down's Syndrome*. London, 21 Press.

18  Karin Paulsson, personal communication, Stockholm, 1991.
19  King, J. (1986) Informed consent: A review of the empirical evidence. *Bulletin of Medical Ethics*, Supplement 3; Kaufman, C. (1983) Informed consent and patient decision-making: Two decades of research. *Social Science and Medicine*, 17(21), 1657–64.
20  The arguments, such as that anxiety and anger can further, instead of restricting, understanding, are listed briefly here because they are discussed in Alderson, P., op. cit., note 2.
21  Kennedy, I. (1988) *Treat Me Right*. Oxford, Clarendon Press.
22  Faden, R. and Beauchamp, T. (1986) *A History and Theory of Informed Consent*. New York, Oxford University Press.
23  Dingwall, R. and Eekelaar, J. (1986) Judgements of Solomon: Psychology and family law. In Richards, M. and Light, P. (eds), *Children of Social Worlds*. Cambridge, MA, Harvard University Press.
24  Goldstein, J., Freud, A., and Solnit, A. (1979) *Before the Best Interests of the Child*. New York, Free Press.
25  Taylor, K. and Kelner, M. (1987) Informed consent: The physician's perspective. *Social Science and Medicine*, 24(2), 135–43.
26  The US attack on paternalism was spear-headed by Beauchamp. T. and Childress, J. (1983) *Principles of Biomedical Ethics*. New York, Oxford University Press, with numerous other critics.
27  Aries, P. (1962) *Centuries of Childhood*. Harmondsworth, Penguin.
28  Solberg, A. (1990) Negotiating childhood. In James, A. and Prout, A. (eds), *Constructing and Reconstructing Childhood*. Basingstoke, Falmer Press.
29  Schnell, R. (1979) Childhood as ideology: A reinterpretation of the common school. *British Journal of Educational Studies*, 27, 7–28.
30  Hendrick, H. (1990) Constructions and reconstructions of British childhood: An interpretive survey 1800 to the present. In James, A. and Prout, A. (eds), *Constructing and Reconstructing Childhood*, p. 47. Basingstoke, Falmer Press.
31  Piaget, J. (1924) *The Language and Thought of the Child*. London, Routledge.
32  Bradley, B., op. cit., note 10, p. 86.
33  Piaget, J. (1972) *The Moral Judgement of the Child*. London, Routledge, Ch. 1. Piaget's interviews play out his assumption that competition is as basic to games as to 'discussion in words'; he insistently questions children to trap them into proving his theories, not to listen to their views on their own terms. His theories and methods ignore power discrepancies between researcher and researched.
34  Kohlberg, L. (1981) *The Philosophy of Moral Development*. New York, Harper and Row.
35  Faden, R. and Beauchamp, T. (1986) *A History and Theory of Informed Consent*, p. 257. New York, Oxford University Press, introduce the term 'noncontrol' to emphasize that non-interference is essential.
36  Donaldson, M. (1978) *Children's Minds*. Edinburgh, Fontana.
37  Siegal, M. (1991) *Knowing Children: Experiments in Conversation and Cognition*. Hove, Lawrence Erlbaum Associates, reviews numerous experiments and observations

which disagree with Piaget's findings. Siegal's thesis is that Piaget's questioning broke quantity and quality conventions expected in adult conversations, which Piaget did not think that children would expect. However, the children's sophisticated response to the broken rules confounded his simplistic analyses.

38 Dunn, J. and Kendrick, C. (1982) *Siblings: Love, Envy and Understanding*. Cambridge, MA, Harvard University Press.

39 Piaget, J. (1972) *The Moral Judgement of the Child*, p. 53. London, Routledge.

40 Gilligan, C. (1982) *In a Different Voice*. Cambridge, MA, Harvard University Press.

41 Piaget, J., op. cit., note 39, p. 87.

42 Erikson, E. (1971) *Identity, Youth and Crisis*. London, Faber.

43 Apter, T. (1990) *Altered Loves: Mothers and Daughters During Adolescence*. Hemel Hempstead, Harvester Wheatsheaf.

44 Piaget, J. (1957) *Logic and Psychology*, p. 7. New York, Basic Books.

45 Perrin, E. and Gerrity, S. (1981) There's a demon in your belly: Children's understanding of illness. *Pediatrics*, 67(6), 841-9.

46 One large and important area of research which there is not space to review is that on children's understanding of health and illness and their social construction of illness. This is comprehensively reviewed in Wilkinson, S. (1988) *The Child's World of Illness: The Development of Health and Illness Behaviour*. Cambridge, Cambridge University Press.

47 National Commission for the Protection of Human Subjects of Biomedical and Behavioral Research (1977) *Research Involving Children: Report and Recommendations*. DHEW, 77-0004, Washington, DC; Melton, G., Koocher, G. and Saks, M. (eds) (1983) *Children's Competence to Consent*. New York, Plenum Press; Gaylin, W. and Macklin, R. (1982) *Who Speaks for the Child?* New York, Plenum Press; Kopelman, L. and Moskop, J. (eds) (1989) *Children and Health Care: Moral and Social Issues*. Dordecht, Kluwer; Nicholson, R. (1986) *Medical Research with Children: Ethics, Law and Practice*. Oxford, Oxford University Press.

48 Buchanan, A. and Brock, D. (1989) *Deciding for Others: The Ethics of Surrogate Decision Making*, p. 220. New York, Cambridge University Press, quoting Piagetian psychologists; Grisso, T. and Vierling, L. (1978) Minors' consent to treatment: A developmental perspective. *Professional Psychology*, 9, 412-27.

49 Robinson, R. (1991) Consent and confidentiality for adolescents in the US. *British Medical Journal*, 303, 539.

50 Oakley, A. (1981) Interviewing women: A contradiction in terms? In Roberts, H. (ed.), *Doing Feminist Research*. London, Routledge, explains the irrelevance of detached rigorous interviewing methods when researching personal stories. The same applies to interviews with children.

51 Holt, J. (1964) *How Children Fail*. Harmondsworth, Penguin; (1967) *How Children Learn*. Harmondsworth, Penguin. Holt was inspired by the meticulous childhood study movement, following Darwin and, in 1900, Shinn, M., *The Biography of a Baby*. New York, Houghton Mifflin.

52 Robertson, J. (1958) *Young Children in Hospital*. London, Tavistock, describes the films, their purpose and effects.

53 Miller, A. (1983) *Thou Shalt Not Be Aware: Society's Betrayal of the Child*. London, Pluto Press.

54 Axline, V. (1966) *Dibs in Search of Self*. London, Gollancz.
55 Judd, D. (1989) *Give Sorrow Words: Working with a Dying Child*. London, Free Association Books.
56 Bluebond-Langner, M. (1978) *The Private Worlds of Dying Children*. Princeton, NJ, Princeton University Press.
57 Hill Beuf, A. (1979) *Biting Off the Bracelet: A Study of Children in Hospitals*. Philadelphia, University of Pennsylvania Press.
58 Oswin, M. (1971) *The Empty Hours*. Harmondsworth, Penguin.
59 Noble, E. (1967) *Play and the Sick Child*. London, Faber.
60 Royal National Orthopaedic Hospital School (1981) *Now This Won't Hurt?* Stanmore, RNOH.
61 Bearison, D. (1991) *'They Never Want to Tell You': Children Talk about Cancer*. London, Harvard University Press.
62 Krementz, J. (1990) *How it Feels to Fight for Your Life*. New York, Victor Gollancz.
63 Gardner, R. (1989) *Who Says? Choice and Control in Care*. London, National Children's Bureau.
64 Tizard, B. and Hughes, M. (1984) *Young Children Learning*. London, Faber.
65 Stacey, M. (1988) *The Sociology of Health and Healing*. London, Unwin Hyman.
66 These points are developed through a range of disciplines in James, A. and Prout, A. (eds) (1990) *Constructing and Reconstructing Childhood*. Basingstoke, Falmer Press.
67 Baum, J., Dominica, F. and Woodward, R. (eds) (1990) *Listen, My Child has a Lot of Living To Do: Caring for Children with Life-threatening Conditions*. Oxford, Oxford University Press.
68 Wyke, S. and Hewison, J. (eds) (1991) *Child Health Matters: Caring for Children in the Community*. Milton Keynes, Open University Press, including the chapter by Mayall, B., Ideologies of child care: Mothers and health visitors, pp. 53–66.
69 Glaser, B. and Strauss, A. (1967) *The Discovery of Grounded Theory*. Chicago, IL, Aldine.
70 Dent, H. (1992) The effects of age and intelligence on eye witnessing ability. In Dent, H. and Flin, R. (eds), *Children as Witnesses*. Chichester, John Wiley.
71 Goodnow, J. (1977) *Children's Drawing*. London, Fontana.
72 Rubin, J. (1978) *Child Art Therapy: Understanding and Helping Children Grow Through Art*. New York, Van Nostrand Reinhold.
73 Solberg, A. (1992) *Research with Children*. Paper presented at the University of London, 3 June.
74 Berry Mayall, Institute of Education, London University, personal communication about her interviews with 5-year-olds.
75 Dreitzel, H. (ed.) (1973) *Childhood and Socialization*. New York, Macmillan; Denzim, N. (1977) *Childhood Socialization*. San Francisco, CA, Jossey-Bass.
76 Stern, D. (1977) *The First Relationship: Infant and Mother*. London, Fontana; Wilkinson, S. (1988) *The Child's World of Illness*. Cambridge, Cambridge University Press.
77 Dunn, J. (1977) *Distress and Comfort*. London, Fontana.
78 Solberg, A., op. cit., note 73.
79 Yule, W. (1992) Post-traumatic stress disorders in children. *Current Opinion in Paediatrics*, 4, 4.
80 Hill Boef, A., op. cit., note 57, p. 9.

81 'Anecdote' literally means unpublished, so the examples in this book are not exactly anecdotes.
82 Pickering, W. (1992) The negligent treatment of the medical anecdote. *British Medical Journal*, 304, 1516.
83 Tannen, D. (1991) *You Just Don't Understand: Women and Men in Conversation*. London, Virago, shows how topics which women tend to value in conversation tend to be dismissed as trivia by men. Chapter 10 considers relevant details.
84 Stainton Rogers, R. and Stainton Rogers, W. (1992) *Stories of Childhood: Shifting Agendas in Child Concern*. Hemel Hempstead, Harvester Wheatsheaf.

# 6

## HOPING FOR BENEFIT: CHILDREN'S REASONS FOR HAVING SURGERY

*Children can't possibly decide whether they need an operation. They'll all say "no" because they're frightened.*

*(Surgeon, 1991)*

*Children have no idea about long-term goals. They live in the present, whereas adults can put up with treatment because they understand that it will benefit them in the long run, for years ahead. Children can't see that far ahead.*

*(Hospital teacher, 1991)*

*Well, I might let my son decide about something minor, but certainly not about anything life-threatening, such as if he had appendicitis.*

*(Mother, 1990)*

These were common responses when we asked adults about children's consent. Are they well-founded? The views quoted above imply that children cannot understand adults' decisions, or appreciate their own present or future interests. Yet many young children seem to understand rational explanations, and actively cooperate with their treatment. This suggests that they have to come to an inner decision that it is worth cooperating. Such a decision involves quite sophisticated processes of absorbing, evaluating and comparing information and options. The theme of this chapter is young patients' ability to understand and accept the need for surgery, and their reasons for wanting or refusing treatment.

### Children's understanding of the need for surgery

We asked the 120 young people and their parents before the operation how they hoped it would help, offering a list of possible benefits. The replies are summarized in Table 4. Meanings of 'mobility' ranged from being able to run faster, to being taller so that they could reach high shelves, or to sitting more comfortably in their wheelchair. Some chair-bound children with scoliosis leaned heavily on one arm continuously to balance themselves, and they looked forward to being able to use both hands again freely.

One-third of the children had missed one month or more of school in the

**Table 4** Hoped-for benefits of surgery (totals who replied 'yes')

| Hoped-for benefits | Children (n = 120) | Parents (n = 120) |
|---|---|---|
| To improve: | | |
| Mobility | 81 | 87 |
| School attendance | 25 | 20 |
| Skill in sports | 55 | 45 |
| School integration | 33 | 36 |
| Friendships | 21 | 20 |
| Appearance | 51 | 70 |
| Hopes for career | 20 | 23 |
| To relieve: | | |
| Pain | 82 | 84 |
| Embarrassment | 35 | 45 |
| Anxiety | 40 | 46 |
| Deteriorating condition | 60 | 73 |
| Long-term deterioration | 20 | 26 |

past year, 13 had missed three months or more and one of these had been absent for nine months. Although they were not all keen to attend school, they hoped to be less house-bound. Some longed to be more agile. Wendy, aged 13 years, had scoliosis and came from a 'sports-mad' family. She described herself as a 'gymnastics fanatic' and had sat for years watching her twin sister become an expert gymnast. Others were glad of an excuse to miss games and PE, but their replies suggest that they were also limited in other daily activities which could inconvenience or isolate them. 'School integration' meant being able to join in more activities at school, mainly sport for boys and gymnastics or dancing for girls; two girls who could not bend their legs were embarrassed to sit on a chair when everyone else sat cross-legged on the floor. Krishna wanted to be able to bend his leg when the family sat to pray each morning.

Pain before surgery varied from aching when tired and pain during exercise, to prolonged or continuous severe pain. Helen was too weak to speak above a whisper. Her disability from spina bifida and hydrocephalus had been exacerbated by a brain tumour. After surgery for the tumour she had lost the use of her hands and could scarcely move. Helen's mother said that Helen had loved to write and draw, and after more than 60 operations during Helen's 14 years, her mother was very reluctant to try surgery again. However, the surgeon had suggested trying an operation which might relieve Helen's pain. Helen very much wanted to accept this offer, and so did her father. 'He's fed up with me getting up all through the night to turn her because her pain is so bad', said Helen's mother. Helen smiled and nodded to show her agreement. She had an impressive serenity and despite her experiences she seemed to have retained all her hope and courage. Months later when I 'phoned to ask to visit,

Helen's mother said she did not want an interview. She described the disappointments which some children had to try to accept:

> Nothing is worth it. I've lost faith in everything. I've been waiting three months for her to go in again, but we never hear. She's in constant pain. Her wound is still haemorrhaging and has to be packed. She's lost the ability to sit up now and keeps falling out of her chair. The operation was not a success. It was supposed to relieve pain and it hasn't.

The boys with Perthes also wanted relief from pain. David's mother described months of treatment at his local hospital:

> He was on traction to try to ease the pain. He came home for two days but went back into hospital because he was in so much pain. They gave him a new kind of calliper, a horrific iron frame strapped very tightly at an angle of 35 degrees. He could only keep it on two or three hours at a time, crying with pain. He couldn't go to school. We tried to persevere, to avoid an operation, and I tried to give as little pain killers as possible because they cause stomach ulcers. But we had to ring to make an earlier appointment, and the X-ray showed that in those three weeks on the calliper, much more bone had worn away. We think the calliper had done that. My husband said, "You've used David as a guinea pig", and the surgeon said "We have to try these things out". We'd known it was a new design, but afterwards we felt it was an experiment drawn out too long.
>
> By chance I heard of the Perthes Association. They told me about the leading world specialist at this hospital, so we got referred here. We saw him on a Tuesday, and on the Wednesday David was in here having an arthrogram. The specialist wasn't too pleased with what had been done. He said two or three more weeks could have worn the bone down to nothing. David's lost a lot of confidence, he gets panicky. But this surgeon gives you so much confidence, he sits, and explains and tells you, whereas the other hospital wouldn't give you any answers. There are three other boys there with the calliper and their mothers asked me what to do. I said, "Don't hang about, get a second opinion".

David, aged 10, said that he very much wanted to have surgery. 'Perthes stops the blood going to the bone so it wears away. They're going to build up my hip bone, or I'd have to be in a wheelchair until I'm 20 and then have a bigger operation'. Like other boys with Perthes, after unhelpful treatment elsewhere he was still hopeful, and trusted his new surgeon: 'He's the greatest, the real expert'.

Many children said they hoped that surgery would improve their appearance. Some talked of intense embarrassment about, for example, their limp or a crooked back. 'I do want it doing', said 15-year-old Penny, 'I have a really bad limp, and I can't go to the disco or anything without people skitting me.

The lads are the worst, even the ones that know me'. Eleven-year-old Julie's mother commented:

> I've had absolute hell with her. She's deteriorating so rapidly. She's been frustrated, angry, sad, the lot. It's terrible. Such awful trouble with clothes. Her spine is like a "C", it pushes out her right shoulder and her left hip. You can tell her till you're blue in the face she looks all right. She said, "If I don't have it done, I won't go out of the front door any more". She feels like a freak.

Some hoped that the good effects of surgery would enable them to join in more activities with their friends. Others said that disability made little difference to loyal friendships. Some children said they looked forward to being cured so that they would not have to be anxious any more about their orthopaedic problem and its effect on their life. Others were less willing to discuss anxiety and embarrassment with us than their parents were. Regarding the future, some hoped that surgery would improve their career prospects, such as their chance of finding work, or of having the career they wanted, like 'joining my dad's building firm'. Half the children thought that surgery would prevent their condition from becoming worse in the short term. Some had seen successive X-rays of worsening defects or could feel their condition deteriorating. Children with atrophies and dystrophies were informed about the threat to them of scoliosis. As one said, 'You must have it. Otherwise you'll bend right over and squash your heart and your lungs. And you'll die!' Problems in adulthood which children hoped would be prevented included arthritis, or hip and spine problems resulting from unequal leg length.

During the interviews, some young people seemed reluctant to say that they had problems with friendships or achievements. We sensed that many more interviewees than the overt replies suggested hoped that surgery would enable them to become more popular and successful. Yet we felt that it was wrong to probe. Our research interviews were not therapy sessions and the children had nothing to gain by admitting to us their sense of weakness and failure. Not everyone accepts the tension between research and therapy. A psychiatrist reported revealing replies to his research interviews with children on their depression. When I asked whether the children had found the interviews upsetting, he replied: 'Any interview with me is therapeutic because I'm a psychiatrist'. Yet a psychotherapist who conducted long research interviews with lone twins (whose twin has died) described how devastating such encounters can be. She spent hours after some interviews, helping people to come to terms with the feelings that had been stirred up. She was critical of researchers who depart promptly with their data and 'don't think about the aftermath'.[1] A health visitor researching the sexuality of young people with spina bifida similarly spent long post-interview recovery sessions with many of them, and offered a follow-up telephone service and referral to a specialized counselling service.[2]

We did not have the skill or resources to help people to recover from intrusive interviews, and we left respondents to decide how much they wanted to say. Some spoke willingly in great detail, others said little. Trying to respect privacy presents two main problems. Some young people may have wanted encouragement to say more and have found relief in doing so. And the results of our research probably look unduly bland, underestimating much of the distress which drives young people to want surgery. Like all research findings about people's immeasurable feelings, this report needs to be interpreted cautiously taking the context into account. Many disabled children expend much effort on 'being normal', perhaps to the extent of not consciously acknowledging their hopes for a better life. Some of them seem to cope by casually saying 'dunno' or 'don't mind', to avoid having to think about what is to them unthinkable.

Another complication is that some people attribute their loneliness or failure to a physical defect; they long for surgical correction but afterwards find that they are still lonely for reasons which go deeper than the defect. Our interviews touched the surface of such responses. Six girls said that they hoped that surgery would improve their future relationships, and spoke of their worry that boys were not interested in them, but others may have been too shy to express such anxieties. After she had emphasized that she had no interest in boys or what they thought of her appearance, 15-year-old Bridget was told that she would have to wear a spinal jacket for six months. She looked horrified, and immediately said, 'Then I can't go to the autumn dance!' Monroe, who had further surgery just below the knee where his leg had previously been amputated, denied being affected by his leg. He stumped around on his prosthesis playing football frenetically despite bleeding sores, and he was very keen to talk about football but not about his leg. If the young people had known us better, or had been asked more insistently, it is likely that there would have been fuller discussion of problems and of the hope of relief.

When children and parents shared interviews, their replies possibly underestimated their worries and hopes. We avoided dwelling on parents' responses to topics likely to embarrass or worry the 76 children who were present during all or part of their parents' interviews. Remarks such as 'she is embarrassed but she hates to admit it', or 'he's very worried, you can tell by the way he twiddles his hair, but he insists he's not' were fairly common in the children's absence. During the children's interviews, 39 parents stayed for all or part of the time, which probably affected how much the children wished to talk about their worries. However, some other family members were helpful witnesses. When Amy said, 'Yes, it does hurt quite a lot', her mother added, 'It's agony'. This kind of response encouraged children to speak more fully. Elizabeth's problems with her leg for eight years followed a cardiac catheterization inserted through the groin in her second year. She also had a barely visible harelip. She asked to have extra interviews because she enjoyed them, although she said little about her achievements or anxieties. Her sister told me how well Elizabeth succeeded at school despite opposition. 'She gets "A"s all the time. But all the kids in our street used to shout out at her, "Ugly! Peg leg!" I used to get mad with them and fight them all. It got so bad in the end we had to move to another town.

Elaborating on topics could elicit differing replies. When asked, 'Do you think that having this operation might help you when you go to work in a few years time?', Terry replied, 'No'. Yet later, while talking about becoming a car mechanic, he said, 'Well I suppose if my spine is straighter I will be more fit, and it will help me to do my work better. I am good at gardening now but I have to be careful because of my back'. Semi-structured interviews offer people time to have second thoughts. This raises complications for analysis. The initial quick response could be the best guide to young people's conscious hopes about surgery. Their later thoughts might refer to less conscious hopes, or prompt new motives as they spoke. Simply by asking questions we started new ideas. Table 4 is not therefore presented as a precise summary of 120 children's hopes about surgery, but as some indication of their complex hopes.

Even so, the replies indicate that many children had informed views about how they thought surgery might help them. Orthopaedic problems, being often visible, painful or disabling, are easier for children to understand than certain other conditions. Yet other disorders, though less visible, can make children feel seriously unwell, weak, breathless or sick, so that they long for urgent relief. The 82 young patients who hoped for relief from pain suggest that children needing appendectomy will plead for surgery and not, as the quote heading this chapter assumes, resist it. Some children appreciate their future needs. Ruth, aged 9, said, 'My hip feels all right, but I need to have an operation, or when I'm grown up I'll get arthritis'. Louise who was 8 years old said, 'I hope that when I'm 18 I will look like everyone else'. Amy coped with years of leg-lengthening treatment by 'thinking what it will be like when I'm taller'. Meg, aged 12, believed, 'This operation affects the rest of my life. I want to be able to *do* things'. One father said, 'Of course they can't think a few years ahead, they live in the present. Now I'm pushing forty I'm slowing up and I'm beginning to take more care of my health. Adults can do this, children can't'. Yet this father's concern seemed only to begin when he experienced problems, whereas many children we met were thinking about long-term future plans. One surgeon said:

> I use the analogy sometimes that if you save money you can't spend it now, but you've got it in the future. You're treating the future, not the present. A lot of children can accept that, that it's going to make them better able to deal with things.

However, understanding the need for surgery is not the same as accepting the need, which the next section considers.

## Children's acceptance of the need for surgery

Accepting something as necessary involves some estimation of its worth, and may involve deciding that the risks and pains are worth undergoing in order to obtain the hoped-for benefits. Mentioning benefits differs from wanting the benefit enough to undergo surgery. To gain some measure of their acceptance, we asked parents and children about their views on the timing of the proposed operation, the child's medical and personal need for it, and their willingness to agree to the operation.

One other indicator of acceptance was certain children's referral route to hospital. Referral was usually initially suggested by consultants or family doctors. Yet 17 parents, like David's mother concerning Perthes, thought that 'parent request' was the main reason that the child was referred. Five parents thought that 'patient request' was the main reason. These were two girls who wanted leg lengthening, two girls with scoliosis who persistently asked their parents to request referral, and Elizabeth who had asked not to be referred on to another hospital, but to stay with the consultant she knew.

## Preferred timing of surgery

Most children and parents said that they thought the operation should be 'now' because of the surgeon's recommendation, the child's need or the convenience of the family (see Table 5). Some who replied 'now' had waited a long time, but they thought that this had not harmed the child, and that 'other people are in greater need than we are'. Those who wanted the operation sooner had been on a long waiting list, or had taken months or years to persuade a local orthopaedic surgeon to agree to refer the child for more specialized help. Of the two parents who thought that the operation could be 'later', one said there was no urgent need, and Helen's mother was against her having more surgery.

The asterisk against 'never' in Table 5 denotes that we did not ask this question, but some interviewees spontaneously gave this reply. We avoided asking questions which might sound too negative to families shortly before the child's

**Table 5**  Preferred timing of surgery

| Preferred timing | Children (n = 120) | Parents (n = 120) |
|---|---|---|
| Now | 69 | 78 |
| Sooner | 36 | 39 |
| Later | 7 | 2 |
| Never * | 1 | 1 |
| Don't know | 7 | — |

operation. The results may therefore be more pro-surgery than some respondents actually felt. The mother who volunteered 'never' had two boys, both with spinal atrophy. The elder boy had had a spinal fusion and now Colin, aged 8, was waiting for his. He was 'much less robust than his brother' his mother said, and he looked extremely thin and nervous. She agreed that he needed the operation, but she was exhausted by the effort of supporting him through the experience. Months later, I went to see them at home and his mother told me that she had heard a few days earlier that, as Colin's spine was bending again, further surgery was needed. Later he arrived home on the school bus, like a fragile parcel protected from jolts by polystyrene wedges. After she had unpacked him, we watched television and then his mother broke the news to him. He cried bitterly for a while, then peeped at her through his fingers and asked for an extra, and usually forbidden, biscuit, and they laughed at his opportunism. His mother seemed to have chosen to give the news while I was there as an outsider as a kind of constraint at such a difficult time for them both.

The children who said they 'did not know' left the question of timing to the adults, or they had not been given enough information. Some were still waiting to meet the consultant on his ward round to hear the final decision as to whether they needed surgery and, if so, of what kind. Moira, aged 14, said that she 'never' wanted to have the operation (see Chapter 9). Moira's surgeon agreed with her decision. Children who wanted surgery 'later' did not see any urgency or wanted more time to consider or did not want the operation. Ten-year-old Mike, after 12 operations and many more stays in hospital, said that he hated having operations, and his mother agreed that he was terrified of them. Tony also replied 'later'. He was 15, and had Duchenne's. From other pupils at his school, Tony knew something of what to expect. His mother said:

> He needed a lot of reassurance, 24 hours a day. He was pleased when they cancelled just before the first operation, it gave him another week to build up relations with more people in the ward. They wanted to do a heart scan. They said, "Maybe because of your weak condition you may not be able to take major surgery". He was desperately nervous. He's lost two of his friends since Christmas.

Tony looked very wasted and spoke in a breathless, low voice. He told me:

> I'm so bent over and squashed up, it [the spine] had to be lifted up, but I wanted to put it off to give me more time to get used to the idea. But that may have got my mum anxious. One girl at school had a Stryker bed, a bed that turned upside-down, with a halo and bolts at her feet to straighten her, I was expecting that but I didn't have it.

## Continuing acceptance[3]

Spinal fusions are done in one, two or occasionally three operations a few weeks apart. The young people's courageous acceptance of surgery was clear when they went for the second or third stage. Tony told me, 'My friend had a two-in-one operation. I'd like that. I wish they'd done it to everyone. It's not nice waiting for the second operation, but at least the first was not as bad as I expected'. This is not to say that everyone maintained a heroic calm. They complained, but actual resistance seemed rare. Tony's mother said later:

> We've been together in here for 12 weeks. It's a great strain, and you need lots of tolerance and patience! He moaned a lot, he wasn't well between the ops, he needed turning every half hour because he developed sores. In hospital he was a totally different child, I didn't know him. He was so independent before, but in there it was "Where are you? Where've you been?"
>
> After the first operation it was very, very upsetting. He woke up in intensive care, no epidural fitted on, no pump. He came round in a terrific state of shock, screaming and shouting, with no pain relief because apparently only an anaesthetist could set it up. He was screaming the place down, "Mum, do something, don't just stand there!" Eventually an anaesthetist came, and it took ten minutes more to set up. She apologised, but I've never spent such a traumatic hour in my life. I wondered how Tony could face a second operation, but later he woke up and asked who was shouting. He could hear it, but didn't know it was him. For two days he was pain-free and confused and comfortable, and amazed it was painless. The second time he woke up peacefully, I made sure the pump was there.

Besides surgery, some children feared X-rays, having plaster casts put on and taken off, stitches taken out, and journeys on the trolleys. Tony was extremely worried that: 'my sore could break. They don't come to turn me in the night when I call. I might lie on my back for hours and find it's all broken up. It could so easily break and I'll have to stay in for months'.[4]

The hospital was scattered over a large campus, and Tony dreaded the ride on the hard trolley to other departments. His mother said:

> They go bumping over the drains. It made him vomit and he was in a lot of pain with his sore back. He was complaining loudly. The X-ray lady said, "Be quiet!" There were moments when I felt completely helpless. I couldn't believe why it was taking the porters so long to fetch him back to the ward. Two minutes can seem like 30, it was actually 15 minutes we waited. Next time, I insisted he went on a foam mattress on the trolley. I had to reassure him over and over again. Because of his condition he finds himself so vulnerable. I was vulnerable too every first

time until I got wise. I learnt I can put my foot down. If you say everything with a smile the staff are willing to listen.

Children with muscular dystrophy were afraid of being lifted painfully by the radiographers without support for their legs. 'I shouted at them to stop, I wanted my mum to come in and tell them how to do it, but they took no notice', Kerry said. She was also scared of the plaster frame.

When the kids go to plaster [room] it's done on a frame and it's only got thin bits of leather across it, and I was thinking, "Oh, no, I'll fall through that". I can't support my neck, so the weight just goes flat against whatever I'm lying on. So when they roll me on my front on the bed, I can't breathe properly.

David, like many others, was critical of the bumpy trolley rides and routine use of an oxygen mask. He said:

After the operation, the oxygen mask made me sick. The air had a minty sickening taste, you feel hot and clammy. And then on the trolley there are so many jerking bumps, and that started me being sick. I was sick all night and the next day, and every time I leaned over the bowl blood soaked along the wound and my stitches pulled and hurt. You'd think they would take away that bump at the operating theatre door.

Other children attributed their nausea to the oxygen mask, which was used routinely in only one hospital. The strength of children's overall acceptance of the need for treatment is partly indicated by their endurance of numerous distressing incidents, and the way hospital staff could generally take their compliance for granted.

## Medical and personal need for surgery

The children were asked how much they thought they needed the proposed operation (see Table 6). The six who thought it was optional ('it wouldn't make much difference if I didn't have the operation') included children who

**Table 6** Medical and personal need for surgery

|  | Very necessary | Necessary | Optional | No need* | Don't know |
|---|---|---|---|---|---|
| Parents' views on medical need ($n = 120$) | 75 | 32 | 13 | — | — |
| Parents' views on child's personal need ($n = 120$) | 86 | 28 | 3 | 1 | 2 |
| Children's views on own general need ($n = 120$) | 69 | 39 | 6 | 6 | — |

were having repeated surgery and two who were having plates removed from their hips after successful treatment for Perthes. The six who said there was no need for surgery were: Efua who said no-one had explained her arm lengthening to her; Moira; Eric and George both aged 12 who had repeated operations for congenital scoliosis and did not want a second period in a Stryker bed and halo; and Sharon (see Chapter 2).

Questions to parents divided 'need' into medical need and personal need which took the child's wishes and welfare into account. The operation thought to be personally unnecessary was for preventive hip surgery, and two did not know how their child felt about surgery. Differences between medical and personal need partly reflect parents' views on the differences between adults' and children's values. Some parents felt convinced by the surgeon that the operation was medically necessary but did not feel that their child was convinced. The higher rate of personal over medical need is linked to the cosmetic aspects of much orthopaedic surgery. Leg lengthening to increase height is intended to improve the child's personal life, but does not offer medical benefit.

## Willingness to agree to surgery

We asked parents and children about their emotional commitment, how willing they were or how much they 'wanted' the operation (see Table 7). Some people were angry at the mention of 'wanting'. 'How can you possibly want an operation? They're horrible things!', said Mike's mother. Yet after talking she agreed that she wanted even less that her son should not have surgery. Mike had a genetic disease 'which would have turned him into a vegetable, a physical and mental wreck, by the time he was three'. He had bone marrow transplants to prevent the syndrome from taking full effect. As he told me, 'I had my dad's bone marrow first but it was no good so then I had my mum's and that was good'. At 10 years of age, Mike was quite severely physically affected, with short, tight tendons that pulled his body towards a fetal curve, so that he could not stand upright. He was mentally alert, and when we were talking about the family having chicken pox, he said cheerfully, 'Yes, we've had

**Table 7**   Willingness to agree to surgery

|  | Very willing though anxious | Willing | Not willing | Not sure |
|---|---|---|---|---|
| Parents' own willingness ($n = 120$) | 88 | 16 | 1 | 15 |
| Parent's view of child's willingness ($n = 120$) | 70 | 31 | 3 | 16 |
| Children's stated willingness ($n = 120$) | 65 | 39 | 6 | 10 |

everything except AIDS'. Mike had scars from his many operations but he said he did not mind scars except on his face and hands. Sadly, by his next interview, he had scars on his hands. He hated having operations. His mother said, 'He's one of the first to have this bone marrow surgery and that has helped him to live. Once you've started you've got no option, you have to go on having the operations', and she agreed that was what she 'wanted'. She was worried about what would happen when Mike was old enough to consent to, or refuse, surgery.

Parents were asked about their own wanting or willingness (Helen's mother was not willing), and about their perception of their child's willingness to have surgery. Sharon, Moira and Eric were seen as unwilling and seven parents were not sure how their child felt. The six children who said they were unwilling were Sharon, Moira, Efua, Eric, George and Sam. Sam, aged 12, had been wheelchair-bound since a traffic accident five years earlier. He commented, 'I didn't really want it doing. *They* can all have peaceful and lively lives, I can't. The doctors only talk to mum and dad and don't include me'. These children reported lower rates of willingness than their parents said they perceived.

Most children gave several reasons for wanting surgery, but the two reasons most closely linked to 'willingness' were to relieve pain and immobility. The least acceptable operations were those intended to prevent a future or present problem which hardly bothered the child, or which involved full length traction, or amputation, or when the child felt hopeless. Not everyone had firm, consistent hopes; some felt ambiguous, as Jenni showed (Chapter 2).

In a survey of school pupils,[5] we asked how they would negotiate a range of decisions, including two surgery decisions. One operation was for 'your hip which feels and looks fine [but] will be very painful by the time you are 25. The doctor says you need an operation, and your parents want you to have it, but you feel scared'. The other was a knee operation: 'The doctor says an operation *might* help, but it would be better to do more walking. Then your knee might get better on its own. Your parents don't want you to have an operation. You know that your knee is very painful and that walking makes it worse'. Whereas 80 per cent of the students said that they would agree with their parents and have the hip operation, only 24 per cent said that they would accept their parents' view and not have the knee operation; 76 per cent would try to change their parents' mind in favour of surgery. The survey suggests that, at least for hypothetical surgery, young people are predisposed to believe in its benefits, and are far more likely to consent than to refuse.

The benefits of having surgery, and the converse risks of not having it, are often seen as details which doctors explain to patients. As this chapter shows, many harms and benefits are already of intense concern to patients before they discuss them with doctors. However, hoping for benefit is only part of consent which includes being informed, as considered in the following chapters.

## Notes

1 Woodward, J. (1991) Research with twins, triplets and more. *CERES News*, 9, 3–4.
2 Blackburn, M., Bax, M. and Strehlow, C. (1991) Sexuality and disability. *European Journal of Paediatric Surgery*, 1(1), 37, and personal communication.
3 Compliance or coercion could be more accurate words, yet they reinforce the concept of the passive patient. This chapter is about active patients who, whether through compulsion or choice, at a certain point decide to accept interventions.
4 Tony's fear of his body breaking up may have alluded to his fear of dying. The link was expressed by a father who wrote of finding an abscess in his dying baby's hand 'intensely dispiriting for reasons I can't quite fathom'. He felt that it stressed 'that unless she got better, she would get worse. It also brought home the idea of decay'. Alderson, P., Rees, S. and Comer, B. (1986) *Care of Children Who Died at the Brompton Hospital and Care of Their Families*. Unpublished paper.
5 Concerned that many of the youngsters in hospital had chronic conditions which made them very dependent on their parents, we wondered how their answers might compare with school students aged 8–15 years. We used a 17-part questionnaire to ask how they negotiated decisions and disagreement with their parents in everyday decisions, how they might decide about two kinds of proposed surgery, when they thought they were old enough to see their general practitioner on their own and, finally, when they thought they were old enough to decide about surgery. Four secondary schools and three primary schools returned 983 replies. Alderson, P. (1990) Everyday and medical life choices: Decision-making among 8- to 15-year-old school students. *Child: Care, Health and Development*, 18, 81–95.

# 7

# GIVING INFORMATION: ADULTS' VIEWS

*We knew nothing of our physical condition – visiting surgeons spoke in whispers at the bottom of the bed so we were ignorant of what was happening. The nursing staff were usually far too busy to talk much.*

*(Patricia, a child patient in the 1920s[1])*

*However hard children find information, they find it a lot harder if they think there are secrets.*

*(Family care worker, 1991)*

*I think there can't be a greater shock to a child than to have all these invasive procedures done without any explanation or psychological preparation. Never tell lies. If you do you can't expect children to cooperate in future. Parents can be surprised if they are honest, how well their child reacts.*

*(Clinical nurse specialist, 1990)*

*They can understand about the operation really as young as two, and possibly even younger. If they are going to have an amputation, at two we tell them a story to do with why they are having it, about having a bad leg, or we might go through it with a toy. We discuss it very carefully with the play specialist because it's very tricky. They seem to take it well, and it doesn't seem to be a shock at the time.*

*(Senior psychologist, 1990)*

Before patients can consent they need to be informed. This chapter considers who informs children, when children are old enough to understand medical information, and professionals' reasons for giving information. The professionals' views are drawn from interviews with 70 health professionals (listed in Table 8) working at least partly with orthopaedic cases, with a few exceptions.

## Who gives information?

Since Patricia lived in hospital in the 1920s, attitudes towards informing patients have changed. The *Patient's Charter* states every citizen's right 'to be given a clear explanation of any treatment proposed, including any risks and

**Table 8**   Health professionals interviewed ($n = 70$)

| Discipline | Number |
|---|---|
| Surgeon | 6 |
| Physician | 10 |
| Senior nurse/nurse manager | 15 |
| Ward nurse | 6 |
| Therapist | 4 |
| Social worker | 5 |
| Chaplain | 2 |
| Teacher | 12 |
| Play specialist | 4 |
| Psychologist | 5 |
| Child psychiatrist | 1 |

any alternatives, before you decide whether you will agree to the treatment'.[2] One surgeon said:

> In order to give informed consent, the patient, or parent, must have as much information as possible about every aspect – the actual procedure and exactly what it entails, the aims of the operation, the success rate, any likely complications or risks and the balance between these and the possible benefits. Some of the operations are mainly cosmetic. Everyone must think long and clearly, and make it absolutely clear that this is not for life-saving reasons.

Yet there are no formally agreed methods of informing patients and standards vary widely between consultants: 'Consent is more often honoured in the breach than the observance'.[3]

Whereas adults may be informed in terms which they find hard to understand,[4] great care is often taken by children's ward staff to present clear information, through play, and using toys and pictures to explore children's hopes and fears. They also use wall posters, stories,[5] photograph albums following a child through treatment, hospital play sets, dolls wearing medical equipment, puppets, and so on. Information is combined with reassurance, as when a play specialist illustrated the story of a child going through surgery with photographs of her own small son and daughter as the parents caring for a doll patient. Twelve-year-old Heidi said of her play specialist: 'Angela told me all about the tubes I'd have, and how they'd be taken out afterwards. She showed me on a doll. It was really good'. Later, Heidi said in a pleased tone, when asked about her surgery scar on her back, 'Angela got a mirror and showed me. She said it's a beautiful scar'.

Information is given throughout the treatment by a range of people. Surgeons, nurses, social workers, occupational and physiotherapists, anaesthetists and junior doctors, play specialists and, in cases of difficulty, psychologists and psychiatrists, all give details relating to their specialties. Yet there were often gaps if staff were too busy, or absent, or assumed that someone else had given the details. One father said: 'I told sister we didn't know what was going on. She said, "Everyone comes in to visit beforehand, and they're told then". But loads of kids I've talked to haven't and they don't know what's happening either'.

Less than one in six children said that they had made such a pre-admission visit, either because this was not suggested or the journey was too difficult, or they had already stayed in the hospital, perhaps years earlier. Those who had made a visit found it very helpful.

Much depends on the surgeon's attitude. One surgeon explained:

I am very keen on pre-admission visits. I like to go with the family and introduce them to the ward staff and, if possible, get them to meet another family with a similar problem. I keep a list of families who I know will be happy to be contacted about particular problems, such as amputation. The families are always encouraged to 'phone the ward or clinic with any queries or worries.

I never mention all the possible problems on their first visit. It is too much for them to take in. I mention the possibility and outline of the surgery and encourage them to think of lots of questions before their second visit. I am very careful to note everything that has been discussed so that nothing gets forgotten. I dictate what is going on in the notes in front of parents so they have a chance to hear it a second time.

The surgeons were very helpful to us, in discussing their work and allowing us to observe out-patient clinics and ward rounds. Some consultants felt that other hospital staff understood little. One commented:

The difficulty is that only one person can tell patients and that is the doctor. The nurses, try as they will and well informed as they are, don't know exactly what's going to happen, so perhaps their information is not as accurate as it should be. The senior registrars are probably not as well informed as the nurses. They come not knowing anything about children's orthopaedics and at the end of their six months they *might* be fairly helpful.

The surgeons we observed treated the most complicated and intractable cases. They had exceptional skill and ingenuity at trying out new techniques. Some surgeons were the only specialist of their kind in the hospital, and so were unable to share their patients with consultant colleagues. Many worked in several hospitals, most days packed with teaching and ward rounds, an out-patient clinic, operating, hastily fitting correspondence and meetings into any gaps. They had little time to talk to patients and other staff. Junior doctors were then unable to inform families until the consultant arrived to make decisions shortly before, or even during, the operation.

Some surgeons used a colleague such as a social worker in the clinics to deal with questions. However, a surgeon who told us that he did so was surprised to learn that the social worker had left three years previously, and that families did not have the basic information which he assumed they had. In another hospital, the social workers had formerly taken a large part in informing families and one continued to do so. She arranged pre-admission visits and gave much medical and practical information. Her colleagues criticized this approach, saying that the local authority who employed them had neither the resources nor responsibility to provide such a service, and forbade them from giving medical information because they might become liable in costly litigation cases. Legal writers in nursing journals give similar warnings to nurses not to enter the dangerous arena of medico-legal information, but to leave that to the doctors. A few hospital teachers helped children to do detailed projects on their treatment, but most referred any medical questions back to the nurses.

Parents and children very much appreciated having clear written information. Some were misled, such as about parents' access and accommodation, when they received only a general admission leaflet for adult patients without the extra one for children, or received no leaflet at all. Some mothers were so exasperated by the lack of information that they offered to write leaflets. Much standard information can be recorded in leaflets about the conditions and treatments, the equipment likely to be used, time in hospital, and so on. Leaflets can save staff time and give people something to refer to at need. Some surgeons worried that leaflets could be misleading. Yet the text can emphasize that average or approximate details are given, and that leaflets supplement, and do not replace, discussion.

Children were informed from several sources – from having previous surgery, from the experiences of siblings or friends, and from television. Eight-year-old Linda was 'so hooked on *Jimmy's* [the series about the Leeds hospital] that I have to video it for her if she's out', said her mother. One mother referred to a television documentary about a British boy with cerebral palsy who flew to America for surgery; the surgeon was guided by a computer which informed him precisely which muscles to treat. 'The programme last night was about the same operation which Frank is having today – but without the computer'. Another mother described how,

> We were told that Bridget would have to have spinal fusion with a single rod, her whole spine would be rigid. Then I read in *Woman's Own* that a surgeon here used two rods so that girls could bend their back afterwards. We were terribly relieved that we were able to arrange to fly over here from Ireland.

Several families belonged to voluntary organizations for their child's defect or disease – STEPS for talipes, Scoliosis Association UK, Duchenne Family Support Group, Restricted Growth Association and others. These associations publish detailed newsletters and handbooks written by professionals and parents. At their conferences, families meet and support one another and exchange much practical information. Some self-help groups played an important part in treatment decisions, as already mentioned, such as when 'the Perthes Association told us that the best surgeon in Britain for Perthes was here. So we asked to be referred here'. While some consultants criticize the groups for offering misinformation, others value the contribution of the self-help groups; they give lectures and write for the groups' newsletters.

## Is it worthwhile to inform children?

Health professionals vary in whether they believe it is efficient or effective to spend time informing patients. There is still controversy over how much to tell adult patients, although the medical profession is gradually becoming more informative.[6] Research has shown that when doctors adopt clearer information techniques[7] or give clear written information,[8] patients remember substantially more afterwards. 'Although patients forget a large proportion of what they are told, they tend to remember the most important and relevant parts of the information'.[9] This suggests the importance of helping patients to feel at ease and able to ask the questions which are most relevant to them. Effective communication owes much to the clinician's skill at relating to patients, and belief that it is worthwhile to share information with them.

A few surgeons told us, 'It's well known that patients only remember 50 per cent of what they have been told', adding that therefore it was not worthwhile to say much. The resulting ignorance in the patients reinforces a self-fulfilling prophecy that they cannot understand. Yet some surgeons were resigned to poor communication, assuming that the insuperable problem was patients' inability to comprehend. A surgeon commented:

> You might introduce, two years before a decision is made about leg lengthening, that these are the possibilities, so that they become conditioned to the idea that something is going to be done and have some global concept of what *might* happen. But if you take that down the line to details, immediately you are hitting the block which is that once you mention the word "admission", the parents *cannot remember*. Every other piece of information fades from their mind. If you explain in some detail what the treatment entails first, and *then* say that the child is coming into hospital, about a third to a half goes in, however carefully the doctor explains. Social workers did a very detailed study in my clinic which showed this.[10]

> Once you get to 13 or 14 a lot of girls have surprising understanding. Boys, some at 14. But most of them are rejecting the opinion. They don't want the treatment. What they want is to be normal, and they don't want to face up to that evidence about painful treatment. So the idea of true, informed consent is, I'm afraid, a non-starter.

Many people were grateful, after years of ineffective treatment at local hospitals, to meet this authoritative consultant. Yet when he explained little, the parents had to try to derive confidence from uncertainty while persuading their child to accept a decision. Ruth, aged 9 years, had had years of attempted treatments for congenital dislocation of the hip at the hospital nearest her home 200 miles away. Her father said:

> Well it says here on the consent form which I've signed "exploratory and innominate[11] osteotomy" but I don't know what that means. Ruth's prepared for a correction, but now it's just to be an exploratory arthrogram they say. She had an arthrogram six months ago, and she was vomiting after it and sick for days, so she's very worried that will happen again. We are rather uncertain whether any treatment is necessary, though there was a lot of confidence in what he was saying.

He described Ruth's earlier operations which he believed were unnecessary or 'had failed' and caused her much distress:

> At the time you accept it all, but looking back – that shakes your confidence, we were in turmoil. Today, a nurse came and said, "Would you change the consent form?" Four or five doctors came round but none exactly knew what would happen. I can see the value of him doing the arthrogram himself but it's disappointing that we have to go home and come back in two weeks for the operation. He's not sure if she'll be at home in plaster for four weeks. But she might be on springs and have to stay in bed here for about eight weeks.

Later, Ruth said quite confidently:

> I'm going to have an operation so that my hip bone will go back into place and to make my left leg a little longer, and to take bone from my right hip and put it in my left hip. It will stop me having a slight limp. I don't feel it, but the doctors say I have it, and I'd get pains in my hip when I'm 15 or 16. I think it's better to have it done now. It would be harder to do when my bones have grown. I'm going to have an arthrogram and an operation with a very long name. Last time, the premed tasted horrible, disgusting, like washing up liquid. I'm going to have an injection this time.

Ruth's example illustrates points which apply to many other children we met. She could discuss the 'mechanics' and purpose of the surgery. She was interested in the effects she would experience, such as with the premed. Similarly, 8-year-old Alan reported some understanding of surgery technique and a strong interest in his likely experiences. He had seen his series of X-rays showing differences between the normal and the affected hip. His mother said, 'the ball and socket keep slipping in his left hip. They'll build up the bone. There's a lump on the bone that's not in the right position'. Alan explained:

I kept limping and my hip hurts a lot. It was like Perthes, not quite the same disease, but exactly the same treatment, the doctor said. I'm going for my operation today. They're going to break the bone and then reset it to stop the pain. I've got this big lump on my left hip. I'll have a plaster from here to here [points to ankle and armpits]. I'll be in hospital a week and then go home for 5 weeks. Then they'll break the plaster and I'll have physiotherapy and I might have to stay in hospital. The operation will clear it up completely and when I'm better I'll be able to do more things, run faster and ride my bike again as fast as my friends.

Weeks later Alan said, 'It was sort of useful that they told me what they were going to do in the operation. But I was asleep then so it didn't matter much'.

Ruth's and her parents' ignorance appeared to be due to medical uncertainty rather than to their own anxiety, confusion or denial. The surgeon's view that they would be too anxious to understand suggests that they would remain in a state of suspended rationality for weeks. Although people described initial shock, prolonged emotional confusion was not shown by the parents and children we met. Despite medical uncertainty and earlier failed treatment, Ruth shared the optimism of many interviewees.

Some professionals were concerned that children's insight was limited by the adults concerned. A senior sister said:

I get very frustrated with both doctors and parents. The parents must ask more. They never say, "I don't really understand, can you say that again? Let me think about it". They are slowly getting more confidence, but they will not use their rights. A father recently never asked questions but he was obviously very unhappy with the situation. I couldn't persuade him to talk to the doctor. But the doctors make me cross as well. It is up to them to help the parents ask questions. Most of them don't see it as their responsibility, certainly not a priority. One consultant is different. It's definitely part of his philosophy, he *always* has time to talk to children and parents, and in real practical terms they can understand.

### At what age can children understand?

We did not attempt to test the young patients on their levels of knowledge. There were too many different conditions, procedures and methods of informing them. Instead we asked the adults for their assessments. Parents were asked: 'At what age do you think your child was or will be able to understand the details about the operation about as clearly as you do?' If the parent was a health professional, we added: 'Or about as clearly as an average adult?' We also asked the health professionals stressing that we wanted them to discuss actual cases, not children in general. We wanted to elicit an age when the professional would consider the perhaps rare possibility of mature understanding, rather than

**Table 9**   Adults' views on when certain children can understand medical
information

| Year group cited | Number of replies from: | |
|---|---|---|
| | Parents (n = 120) | Health professionals (n = 70) |
| under 6 | 8 | 17 |
| 6–10 | 49 | 30 |
| 11–15 | 45 | 15 |
| 16+ | 10 | 1 |
| Don't know | 8 | 7 |
| Mean[a] | 11.9 years | 7.3 years |

[a]Mean scores exclude the 'don't knows'.

dismiss it as impossible. We asked: 'What is the youngest age that you have found *some* of your patients can understand the relevant information in a fairly adult way?'

Some adults would reply, 'What do you mean by relevant?' and we asked them what the word meant to them. We were interested in the meanings behind the replies. The question was easier for parents because it was about their own child and the current treatment, and came at the end of an interview about relevant issues. For busy professionals, their often short interview opened with the questions which parents found most difficult (see Table 9).

The ages stated were complicated by:

• many adults not having thought about the issue before, and being surprised by the question;
• many adults preferring to give an approximate rather than a specific age;
• the view that understanding develops gradually so that it is hard to pinpoint a precise time of 'adult' understanding;
• difficulty for parents in remembering how an older child might have understood a few years earlier, especially if they had not had surgery for some years previously;
• difficulty in imagining how soon a younger child might mature;
• uncertainty about how to define and assess understanding;
• beliefs about what children generally ought or could achieve, such as 'not until they start GCSEs'.

The examples of Brenda and Anita illustrate the widely varying views of children's understanding, and how these depend on the adults' working definitions of 'understanding' as well as the child's comprehension. Brenda's mother thought that Brenda could understand about her treatment 'when she was six', at the time of her previous operation. Now aged 9, Brenda was having her third hip operation. 'We took a lot of trouble to explain everything', said her mother. During the interview, the anaesthetist arrived, and before he spoke Brenda said, 'Please can I have gas? I don't like the injection and please can I have the mint flavoured gas like I had last time?' The interview later continued:

> *Int.*: What is the matter with you?
>
> *Brenda*: When I was a baby I had persecuted [dislocated] hips and so I had to have these operations to help me to walk properly. After the first and second operations they put a tube [plate?] in my leg and I think one in my hip as well, and then they put a large plaster on, and I had to lie flat for ages.
>
> *Int.*: What do you feel about having another operation?
>
> *Brenda*: Well it will be worth it if I can do everything my friends do – run, jump, skip. I really like PE but I can't do it properly and they laugh at me and make fun of me. I get out of breath and it hurts and itches if I walk a long way [Brenda was over-weight].
>
> *Int.*: Do you think your operation is necessary, or very necessary?
>
> *Brenda*: It is necessary. I didn't want to have the operation done, Mum persuaded me. I don't know how long I'll be in hospital. I'll be in plaster about six weeks because the older I am, the longer it takes to heal. Carolyn [nurse] told me I'll have a plaster on both sides to my ankle on the left and to my knee on the right.

While some people would say that Brenda's grasp of the technical terms and details was too hazy, others would say that she had a reasonable understanding of the purpose, nature and hoped-for benefits of the treatment.

Anita's mother was a radiographer and Anita, aged 15, planned to be a doctor. She had syringomyelia and had undergone neurosurgery the year before. Her mother said:

> Syringomyelia is caused by Arnold Chirari Malformation [ACM]. The cerebella protrude through the foramum magnum, where the spine is attached to the cranium. ACM causes the flow of cerebrospinal fluid to be interrupted, which causes a cavity in the spinal cord, a syrinx, which causes muscular wastage, sensory loss and maybe scoliosis – it affects people differently. Normally, it presents at 30 to 40 years. It is rare to have it so young as Anita.

Anita also had scoliosis, which recently had become much worse, and her surgeon advised that she needed surgery urgently. Anita was upset about having another major operation, but was in continuous pain. She hoped that surgery *might* relieve the pain, but knew that the doctors were uncertain whether it would. Anita might be thought to be highly informed because of her experience, intelligence and interest in medicine. Her mother was, however, sceptical about informed consent:

I think 16 is as good an age as any to sign the form. But all consent forms are ludicrous – they have no legal basis, doctors can always claim that *everything* was explained. Even adult patients or parents are in no fit state to ask important questions – if they know what these are. And they can't remember the explanations later.

At each clinic they saw different doctors, who gave conflicting and confusing information until Anita's mother, because of her position in the hospital, was able to arrange that they always saw the consultant. The information greatly improved. When asked, 'When do you think Anita was or will be able to understand the relevant medical information?', her mother replied, 'It's very difficult to think back', and then decided '15', but added:

> When Anita was nine, scoliosis was diagnosed. Shortly afterwards, when we were talking in an informal family gathering Anita said, "I want to be an orthopaedic doctor, because I will know what it feels like to be told you have scoliosis". We were shocked, as she hadn't seemed at all bothered about the diagnosis, but she obviously felt very strongly about it.

Anita thought that she was as fully informed as her parents were, and the consultant had told her 'a lot'. 'I like to see the X-ray. You can actually see what is happening to *you*, not a general explanation. He always told me exactly what he was going to do and why'.

### Defining 'understanding'

Anita's mother illustrates the problem of defining 'understanding'. She seemed to be highly informed herself, but denied that parents could be. She may have classed herself as a professional who could understand, or felt that she did not meet her own exacting standards of an 'informed' person. Our interview replies ranged from one extreme of the surgeon who thought that even his senior registrars could not be properly informed, to the other extreme of people who accepted a grasp of basic principles as adequate. Among this group, a psychologist mentioned an 'exceptional, brilliant' 3-year-old with haemophilia.

> *Psychologist*: He explained the nature of his illness and how he could do his injections himself, and what they meant and why he was doing it. He trotted it all out.
> *Int.*: Might he just have been fluently repeating adult phrases?
> *Psych.*: Oh no. I asked him questions to check that. It's not enough to be given information. I asked, "What do you do that for? What would happen if you didn't do it?" So I knew he had grasped the implications. If he'd said, "Because the doctors told me to", or "I'd be naughty if I didn't do that", that wouldn't count. But he really

understood. He told me, "Because if I cut myself my blood is going to keep coming out and I'll get ill". I asked him what "ill" meant and he told me.

One senior house officer (SHO) described a 4-year-old who was:

. . . very interested to see how his fracture was mending in each of his X-rays. Many children of three and four know the parts of their body and how they relate to each other, about their muscles and bones, and about things breaking and needing repairing. When my son was seven he had re-implantation of his ureters. I went to great lengths to draw and explain what was wrong and what the surgeon was going to do. I know he understood exactly what was going to happen so he wasn't frightened. I'm sure other 7-year-olds are quite capable of understanding all the relevant information, as long as it is explained properly.

During discussion, some people revised their opinions, as if they associated 'understanding' with adolescence, and then began to reconsider. In a group of psychologists, someone began, 'A competent 12- to 13-year-old would be able to understand'. Gradually, they described younger examples, until someone said:

A 3-year-old understood his liver biopsy as well as some adults. He knew that a piece would be taken from his liver, a little piece so it wouldn't matter. And it would be looked at under a glass (he didn't seem to know the word for microscope) to see if it was good or not. He seemed to understand that it was for investigation only, not for cure. He knew that his liver was near his stomach. His mother was a nurse and she spent ages preparing and explaining.

Another psychologist added, 'One 10-year-old kept forgetting about his liver biopsy. He was intelligent enough to understand but there were reasons why he kept "forgetting" although we kept telling him'. The replies show how 'understanding' is affected in how it is nurtured, defined and assessed by adult expectations.

The 10-year-old who 'forgot' introduces another vital aspect of understanding. It is not simply handling facts, but includes emotional awareness, coming to terms with shock and fear. This boy seemed too overwhelmed to cope with his emotions at the time, but emotions contribute to true understanding of medical information. Although Anita's mother defined understanding in intellectual terms, she recognized that Anita also 'knows what it feels like', through personal experience. Patients have unique, direct knowledge of their own case, which complements general professional knowledge. A sister in a heart–lung transplant unit described this crucial aspect of understanding.

*Sister*: Children who have a chronic illness have an above average awareness of illness and what it means. A little girl of five who was dying of cystic fibrosis [CF], certainly knew 100 per cent that she had a lung disease, exactly why she was in hospital, that her lungs could no longer function, that in order to be well she needed lungs to come from somewhere else, that they came from somebody else who had died, who was on a machine and no longer needed them, and if she didn't get them she would die. She knew that death meant total separation from her parents. She knew that no-one could tell her where she went to, but she never came back. Her hopes were that her parents would someday join her. So for a 5-year-old she had total understanding of all that, and certainly they can take in a lot of information about the surgery . . . Children who have an acute illness [often do not understand much because] their parents can protect them. But with children who have a debilitating illness, parents have to deal with them on a day-to-day basis of why they have to undergo various treatments. They have an understanding greater than mine.

*Int.*: Are you saying that suffering and all the treatment, which might look from the child's view like abuse, increase their understanding? That is the opposite to the usual ideas about cognitive and emotional delay in chronically ill children.

*Sister*: It does vary, but we have seen almost 100 CF children who come for transplants, and the ones who don't know much stick out. Because if they don't understand about their illness, and its terminal nature, then they won't look on the transplant in any way as a positive experience. Only about ten children or less have been so protected from knowing how seriously ill they are. It's their armour. It isn't right for us in four days to take away that protection from them. Parents usually agree to go home and prepare their child. It's part of the role of the parent to protect children, but it depends how you decide to protect them. Thirty to forty per cent know about the genetic component, and that it's inherited from their parents. They know they carry the gene, that boys are likely to be sterile, they know all these problems.

Developing inner awareness is an invisible, very personal process. It is usually ignored in studies of consent which attend to intellect rather than emotion, to overt measurable data, and to professionals' academic knowledge rather than patients' experiential knowledge.


### Levels of informed consent

There is disagreement over the level at which consent can be informed. Some people say, 'Nonsense, there is no such thing as informed consent'. Others insist that there is. The debate can be compared with looking for a needle in a haystack. Evidence of the needle/informed consent is more convincing than assertions (which can never be proved) denying its existence. Yet evidence of informed consent is likely to be dismissed by critics as an illusion. The debate is not just about the needle, but about the haystack or context, and people looking at different haystacks will not agree on their contents. They are discussing different definitions of consent and also different value systems, such as whether information is confined to esoteric clinical details or includes patients' feelings and interpretations, whether consent relates to an overall major decision, or also to all the interim stages. A play specialist commented:

> *Play specialist*: First, there's the parents' and child's or layman's level, of what's going to happen to them, the general process of hospitalization, medical treatment and so on. Then second there's the level of the doctors and nursing staff, and the language they use. There is a huge gap in between, and to try to cross over that gap depends on communication between one group and the other.
>
> *Int.*: Are you saying families can reach a certain satisfactory, lay level? And we should stop talking as if informed consent's all one level, and think instead about wanting to bridge the two levels to a reasonable extent. You can't merge the two, but it doesn't matter?
>
> *PS*: You have to bridge it to the extent that patients are satisfied and know what is going to happen at each stage – through a lot of play preparation, discussion of what medically will happen, each stage of treatment, how they will feel afterwards. And preparing for the emotional and social aspects and the medical side as well. Sometimes it's very complicated trying to sort out what they've heard. A child hears the doctors say "pyrexia" and thinks there's something terribly wrong. A 6-year-old was very worried that "taking blood" meant taking all the blood, so we looked at a body book, and he could see that it wouldn't be dangerous. I like them to be familiar with what will happen. This morning I had gone through things like EMLA cream with an 18-month-old child. When we'd gone down to theatre, the anaesthetist was wiping the cream off and, in so many words, the child said, "Oh, we'll wipe that away, this is numb, I won't feel anything now".

## Information and trust

An argument against informing patients is that they will become overemotional, anxious and untrusting. However, those professionals who treated young children as rational found they responded rationally. These professionals also tend to respect emotions, such as trust, as partly rational. The play specialist commented:

I see very much, hospital staff thinking that they know better and parents will trust them because of their knowledge, and that consent is to do with trust rather than with understanding. That is very contentious because I don't think you can trust someone fully until you know fully what they are going to do.

Doctors who see patients as mainly irrational tend to see questions as emotional expressions of anxiety which require reassurance; further explanation could excite alarm. Trust is seen as relinquishing responsibility, a state of feeling not thinking, such as by a surgeon who said:

> Adults and adolescents can take part in informed decisions for themselves, but the moment you talk to adults about their child they cannot appreciate what was actually said. They are too anxious. What parents are consenting to is your treating their child in whatever way you recommend. Under 10 or 12, children need to know globally, but they don't need to know the details unless they specifically ask. In which case you tell them in very simple terms that they need an operation which requires a cut in the skin, and a plaster or traction. They don't understand the mechanics if they haven't done anatomy at school. They want to know the effect on them. I don't think that the explanation should be made more complicated than that for either parents or children because beyond that they get confused. Caring as many of them are, parents don't ask sensible questions. You have to pose the questions for them, which you then answer. At the end when you say, "Have you got any questions?", they say, "Well I think you've probably covered all we need to know". Sometimes the parents will be positively involved, but the majority can't be.

Other professionals aimed for children to have a reasonable understanding, beyond unthinking trust. They encouraged children's questions, such as the surgeon who said:

> True competence is to answer me back and query things. I think – understanding *as well as* an adult – children vary enormously but a typical child will understand somewhere around the age of eight. But they'll understand the basic outline earlier. I spend a lot of time talking to the children. I'd talk to an 8-year-old as though they are an adult, softening bits. I'm very unhappy if I don't think a child understands *why* I'm doing something and what I'm trying to do. So the bottom of it is really, comprehension starts at 18 months upwards, as long as you couch it in very simple terms. I think you have to take each one on its merits. They are all very different.

A senior sister on a girls' ward saw information and trust as complementary and time-consuming:

Parents need a great deal of information to give informed consent, but they also need to trust the surgeon and these two go together. If everything is explained fully, the parents are happy and trust in the whole team. You need time to set the girls at their ease, and gain their confidence. The evening is a good time to chat, when you'll be less interrupted.

Yet she felt there were difficulties in balancing honesty with encouragement.

Sometimes we try too hard to "play down" the difficulties, we're so keen to have the family feeling happy about it. Then wham – reality hits – pain, drips, restricted life-style, depression.

And a surgeon who felt that the main fear was often of pain and needles discussed pain relief in detail with children but had to warn that 'at the time there *might* not be an anaesthetist to set up the technique'. Many nurses felt that information could increase confidence:

They come in a few days before their spinal fusion for a work-up. We go through everything that is going to happen – they practise using a bed pan, log rolling, they go to see the recovery ward. It is very important to make sure that they know exactly what is going to happen to them.

### Assessing understanding

Many interviews illustrated adults' growing practical respect for young children's understanding. There is not space to describe the scores of replies about children's understanding, but through their variety they illustrate the following conclusions. Understanding is partly hidden in the thoughts and feelings of the patient and perceived through the prejudices of the observer. Yet it is not entirely relative, arbitrary and therefore unimportant. On the contrary, because it is so important, understanding must first be recognized as a changing experience and more than a static fact. It is a mutual process in the minds of the child and the informer, the doctor and the patient.[12] It grows or withers through the relationship between them, and thrives on reasonably high expectations.

Definitions of understanding are influenced by the definer's respect for professionals, parents and children.[13] The same applies to informed consent. Those who define it narrowly, as based on highly technical, academic knowledge, trust the professionals. Those who believe that 'an adult of sound mind'[14] can be reasonably informed trust parents. People working closely with children are realizing how comprehensive and profound their grasp can be when they are experienced and have been skilfully informed, despite their sometimes naive language.

### Professionals' reasons for informing children

The consent literature tends to imply that professionals inform patients in order
to obtain their consent. However, much information is given for other reasons,
and only indirectly relates to consent. This section gives examples illustrating
why health professionals inform child patients.

#### To explain planned treatment

All the professionals we interviewed believed that children should be informed,
but varied in how much detail they would give. Some surgeons gave brief
explanations seemingly as a courtesy, or to enable patients to comply with treatment plans.

#### To observe the law

A spinal surgeon who spent much time talking with children said:

> It is a difficult balance between reassuring and yet mentioning the possi-
> bility of paralysis but the word must be used. There was a famous case
> of litigation which cost £50 000 because the word "paralysis" was not
> used.

#### To give warning of risk

Professionals varied very much in whether they thought it important or even
possible to explain risks to children. Some thought that children could have
no concept of risk, many believed that it was unfair to burden children with
worries which might never be realized, while others believed that children must
be warned and prepared for possible serious harms. Here are views from two
surgeons explaining opposite ends of the spectrum.

> I wouldn't begin to talk to a child about risks. I don't know when a
> child normally understands the concept. You'd have to ask a psychologist
> that. Most children under ten have no idea of risk; they rebreak their
> fractures after you've taken the plaster off, because they're not worried
> about breaking their arm, even when they've done it a few weeks ago.
> Whereas an adult is so careful. Obviously you wouldn't want to frighten
> a child about their prognosis either, that they might get early osteoar-
> thritis if nothing is done about it. It's better to wait until they ask about
> risk, and that's usually not until they're 17.

Another surgeon said:

> You can give children down to 5 or 6 years old having spinal surgery
> some idea of what spinal cord injury means. Even though the risks of

paralysis are so small, if it happens it totally destroys a child's life. And I explain, "Well, you can't cross the road without some risk", and I say, "It's very rare", or "very very rare". The risk varies. You can't operate on a 12-year-old with a 25 per cent risk, without making sure the child has understood what paraplegia means. And that takes time. If we don't inform children, and they then have to face something they weren't expecting, that's something they carry with them for the rest of their lives. They're resentful, and rightly so. I'd never ever operate on a child whose parent says, "Don't tell my child about spinal cord injury".

This surgeon also told children about the 'wake up test', when children were asked to wriggle their toes towards the end of the operation to check against damage to the spinal cord. I saw one girl do this during surgery, and she was barely conscious and showed no sign of feeling any pain. Children were assured this would be so, but they worried a lot about it. The surgeon commented: 'Explaining the "wake-up" test always terrified children, no matter how I tried to explain that they wouldn't know anything about it. We now have a machine to monitor the spinal cord and I explain how that works'.

### To reduce anxiety

Professionals who were aware of children's many questions and worries believed that informing them, rather than introducing new worries, helped to resolve anxiety which already preoccupied them.[15] A senior ward sister said:

I usually say to the child, "What do you want to be told?" Sometimes the teenagers say, "Everything", but then you can see them edge away as if what I am saying is too much for them. I don't leave it at that. I say, "What is it upsetting you?" I make sure that before the day of surgery they have an opportunity to voice their fears and uncertainties. These girls can be very protective of their mothers. They don't want to upset them by showing how worried they really are, and they put on a brave face when others are around.

Sometimes it is important that they know more than they have asked for. I try to edge them forwards to accept a little more information each time we have a chat. I watch carefully to see how successful this is being – and I ration it out, particularly if they seem very anxious, only telling them one main thing at a time. It can become obvious that the child doesn't really want to have the operation done – they have been persuaded by the parents – and these children can just switch off and avoid getting involved. They just won't listen to the information, and rarely ask questions.

*To ensure high standards of care*

Through talking supportively with young patients, professionals were able to provide appropriate care. For example, the senior sister just quoted discovered that one girl aged 15 was taking a contraceptive pill. The operation was postponed for three weeks while she stopped taking the pill. The girl did not want her parents to be informed, so they were told that the delay was due to administrative reasons. The sister continued:

> Many parents want to shield their child. Some can't bear to hear things being said to the child that *they* can't accept. In fact most children can accept more than the parents can, and surprise their parents in how well they can cope. It's no good going against parents' wishes to protect their child. You have to spend time trying to explain what is good for the child, that they know what to expect. I have seen very bad reactions after surgery when children haven't known – and lack of trust. The child suffers more pain because they haven't been properly prepared. Often parents who don't want a child told haven't given any thought to how the child will react afterwards, to the consequences of not being truthful, when they wake up to find drips, a wound, and so on. After spinal fusion girls tend to get very depressed, even if they were keen to have it done. It's much worse if they weren't involved and prepared for all the possible setbacks and problems. They must be willing to accept these as well, not just the surgery.

*To prevent resentment*

We were given several instances of resentful, angry children who felt that they had been deceived through not being informed. A staff nurse reported:

> A 9-year-old thought they were just "going to look" at her knee, not operate on it. When she came back with a plaster and drainage tubes and a drip she was dreadfully upset, and then quite aggressive to everyone. I didn't blame her. Of course she felt cross with all of us.

*To prevent harm from surgery*

Several nurses criticized doctors for not discussing with parents the possibility of the harms of treatment exceeding the benefits. They felt that such discussion could help to prevent avoidable distress, but they also felt powerless to intervene. For example:

> Parents often aren't told when there's likely to be a series of operations. They think each one is the last. I feel very unhappy when children are mentally retarded and there's no way you can explain to them what is happening. If someone is wheelchair-bound do they really need yet

another operation to correct their twisted foot? Does it make that much difference to their lives? They already have so many problems, are we adding to them? They must be terrified by all the drips and plasters.

In out-patient clinics, many doctors carefully give information about risks, and explain if they consider that a defect is too mild to require surgical treatment or, alternatively, is too severe to be treated safely. Occasionally, we saw young adults whose spines were so severely curved that they could only sit for a few minutes, before having to lie down in order to be slightly more comfortable. Warning them that the harms of treatment would be worse than their present distress was very hard. A spinal surgeon commented:

*Surgeon*: We still get older handicapped ones when it's too late to operate. I don't usually admit them to the ward where everyone else is having ops and they're not. There was only one kid who very much wanted to have surgery, but the respiratory problems and the risks were so high. I did admit him, and by the time it came to surgery he realized. He and I decided together, it was positive. He made his own decision, that he didn't want to take that risk. Otherwise I don't admit them because I don't want to disappoint them. They'll feel something has gone wrong, that they're too bad because "Mum didn't bring me up to the clinic early enough".

*Int.*: Are you treating more complicated cases now than had surgery in the past? Do you specialize in the more difficult ones?

*Surgeon*: Yes. There aren't enough people doing the work. The waiting list is too long, the pressures on us are too high.

*Int.*: So some of these children arrive later that you would wish?

*Surgeon*: Inevitably.

Another surgeon who specialized in treating children with multiple handicaps thought that admitting children for assessment could be very helpful:

I get them in and assessed by the physiotherapist, occupational therapist, the ward sister and social worker. It gives the parents and child the opportunity of understanding more about the process of surgery. Then you sit down and explain why you've made the decision, those parents are more willing to go along with what you say [perhaps] because they've realized that you've actually not done it too quickly. Frequently parents don't want surgery anyway. It allows everybody a chance of dealing with matters a little bit more expertly. The nurses will realize, if there are excessive problems, what they're going to be, and prepare for them, such as having a nurse on special duty.

### To respect and help children

Professionals were critical of parents who did not wish their child to be informed. Almost all the children living in Britain had basic information, but some of those from abroad were misinformed. Nurses tried to cope with children's anger, bewilderment and distress, with the added problem that they did not speak the same language. 'One boy came over here for an amputation, and all his parents would tell him was that he was coming for a holiday'. There was a general feeling that parents who wanted to keep a child in ignorance wanted to protect themselves, rather than the child. A psychologist commented: 'Our policy is that children should know and if their parents don't want them to know, children really worry and carry around secrets that they do know and they pretend that they don't'.

When we asked professionals what they would do if parents did not wish their child to be informed, psychologists spontaneously described their duty to talk honestly with children who had cancer or a terminal disease: 'You must tell them, they usually know anyway'. They were less interested in insisting that children should know about more routine conditions. Yet this implies that if children benefit from being informed about the most frightening issues, they also benefit from knowing about matters such as expected pain.

Professionals' methods for responding to parents' resistance ranged from confrontation ('As a psychiatrist I would insist on telling the child') to acceptance ('Well in the end you can only go as far as the parents want, it's their child'). In between these extremes, many felt an obligation to the child as a member of a family: 'I would discuss it very carefully with the parents and try to get them to think about how much their child already knows and worries about'. A spinal surgeon commented:

> I would always try to bring the parents round to being open with the child. It has never happened to me that I have been in direct conflict with parents over this. Kids know much more than parents realize – parents are often unaware of their child's maturity. I think the child has every right to know – it's their back.

### To help children to recover

Through listening, explanation and play, professionals helped children to recover from fearful experiences. A play specialist stated:

> I didn't have time to play-prep one little blind girl. Afterwards she didn't say, "I've had a nightmare", but just through talking she mentioned that she kept waking up crying, thinking she couldn't breathe. After we had talked, she said the oxygen mask was held on her as she woke up. Being blind it terrified her. It kept recurring through her dream. For a couple of days she kept putting this mask on and off April [a doll the play

specialist had made]. Eventually she could actually put it on herself, and she worked through it.

### To increase compliance

Informing patients enables them to follow medical advice, such as to arrive for surgery or to take prescribed drugs. Knowing the purpose of treatment is likely to increase their cooperation.[16] Preparation methods such as telling a story can also help to free children from fear, misunderstanding and uncertainty, as with the story about amputation mentioned earlier. Play specialists felt rewarded when frightened children found after 'play-prep' that they could cope with having surgery and gained confidence: 'He was happy afterwards, and prepared to trust me, and that was lovely'.

Yet stories can also be used to control children. A psychologist described how a 5-year-old admitted for surgery 'screamed all night long because she wanted her mother to stay with her'. The ward was very unusual in banning parents at night. The psychologist told the girl a story about a kitten who learned to cope without her mother at night: 'She screamed for a few more nights but after that it worked'. One theatre manager was very impressed with an elaborate American operating day programme. A nurse disguised as a huge pink mouse prepared groups of children, and later took them to the operating room. Small children were found to be less upset because they 'trusted' the mouse. A much cheaper, simpler and, for children, preferable alternative, that they go to the theatre with a parent, did not seem to occur to the American team. The artificiality and deception involved (the costume had to be very elaborate so that children would 'believe' it was a mouse) seemed to be a way for adults to retain power by tricking the children into conforming to pre-ordained routines. Many children we interviewed found play preparation very helpful. Yet preparation tends to stress what is definitely going to happen, and how the child will comply with all the rituals around surgery, wearing the theatre gown and riding on the trolley, which many children dread. They are encouraged to express their fears in order to overcome them, such as by playing with a syringe before having injections. In contrast, information for consent is about questioning decisions and discussing possible alternatives. Telling children how they ought to behave (as in much preparation) and offering them choice (as in informed consent) are two very different approaches. The first is about reassuring, and to some extent controlling children; the second approach of learning from children will be discussed in later chapters.

The next chapter complements this one, in considering children's responses to information.

## Notes

1 Roden, P. (1990) The story of a hospital childhood. *Children in Hospital Update*. Newsletter of *Action for Sick Children*, London.
2 Department of Health (1992) *The Patients' Charter*. London, HMSO, although whether the Charter's 'rights' are binding is questioned: Lavery, R. (1992) What is the Patient's Charter? *Medico-Legal Journal*, 60(3), 201–4.
3 Anon. (1990) Consent calls for knowledge. *Hospital Doctor*, 23 August.
4 The average leaflet for patients assumes a sixth-form or graduate reading age, whereas the average reading age for the population is around 9 years. Among many texts examining the difficulty of writing clear leaflets is Mann, R. (ed.) (1991) *Patient Information in Medicine*. Carnforth, Parthenon.
5 Bjorge, G. (1991) Talking with young children about cancer. *Journal of Educational Therapy*, 3(3), 43–52, illustrates the value of explaining to 3-year-olds.
6 Reviews of research on informed consent report studies showing that most adult patients said they wanted to be informed, but most doctors replied that patients did not wish to be informed. King, J. (1986) Informed consent: A review of the empirical evidence, *Medical Ethics Bulletin*, supplement 3. Change in clinical practice is shown by Novack, D., Plumber, R., Smith, R. *et al.* (1979) Changes in physicians' attitudes towards telling the cancer patient. *Journal of the American Medical Association*, 241, 897–900. In 1961, 88 per cent of the clinicians surveyed reported a policy of not disclosing a diagnosis of cancer; by 1979, 98 per cent of clinicians said that they would disclose the diagnosis.
7 Ley, P. (1979) Memory for medical information. *British Journal of Social and Clinical Psychology*, 18, 245–55.
8 Holtzman, N., Faden, R., Churalow, A. and Hoirn, S. (1983) Effects of informed parental consent on mothers' knowledge of new born screening. *Pediatrics*, 72(6), 807–12.
9 King, J., op. cit., note 6, p. 7.
10 Although the surgeon referred to a paper on this study carried out about 20 years ago, I was unable to trace it. 'Admission' in those days would be a far more threatening word, implying perhaps months in hospital with very little visiting allowed. Patients were then much less informed than they usually are today. The surgeons we interviewed prided themselves on keeping up to date with the latest papers on surgical technique, and were unlikely to have based their surgical practice on a 20-year-old unpublished paper. The example illustrates the relative value placed on technical and on social issues by some surgeons.
11 'Innominate' is a hip bone but the Latin also literally means unnamed or undefined.
12 Understanding is also a mutual process for researchers and researched, as Chapter 5 discusses.
13 See Chapter 3 for the section on parentalists, interventionists or child libertarians.
14 Judge Cardozo, the American legal doctrine of consent; see Chapter 4, note 3.
15 There is an extensive literature on preparing children for treatment, among the most comprehensive being the *American Journal of the Association for the Care of Children in Hospital*. I do not deal in this book with the question of proof as to whether children want to know or benefit from knowing which has been amply studied by psychologists. The salient questions seem to be: Who benefits if the child is

not told? How can one be certain that a child does not know and does not want to know? And how can worrying information be given as carefully as possible, in ways the child can accept and cope with? Preparing adult patients for inevitable pain, discomfort and inconvenience can improve recovery rates. Wallace, L. (1986) Informed consent to elective surgery: The 'therapeutic value'? *Social Science and Medicine*, 22(1), 29–33. A study of girls having orthopaedic treatment showed that understanding the benefits improved recovery rates, whereas girls who perceived their treatment as harmful and not beneficial recovered more slowly. Clough, F. (1979) The validation of meaning in illness-treatment situations. In Hall, D. and Stacey, M. (eds), *Beyond Separation*. London, Routledge.

16 Compliance is still taken for granted, to the extent that 31 per cent of 240 new drug treatments were started without parents knowing their purpose. Rylance, G. (ed.) (1987) *Drugs for Children*. Copenhagen, WHO.

# 8

# UNDERSTANDING INFORMATION: CHILDREN'S RESPONSES

*I think they should tell you honestly. You are much less frightened when you know what's going to happen.*

*(David aged 10)*

*Mum kept the information to herself, and she said in the clinic, 'Judy, go out.' I said, 'No.' And the doctor said,' No, children must know what is going to happen to them.' Mum changed after that. She realized it's better for me to be informed, and she started explaining things.*

*(Judy aged 12)*

This chapter reports children's and parents' views about sharing information. The dilemma for adults of whether to respect children by informing them honestly, or to protect them by withholding frightening information is discussed. Ways in which children benefit from being informed are listed. The final section reviews ethical problems we encountered when discussing serious medical issues with young patients.

### Children's and parents' views about sharing information

We asked the 120 parents and children before the operation if they thought that the child was as informed about the proposed treatment as the parents were (Table 10). Parents who said they knew more than their child talked mainly about risks, or anticipating how difficult the treatment would actually be. Three parents of 10- to 12-year-olds thought that their child was more fully informed than they were: 'She's always here, whereas we miss some of the rounds'.

We asked parents whether they thought they had been informed adequately about the nature, purpose, benefits and risks of the surgery (Table 11). Many of the 35 who had not been informed about the nature of the operation felt that no-one was certain: 'Mr X says he'll probably decide finally what to do during the operation'; 'No-one seems to be sure how long she'll be in for, it all depends'; 'We're still waiting to know, because Mr Y hasn't looked at the latest X-rays yet'; 'We'll just have to wait and see, we're not even sure if he's going to have the operation'.

**Table 10**  Children's and parents' views about whether the child was as informed about proposed treatment as the parents

|                      | Children's views (n = 120) | Parents' views (n = 120) |
|----------------------|:--------------------------:|:------------------------:|
| As fully informed    | 87                         | 91                       |
| Less fully informed  | 28                         | 26                       |
| More fully informed  | –                          | 3                        |
| Don't know           | 5                          | –                        |

**Table 11**  Parents' views on information about proposed surgery

|                          | Parents' replies (n = 120) | |
|--------------------------|:--------:|:--------:|
|                          | 'Yes'    | 'No'     |
| Parent was informed about: |        |          |
| purpose                  | 111      | 9        |
| nature                   | 85       | 35       |
| prognosis                | 82       | 38       |
| risk                     | 58       | 62       |

Fifty-eight parents said the risks of surgery generally, or of the particular operation, had been mentioned. The risks of not having surgery had been discussed with 100 parents, such as continuing pain or disability. Some of those who said they had not been informed were critical; others were satisfied: 'We've been through it before so we didn't need to discuss it'; 'There aren't any risks'; 'Well, it's obvious there is a bit of risk with any anaesthetic but he doesn't need to tell us that'. The figures are not typical of all surgical wards,[1] but show that even in specialized centres a significant number of people thought that they were not adequately informed. They may have been given more information than they understood or remembered. However, observing in wards and out-patient clinics, and when interviewing surgeons, we found that the way they gave information tended to confirm what the parents and children said. Most replies concerned fairly basic practical information and not intricate details. Children who had been treated by more than one surgeon contrasted informative with evasive ones.

Children were asked before surgery whom they thought doctors should inform (Table 12). Most of those who wanted the doctor to talk to their parents said this was because their parents explained medical information to them more clearly. Table 13 shows the children's reported satisfaction levels before their operation about how much they had been told. After surgery, 73 children said that something 'unexpected' happened. Some surprises were pleasant, such as unexpectedly rapid recovery, but mainly the surprises led to shock and distress,

**Table 12**   Children's views on whom doctors should inform ($n = 120$)

| Child | Parents | Child and parents | Not sure |
|-------|---------|-------------------|----------|
| 4 | 16 | 99 | 1 |

**Table 13**   Children's reported satisfaction levels about how much they had been told ($n = 120$)

| | Children's replies | |
|---|---|---|
| | 'Yes' | 'No' |
| Enough | 61 | 39 |
| A lot | 17 | 103 |
| Too little | 42 | 78 |

such as prolonged pain or complications, extra weeks in hospital, or the operation being much more serious or the wound much larger than they had expected.

We asked the young patients about the amount of warning they preferred to have before surgery. Thirty wanted two months or more, saying that although waiting was an anxious time, it helped them to adjust and accept the need for surgery; the rest wanted between seven weeks and 'just before'; 20 said they did not know or did not mind. The older ones tended to prefer a longer warning. A common difficulty was that children knew in principle many months ahead, but had only a few days warning of the actual date, so that they could not become gradually, increasingly prepared.

When asked what they would tell another patient, most children would offer reassurance rather than information: 'There's nothing to worry about'; 'I'd try not to get him worried, every operation is different, and everyone worries about different things. I'd just talk about general things like the tele and food', said a 15-year-old boy. After six weeks in plaster, Brenda had just learnt that she would have a new plaster for four more weeks:

> *Int.*: If a girl who is 9 years old was going to have the same kind of hip operation that you have had and asked you what it was like, what would you tell her?
>
> *Brenda*: Be brave, try not to cry, like when you go down to have the operation.

Anita, aged 15, said, 'I'd tell her about the PCA, and say, be patient, don't expect too much too soon'. Robin said, 'I'd explain the procedure and invite questions. Nurses tell you the technical things but patients have been through it. It's important to hear that mixture'. Some children mentioned details they wished they had been warned about: 'Find out what is going to happen and how long you'll be in for'. Being in hospital together seemed to increase their supportiveness towards one another.[2] Several of them spoke warmly of the kindness of other young patients, in contrast to hostility and teasing at school. Mario was horrified after surgery to be fitted with a brace which, he felt, made his humpback look much worse. He went around making jokes against himself about being 'a bloody camel', as if to ward off teasing by being the first to ridicule, but the other adolescents did not appear to taunt him.

### Talking about risk

A common argument against warning patients of risk and pain is that they will refuse surgery because of their fears. Children, especially, are often assumed to be too immature and easily frightened to cope with this information. 'Risk' concerns uncertainty about probability or magnitude – about how likely something is to occur, and how serious it might be. Some doctors said little about all negative aspects of surgery. Their vagueness constructed these negative aspects as 'risks' in the sense that they were then uncertain and unexpected events. These 'risks' were of three kinds: possible harms, such as paralysis or failed treatment; inevitable harms, such as pain and wounds; social costs, such as being in hospital for weeks. The following examples illustrate tensions between respecting children by giving them information and protecting them by withholding it, and how some children responded.

### Protection

Annette's parents wanted to protect her from alarming news for fear that she might refuse surgery. Annette, aged 14, had been treated for scoliosis for seven years, with three previous operations to remove five ribs and insert a Harrington rod. Her father was a barrister. When asked the purpose of the proposed surgery, Annette's mother said:

> I don't really know. My husband got it into his mind last year that he didn't like Annette having this rod in her back if it was no longer needed. When he spoke to Mr Z about removing it, Mr Z said, "That's not a bad idea". But they never discussed it with me or Annette. She'll have the whole length of the old scar reopened to take the rod out – it would only need opening about three inches to do the ribs. I am not very happy about it. Annette was told eventually. We knew if we told her the full extent of the operation she would be very unwilling to have it. We didn't tell her about the ribs until she was in hospital.

Annette's mother said that the risks had not been discussed 'because it's purely cosmetic', and that Annette was 'quite willing, after a great deal of persuasion'. Harrington rods are very seldom removed.

Annette said that her operation was 'to take some bone off the right shoulder blade, remove some segments from the ribs to flatten them, and then remove the Harrington rod'. Her mother agreed to go to the canteen during Annette's interview, but returned after ten minutes. She sat nearby and Annette became more reticent. While her mother was away, Annette said, 'My parents were very keen for me to have the operation because of the hump on my back'. She explained that 'I *do* know that now is the best time' before she started GCSEs.[3]

> But I didn't make the decision – it was made on my behalf and I would have felt much better if I had been involved. At first I didn't want the operation at all – it is only for cosmetic reasons, and also Dad has got this idea he wants the rod removing. Ten months ago there was no talk of an operation in front of me. Mr Z did say I could have an operation any time of my life if I wanted the hump reducing, but I didn't realise Mum and Dad were wanting me to have it soon, and I had no idea Dad was planning to have a "private chat" about removing the rod. Mum didn't know either.
>
> Apparently they have had the date for my admission for ages. The reason they gave for not telling me was that they didn't want me to get upset before my school exams. I can understand why they did it, but I don't like secrets like that – I would have preferred to have been told. Mum suddenly said, "Would you like to have this operation quite soon?" When I said, "No", they really had to work hard persuading me, as I was due in the next week! Then they only told me half of what was going to be done. I know why they do it, they think it is for the best. But I don't like it.
>
> I feel really strongly that doctors should talk to both patient and the parents. It's best if the doctors give their view, then let the parents and the patient go home and discuss it and make the decision together. I don't know why, but I have a horror of people looking inside me when I have been cut open, and messing about with my muscles and bones. I know I'll be asleep and won't feel it but I still worry about it a lot. I really hate intra-muscular injections. I had so many last time – I am really scared when I know I have to have one. Last time, when I had five ribs removed it was excruciatingly painful. I couldn't have morphine through a drip because the nurse took the special key home by mistake. I had to have injections of morphine and they didn't seem to last very long. I was in agony long before I was due to have the next one, and the nurses couldn't give it to me before the correct time. Last time, when I was 12, Mum told me everything she knew and that helped a lot.

When asked what she would tell another girl of 14, Annette said, 'You must be honest. Don't hide anything'. A week later Annette added another worry about repeated surgery: 'I get very depressed just lying on my back. I love walking and I can't walk very far now – I don't know if it will improve or not. If not, I shall just have to live with it'. She seemed able to cope well with the short notice about the operation, yet to share some of her parents' mistrust of her abilities. Asked when she thought she would be old enough to decide for herself, she replied, 'It's too complicated, there are too many things to consider to make the decision on your own before 18. And 16 is a very strange age, you can be very silly then'.

Meg thought that parents should be informed,

> because they have to make the decisions, but the patient needs to know about things to stop them worrying. When I was ten my mum didn't tell me about my last operation. I guessed I was going to have one, because you don't need to go to sleep to have a plaster put on, also I overheard the nurses talking. I was a bit cross with mum to begin with, but she was right not to tell me because I would have worried. I knew she would get upset if I was worried. When you're older you don't worry so much, and you can be told more. I would be angry now I'm 12 if someone didn't tell me if I was going to have an operation. I feel I'm a lot more experienced now, and I'm actually looking forward to it, to get it over with.

It is uncertain here whether the mother or the daughter was most concerned to protect the other.

### Sharing knowledge of risk

Annette and Meg were unhappy that they were not informed about inevitable harms. A more contentious question is whether to tell children about true risks – possible harms which may never occur, and they might never need know about. A hospital social worker, whose daughter Lisa recently had a spinal fusion, described the difficulties. Three years earlier, a boy Lisa knew, with the same severe progressive disease which she had, died after a spinal fusion. The hospital where this happened refused to accept Lisa for surgery, and her surgeon at another hospital was 'very edgy'. Lisa had had other high-risk surgery, and used a wheelchair. Her mother said:

> Her understanding is as good as many adults. But there are issues I'm not sure one gives to a 13-year-old, such as whether she'd die during the operation. Was that fair for her to have to take that on? She went through a lot of pain thinking about that. I could have saved her from that.
>
> As a parent, I feel my child has the right to know if she asks. From the professional view, unless parents go along with it we don't pro-actively tell children, but we tell parents. It's a grey area. We won't go

behind parents' backs, but I do feel children are left with anxieties no-one can reach because their parents can't face it. Lisa is so physically dependent I have to be more active in promoting her independence.

I think they can give reasonably informed consent but not totally informed. They'll never know all the ifs and buts about surgery. But nevertheless I think it is important they know as much as they possibly can, and make a decision. And now that Lisa's around 13 her consent was much more informed. But there were some things I decided not to burden her with, that were informing my consent, such as about the intensive care facilities. Lisa knew that without surgery she could become paralysed and lose bowel and bladder control. She had met some patients with spinal injuries and knew much more than a normal child would know about what paralysis means.

When we saw the surgeon, he dumbfounded us by saying he wasn't sure the surgery mightn't be too risky. Lisa is a bit deaf, so I started telling her afterwards that the surgery might be too risky, and she immediately said, "What do you mean? I might die?" And I hesitated for a moment, but I knew I had to be honest because she would have understood my hesitation, and so I said, "Yes", and she immediately burst into tears, and said, "I never knew you could die from an operation", and was very, very upset.

We talked a lot about wanting to find out about death and heaven, and I read to her about near-death experiences. She wrote a story about going up into heaven and she was running (that was her idea so it was very real to her) and she got to the doors of heaven and she saw Granny and Granddad and they said, "Come in", and an angel said, "No, go back. It's not time. You have a bit more time before you come". Lisa talked a lot about paralysis. This went on for two or three weeks. She summed it all up by saying, "I have a choice, either I have this operation and I might die, or I might go on without it and I might be paralysed". I felt that I should never really have let her know the worry about the anaesthetic. Yet she managed to go on at school quite cheerfully. It was only at intervals she wanted to talk and got upset.

The anaesthetist thought the risk wasn't all that high. So maybe we needn't have put her through all that. Whether it's right to share, I honestly don't know. Yet I think Lisa's survived it perfectly, and she's probably grown in having to think about it to that extent. But if she'd been a less emotionally robust child, perhaps it wouldn't have been right to share so much.

At times Lisa's mother had tears in her eyes, showing the strain of talking about serious risk with children. Many professionals mentioned their own children during interviews, suggesting that their attitudes towards young patients were coloured by personal experiences. Doctors' and nurses' reluctance to explain serious disease, risk and uncertainty,[4] and the ways they evade questioning have been well documented.[5] They are constrained by seeing most patients briefly and seldom, by uncertainty about how each family can cope with bad news, and by the stress of repeatedly caring for patients at risk. One hospital corridor is painted with balloons bearing the names of former patients, sponsored by families in gratitude for recovery or in memory of their child who died. A surgeon remarked, 'It's a nice idea, but when you see some of the names, it's like a knife going through you'.

Lisa's mother thought that, when younger, Lisa had been excluded from discussions about risk, as 'she was not told about the decision to operate until months after it had been agreed, because of not worrying them by telling them too soon. But at 13 she can know a year ahead, she's involved from the very moment you start to talk about it'. This increased her mother's worry that Lisa might refuse surgery:

> If she did not have surgery it would put an enormous strain on us. It would affect the whole family lifestyle and – not wanting to put pressure on her – but she'd thought it through as well. *Every* time she wanted to get off the stair lift, she wouldn't be able to do that on her own any more.

## Motives and manner

When considering whether to share difficult information with their daughters, Annette's parents' main motive appeared to be to ensure their control and her compliance. Lisa's mother's main concern, to protect her from possibly avoidable distress, and to carry that burden for her, was generally held by parents. Mike's mother said, 'You couldn't tell that to a child of ten, although there are things I would tell Mike that I wouldn't tell my mother and she's 70'. So the motive to protect is not simply a matter of age, but of how people perceive their relationship with the patient, and the patient's needs.

Kerry, facing similar risks to Lisa's, showed the importance of the adults' manner and motives when informing children. She had muscular dystrophy, and was aged 12. She wanted 'to have my spine corrected and to be able to sit better in my wheelchair'. Her mother said:

> Fifteen minutes before going to theatre they said the operation was cancelled because of her poor lung function, and they talked about halo traction instead. My mind went a blank, so I signed for the halo without knowing what I was doing. As soon as she woke up afterwards, Kerry said, "Get this thing off my head! I hate it. I want to go home". She went on for several days after that. I feel so guilty. We're putting her through all this anguish and there's no guarantee that it will help.

The hope was that traction, by straightening Kerry's spine, would take pressure off her lungs and improve her lung function enough for her to undergo the spinal fusion. Days later, Kerry said that on waking up with the halo on:

> I could feel the pins in my head, and I was really sore, and I was sick straight away. They had to rush me back to the ward to get some pain killer. It was hurting a lot. I was upset because I had imagined my halo would be much worse. Like the one the social worker showed me weeks ago in her picture, a Stryker bed with someone lying down with bars, and a head halo, and pins through the ankle as well. She said, "It doesn't apply to you". I thought then, "I'm glad I'm not having that". All the doctor said was, "We're going to put a halo on you". I said nothing. I was shocked and I cried.

Kerry was asked when she first realized she did not have the full-length traction: 'I went to sleep and I didn't see it till I got up, into the wheelchair, when the nurse took me to the toilet. I saw in the mirror a little bit'. The halo prevented her from moving her head so she was unable to see herself. Not realizing her misunderstanding about the type of halo, no-one could reassure her, and her expectations seemed to stop her from realizing that her feet were not affected, until she saw her reflection.

A week after having the halo on, Kerry was rejecting all treatment plans. The physiotherapist tried to help her by making her see that it would be more dangerous for her not to have the spinal fusion. Her mother was unhappy about the timing and starkness of the risk-telling, and was uncertain about frightening Kerry into wanting an operation which she would not be able to have if her lungs did not improve. This could leave her worse off than before.

> How's she going to handle it if there's no operation? What will happen to her body? I wanted the physio to talk to her, but not like that. Not to a child. No-one's spelt it out so clearly, that it could collapse one lung, and that puts a strain on the other lung and the heart, and the risk of pneumonia and infection. I definitely decided I did want it done, but Kerry's adamant she doesn't. She was fine before we came in, no nerves. Now she hates me, she hates herself, and everyone. I know they've got to be clinical, but they don't seem to feel our feelings. They don't realise I have to cope afterwards. They tell me to keep her morale up, but I've nothing to base it on with this uncertainty, and who keeps mine up? I've no-one behind me, and the family's so far away.

Later, Kerry's mother said, 'Those seven weeks of waiting to see if she could have the spinal fusion were the worst nightmare of my life', again emphasizing the importance of the manner of carefully informing parents and children, and of supporting the child, as Lisa's mother had done, through the struggle of coming to terms with risk.

Niki stood out as the most streetwise young patient we met. Her body was wasted and twisted with anterior horn cell damage; leaning on her crutches she said earnestly, 'It's so important to be normal', and described how she and her (single, unemployed)[6] mother had fought for access to the local school: 'It's stupid to go to a handicapped school, because I'm normal and that's that. One day I'm going to have to go out into that big wide world and do what normal people do, but in a handicapped school you don't get to do that'. Now that ramps had been built for Niki, other disabled children attended the primary school, and Niki was campaigning to be let into her local comprehensive. Niki's mother said after the first spinal fusion:

*Mother*: Mr V explained it very well. It was sort of between the devil and the deep blue sea. If I didn't have it done, she would get worse, if I did have it done there was the risk. She's got small lung capacity. If he did collapse the lung he might have to put her on the ventilator for longer [describes other risks].

*Int.*: Did you tell Niki?

*Mother*: Oh yes, oh yes, she was there. I wouldn't not, I don't think she could go through it if she didn't know.

*Int.*: Is there anything you wouldn't talk about with Niki?

*Mother*: No. It's her body, her life. Kids can cope. I think they're more likely to take things with a pinch of salt than some adults. I reckon kids understand what you tell them from whenever, there isn't an age. As they get older you're talking more together. You're jointly making decisions.

Niki said she wanted the operation:

*Niki*: I don't want to look horrible. I've got a hump as well. And if your spine's twisted and your ribs go in, it would squash my lungs and all my inside, and then kill me after a while. I'll be going like that [she bent over further].

*Int.*: Yes, I see.

*Niki*: You won't be able to tape that. My sister, she's 8 years old, she says that the hospital is practically saving my life. I said to Mum, "You'll be okay Mum".

*Int.*: Was your Mum worried?

*Niki*: Yes. That's why I said that to her.

*Int.*: Did that cheer her up?

*Niki*: Yes, she started laughing.

Niki described the play specialist's preparation programme in detail and spent hours talking with the nurses. Yet her mother felt that 'Even though it was all explained, she couldn't really know what to expect. I think she got a cruel sharp shock about how much it really hurts. But she's done so well, she's been great'.

## Coming to terms with risk

Shock about risk was the usual initial reaction. Alison, aged 14, described how during an out-patient clinic:

> *Alison*: Mum and Dad and I and two doctors were sitting around talking about my operation, and I fainted. I didn't know mentally what was going on, but I must have known deep down, unconsciously, that I was scared. I'd had three operations before on my ears and it was very painful. To faint, I must have wanted not to know. I was laughing, having hysterics. It was an amazingly relaxed feeling to faint. I had a little cry, but I still wasn't absorbing it. It seemed a long way off. Then, one week before the operation, they sent the information and I went in and it hit me then, but by then it was all right. The only thing I was really scared of was the needles. I'm glad that when I went in a girl said, "I've been paralysed" [after her spinal fusion]. After intensive physio she was walking on crutches very slowly. I'm glad I knew. It was very worrying, but I'd have been really upset if I hadn't known and it happened. The night before, the doctor came round and told me they were working quite close to the spinal cord. There was a one in 10 000 chance of getting an infection.
>
> *Int.*: Did that bother you?
>
> *Alison*: Yes [laughs very nervously]. Just when I got to the anaesthetic room I thought, "I could never walk again". I know it's silly but it just sort of hit me.
>
> *Int.*: Would you rather not be told?
>
> *Alison*: No, I like knowing.
>
> *Int.*: Was that the best time to tell you, or would you rather know sooner?
>
> *Alison*: Yes, a bit sooner so you've got time to get used to it.

Some children do not want to know. When the word 'risk' was mentioned to his mother, Philip, aged 14, and having spinal fusion, said quickly, 'There aren't any'. Others half-heard and worried. Judy, aged 12, had back pain and severe scoliosis. Her father was a painter-decorator. She was on the 'urgent' list for six months. Her mother said that the GP had warned her on the 'phone, so that Judy would not know:

> He said, if her bowels or legs went, go straight to the hospital. I'd be talking to a friend, and Judy would hear and say, "You never told me that". So we began to tell her the whole story. You can't tell them a pack of lies at that age. After waiting for months for the operation, once she sat in the garden for an hour and a half in the dark. We thought she was in bed. She was so cold when I found her, she said she wanted to die. She was afraid of the unknown, and of skits from school. She

slid downstairs on her back, and hit her head, and tried to kill herself. She said she'd rather die now, waiting so long, there seemed no end. Time seems different to a child, it's endless to them. When it was cancelled, she flipped her lid completely. But once the 'phone call came, she was over the moon, a completely different child.

Despite her urgent wish for surgery, Judy was further worried when she arrived in the ward. Her mother said:

They produced the special form about spinal surgery risks. We weren't expecting to see it in black and white, and we were quite upset. I said, "I'd rather think about it". I knew I was going to sign. I can't think how it could be done better. But what condition will they be in when they return, any permanent damage? Knowing about the monitoring machine is a mixed blessing, reassuring that the operation could be stopped, but she really needs the operation, so it's a worry if it's stopped.[7]

The next day, Judy's mother felt ready to sign the form. Children and parents who said they were pleased to be informed, after initial distress, came to accept their fear, through talking it over like Lisa and Kerry or, like Alison, half-consciously absorbing it over time.[8]

Many young patients' ability to cope seemed to be based on mutual support: through children's desire not to worry their parents, and the assurance that their parents' decision expressed loving concern for the child. Elaine was very worried about pain, having to wear a large Milwaukee brace,[9] and the 'wake-up' test. Aged 12, she lived with her unemployed, single mother in a large, close extended family. Her mother described the whole family's worry during the three-month wait, but said, 'Elaine really was the best of us all. After a few tears she was very brave during the time we were making the decision, and afterwards she was as firm as a rock, no second thoughts'.

Children's silence about their fears, to protect their parents, can increase their fear; alternatively, it can perhaps be a helpful form of coping, just as parents get through stressful weeks of treatment by being determined not to 'break-down' in front of their child. Linda's mother was also single and unemployed. Linda, aged 8, had spina bifida, hydrocephalus and kyphosis. Her mother said:

I usually tell her everything. She wants to know exactly what is entailed. Last year her urethra ruptured and she was very upset that she wasn't warned fully about the catheters. I think she has reached the age of worrying about what is happening to her body. She's maturing very quickly and she asks, "Why me? Why is my body made wrong?"

Mr V said, "Ten per cent of these children don't come out of the theatre alive". I thought that was very fair, I wanted to know. It's the lesser of two evils, for her to have a better life. She reads books a lot, she writes down her questions and asks them in the clinic and wants to know, but I haven't told her about that risk. She was very worried when she saw the book of photos about spinal fusion.

Linda was a formidable interviewee, wanting to know the reasons for our questions. Her mother's methods of informing her appeared to sustain Linda's confidence before her fifth operation.

*Linda*: We've been waiting for ages. I say, thank goodness I'm getting it over and done with.
*Int.*: Were you looking forward to anything about coming into hospital?
*Linda*: Seeing the hospital videos again [she smiled], I really go for them!
*Int.*: And anything you weren't looking forward to?
*Linda*: Blood tests! Please tape, "And the children were saying, 'I don't want a blood test,' " [repeated three times in a pathetic tone].
*Int.*: And who do you think the doctors should talk to?
*Linda*: Mummy and me. And auntie should hear too, so she doesn't get worried [Leans over to kiss her aunt]. But particularly me, so I can face up to it if I'm frightened.
*Int.*: Who decided that the operation should be done now?
*Linda*: My doctor and my mummy decided about my operation. They knew what I wanted. After all she is my mum and I do trust her [kisses her mother].

Like many children, Linda hinted at controlled anxiety. Later, when her mother had gone, she said, 'When I get back tomorrow they'll be in tears for me'. Another time, Linda's mother said:

Several people at home said goodbye to her with tears in their eyes, and that worried her. She said, "Why are they crying, if I'm going to be back in a few weeks?" She said, "What if it goes wrong?" She's got the idea that you can have setbacks. I said, "Mr V is the very best doctor to do your operation for you".

Linda returned from theatre unexpectedly in a halo and Stryker bed. She was often distressed during the following weeks and relied heavily on her mother's and aunt's constant nursing. Talking about risk includes coping with setbacks as they arise, 'talking the child through the treatment' with constant encouragement, and working out with children how much they can cope with knowing. Parents and friends can do this when they are well informed.

### Does fear of risk lead children to refuse surgery?

Obviously we did not meet in the wards children who refused to arrive for their operation. Some admission lists showed repeated cancellations made for a very few children. Yet operations were far more commonly delayed through limited resources, or notes being lost or not followed up until parents kept reminding the hospital staff. During our study, one boy ran away from the hospital before his operation. Overall, refusing strongly advised surgery seemed to be rare, such as in the view of one surgeon who warned children about risks.

*Int.*: Do you know of any cases when children have refused surgery?

*Surgeon*: Not when I thought it was right, and they thought is was wrong. Between us, we've decided not to operate, maybe if the risks are too great, or the worries they have [about their condition] are not worth the risks they have to undergo. I've never had a child who refused surgery when I told them strongly that it was necessary, and I've been able to justify that view. They may come back three years later, and say, "Now I'm ready, please do something".

Another surgeon who explained detailed risks said:

I think people turn things down because they're scared stiff you're going to kill them, or maim them, or put them in a wheelchair. If you can take on board those concerns, and explain properly and talk over it. I can only think of one child who's been "allowed to get away with it" [refuse]. I try to explain that what we're doing, although dangerous, can be managed. I use analogies like crossing the road sometimes, i.e. you don't rush across without looking carefully. If you can see you're causing stress, then you've got to back off and start again, in a different way if necessary. If you're truthful, children then learn to trust what you say. If you're untruthful, you're written off just like the rest of adults, as people who use information for their own purposes, and I don't like that.

Warning of risk is likely to induce children to agree to surgery, rather than to refuse it, because high-risk treatment is usually attempted if the risks of the untreated condition are even higher. Lisa and Kerry, through evaluating risks, came to accept that surgery was 'the lesser of two evils'. Kerry only began to reject treatment when she felt inadequately informed and prepared; her confidence returned as she came to terms with her fear. The hoped-for benefits of surgery, explained by many children in Chapter 6, can equally be cited as the risks of not having surgery. Children usually mentioned these calmly, even those like Niki and Sally who thought they might die without treatment did not say they would rather not know, although they spoke to us after they had had time to come to terms with their fear. Earlier, concern at children's 'irrational' fears was mentioned. Yet many young patients' fears are rational, in that they are realistic and also carefully considered. Irrational fantasies are likely to flourish if information is withheld.

## Children's reasons for wanting to be informed

When people argue that patients 'don't want to know', they tend to confuse two very different matters. They usually mean risks which may never occur, very complex clinical details, or a frightening diagnosis or prognosis. In contrast, young patients we met wanted to be told details about, and reasons for, the treatment they would definitely experience, although this could include knowing about diagnosis and risk. The following examples illustrate some children's reasons for wanting to be informed.

### To obtain answers to their questions

New and experienced patients arrived wanting to know about each specific operation. For example, Lesley's mother commented: 'Lesley asked lots and lots of questions, it went on for about an hour, but he [consultant] didn't seem to mind'. Lesley's father was a car assembly worker. Aged 14, she planned to be a doctor, and wanted details about her leg-shortening treatment:

> I was surprised the metal plate was a strip with holes for the bolts. They'll cut down the side of my thigh and remove five centimetres from the thigh bone, then insert the metal plate to join the bones together and give support. I got a shock about the blood test. Why did I need one, and what is it for? It would be a good idea to have a booklet for each condition. I'm scared of all the tubes going into me, and of injections!

The surgeons who were most informative were the most highly liked and praised. For years, Julie, aged 11, had insisted that she needed surgery for her 'terrible crooked back'. Eventually she managed to get referred to a back specialist. Julie's mother said, 'He's marvellous, didn't half make her feel at ease. He put his arm round her and said, "You're totally unacceptable like this, we'll get you right". We both felt different'. Because he had taken so much time to talk to her, Julie felt that she could take up his time with questions. After her operation she was very worried that her back was 'clicking', and was relieved to be able to discuss this with the surgeon.

Barry, aged 10, showed how questions continually arose, for some children at least. Having congenital scoliosis, Barry was an experienced patient. His father was a fitter's mate. When asked whether anything unexpected had happened, Barry described being in the anaesthetic room:

> *Barry*: I had pads on my arms to measure the pulse and other things, and one on my toe. I worked out that it measures the oxygen in my blood. I saw the instructions on the wall. They asked mum to come in at 9.30 one evening. I was having trouble breathing. I had an oxygen mask and I was on 72 per cent oxygen.
>
> *Int.*: Do you wish anything had been explained that wasn't?

> *Barry*: All the tubes, what they were for. They told me there would be tubes, but I had to listen hard to find out what they were. They took a graft off my hip to strengthen my spine. I didn't hear about that until afterwards, and I would prefer to know beforehand.[10]

When asked how much warning he would like before an injection, Barry logically replied, 'An hour, because you have to wait an hour for the EMLA to work'.

### To relieve anxiety

Sheila, aged 14, had spina bifida and gave as her diagnosis, 'My feet are wrecked'. Her father was an unemployed electrician with leukaemia. Her mother described one highly informative consultant:

> You could ask him anything. He was wonderful, so different from the others. He explained everything and was sympathetic, understanding. He didn't rush us to make a decision, but once we decided he had us in the very next week. Her spinal cord was "saved", but it is permanently damaged and it's made her feet worse. We go to see him every year and he's always interested to hear how Sheila is progressing.
>
> But with her feet it's different. She's waiting for her sixth foot operation. All these operations and no success at all. We see lots of doctors but we never know their names. It's helpful to know who you've spoken to. She had a great deal of pain, and it's impossible to buy her attractive shoes.

The foot consultant suggested amputating the large, misshapen big toe. Sheila and her mother were very upset, and he assured them, 'We won't do anything you don't want. I'll discuss with my colleagues what is possible and let you know'. Sheila's mother continued:

> We expected to hear soon but that was five months ago. I kept 'phoning and eventually we got this appointment to come in. Sheila is so anxious. Ever since she was six we've been saying, "Just one more operation". We're not exactly sure what will be done, and how successful it will be.

During this interview, the consultant arrived with about ten students. Sheila's mother was not able to get near her. They examined the foot and conferred very quietly. Sheila's nose started to bleed, and a student found some tissues for her. The consultant appeared not to notice and walked away. He asked the interviewer how our research was going, and she then asked him if he would please explain to Sheila and her mother what he intended doing, as they were very anxious. He looked surprised and sent a junior doctor to explain. Afterwards Sheila's mother said:

> *Mother*: I felt shut out and not in on an important discussion on my daughter's foot. I felt unable to get into the group. But I thought,

he's bound to come and talk to me and tell me exactly what the operation is going to be. Instead a young doctor came to explain, but he could hardly speak English – something about wires and a plaster. He didn't know how long the plaster would be on. I asked the ward sister, and she didn't really know the details, but she was sure that the toe was not to be removed.

*Int.:* How do you feel about the operation now?

*Mother:* It must be Sheila's decision, but if this one isn't successful we don't want her to have any more. She doesn't worry too much about the operations, but she's very worried about injections, especially in her leg. When she was eight, a nurse was testing by squirting the liquid out of the syringe and it went near her face. She's been terrified of injections ever since. She can get quite hysterical and start screaming.

At this stage, they did not know that these injections were no longer given. The example illustrates how two questioners, the child and the parent, can be at a greater disadvantage in the choreography of the ward round than one, when they are uncertain who is going to be informed and when. Months later, Sheila said the operation had not worked and had 'definitely not been worth it'. The family felt that they had been through much unnecessary anxiety, and had not been told honestly about the slight chance of success. Doctors often seemed unaware of the anxiety in young patients, reaching a peak during ward rounds, and their longing to take part in discussions. They would wait anxiously for a week for a decision, only to be told, 'They'll decide in a week or two'.

### To feel respected

Some children who felt under-informed also felt under-respected. Cliff, aged 15, after seven operations, criticized a retired professor:

He never liked me, couldn't be bothered with me. He just wanted to get things done as quickly and cheaply as possible. When I was ten I had to have a knee operation done three times. The first two times he let his registrars do it because he said it wasn't difficult, but they just made it worse and more painful. He then did it himself, and it was OK. He never spoke to me, and only briefly to my mum and dad. The new professor is much better, he explains things to me and asks me what I think about it.

### To be able to cope with the treatment

Some consultants made last minute decisions without discussion with families. Kristie, aged 8, was the eldest of three sisters with congenital rickets. She and her middle sister were both due to have their bent tibias broken and reset 'although they can't guarantee they'll be straight'. Kristie said, 'I'd like to know more about how they are going to break the bones'. Although frightened, she very much wanted treatment because she was teased so badly at school. The paediatrician advised against surgery, preferring medication, but the surgeon advised surgery, leaving her parents uncertain. Her father was a television engineer. Kristie was expecting short leg plasters, but she woke up to find herself in plaster from the waist down. Kristie's mother said that her 3-year-old went to theatre first. The theatre staff 'phoned the ward to say that the surgeon:

> had to do her thigh bones as well, when he saw the X-rays. So we knew he was going to do the same with Kristie. We tried to tell her, but she was sleepy with the premed. I would never have had two girls done at the same time if I knew they were both going to have these huge plasters. How can I manage them both at home with a baby as well?[11]

### To maintain confidence

Many children repeatedly had surgery. Their parents felt that when everyone was well informed, problems affecting present and future treatment could be avoided. Grant, aged 13, had spina bifida and severe club feet which had not worried him until he recently decided to be 'on the go' and become a tourist coach driver like his father. He was haunted by bad memories of earlier bowel and bladder surgery, and though assured that foot surgery would be much easier to bear, he said, 'It's frustrating. They kept changing their minds. We're never sure what they're going to do'. Three consent forms were signed for three procedures on his feet. His mother commented, 'I know some medical terms, and I pick up what the doctors are saying, but I wish they'd use ordinary terms like "heel" '. Lack of clear detail made it harder for Grant and his mother to suppress worrying memories and doubts.

Robert, aged 12, with congenital scoliosis, also had daily growth hormone injections. He felt ambivalent about his spinal fusion, thinking he might prefer a brace. He wished he could read a book about scoliosis, and 'have a talk with Mr Z, just the two of us, not with all the other doctors about, so he can explain the whole thing'. With the interviewer's and his mother's encouragement, he asked the surgeon, 'Can you tell me exactly what you are going to do?', and they had a detailed discussion. Later, while in a halo and on traction he said, 'It's very good here, the people are very good'. Careful medical information could be therapeutic in increasing children's confidence in their treatment.

### To encourage cooperation

Withholding information can frighten children. Simon, aged 11, suddenly developed severe back pain and was unable to stand or sit. After weeks of uncertainty, his parents were told that he had a malignant tumour in his spine and that 'there was no hope'. His mother believed that 'sharing and talking together are important' and that Simon could understand the medical details as well as she could when he was ten. She told him about the tumour, but not that it was thought to be malignant. She said:

> It was harrowing, not knowing what it was and thinking the worst. They put him on valium which totally changed his character. For any child, they expect to be made better. But to be told "We don't know what's wrong with you, we don't know how to treat you", to wait for five weeks, in terrible pain, flat on your back, totally bored and frustrated, I think the whole thing made him completely untrusting of hospitals.

Simon later said: 'The professor just walked past my bed. He didn't know what to do and he was frightened. He talked to other patients but he was too scared to talk to me'. Later, Simon was transferred to the hospital where he was interviewed. His mother said:

> When we arrived here, he covered his mouth, and said, "You are not treating me, you will not feed me, I've had enough". It took a fortnight to get him having any faith in this hospital. They found it difficult to deal with him, because he was just stroppy about everything. But within 24 hours they'd controlled his pain. They discovered that the tumour was benign, but would have to be removed by surgery because it was growing all the time into his spine. It was six inches long, and causing the nerves to be squashed against his spinal canal and causing paralysis and pain in the legs.

### To make sense of their experience

Knowing their treatment plan helped children to appreciate the logic and good intentions underlying painful, frightening procedures. X-rays, scans and the experience of their illness or defect yielded confusing and alarming evidence which medical explanations helped young patients to understand. Simon said: 'I wanted to have the operation to get rid of the tumour in my back, well from the inside really, inside the spine. I couldn't feel the tumour, but I could feel what it was doing, squashing the nerves, and I saw it on the scan'.

He was talking during the four weeks between operations, and the pain became so severe that we stopped the interview. Simon was very worried that he might never walk again, or play football every evening with his friends. He said that once his friends came to see him at home, 'and they jollied me to get up, when I had to lie on the floor. My friend yanked my legs to lift me up. I screamed, and then I covered up for him when my Mum came and I said I fell down'. It was as if Simon had moved into a world of pain that his friends could not understand. Six months later, Simon was almost fully recovered.

## To 'take courage'

In 1767 a judge said, 'It is reasonable that a patient should be told about what is about to be done to him, that he may take courage and put himself into such a situation as to enable him to undergo the operation'[12] – or the weeks in traction or plaster. As Lisa, Kerry and Alison showed earlier, children need information and time in order to be able to 'take courage' to come to terms with major decisions.

## To receive continuing explanations and support

The idea of informed consent can wrongly stress that all information must be given beforehand. Yet many decisions are made during, as well as before, the course of treatment and as the child's state of health changes. Meg's mother said:

> It'll be an incision in the left groin, the aim is to cut through muscle tissue to release the leg, so the heel can touch the floor. Originally it was to be the tendons. I was surprised, worried by the change. They said she might go in a plaster cast. Meg was very worried about this. Later a message came via a nurse, no plaster but maybe traction. We don't really know what that involves.

Judy's mother said: 'They've told us the second operation isn't necessary. We don't *really* know what's going on. It's helpful if someone comes to update you each day'.

There was also time to get to know helpful professionals during their stay in the ward and to learn many more details from them. Kevin spoke for many others when he said he was pleased that, 'After the operation they told me all that they'd done, and showed me the X-rays showing that it had worked'.

## To avoid misunderstanding

Informed consent is usually assumed to centre on the surgeon's activities. In contrast, young patients usually wanted to know about their own likely activities, such as how long they would be in pain, in hospital or in plaster. Jane, aged 15, was extremely distressed about her short stature, and was very keen to have leg lengthening. Her growth was affected after she had treatment for a brain tumour, eight years earlier. Jane appeared to have been given a surgeon's rather than a patient's view of what to expect. 'They told me they'd sort of break my legs and put a metal thing inside and wind the bones apart, about six months for the tops, and six months for the bottoms'. The surgeon does fix the distracter to the bone inside the leg, but Jane had not realized that the main part of the distracter would also be outside, with open wounds during the lengthening. Many children told us of this misunderstanding, compounded by the logical medical term 'internal traction', which a photograph would have prevented.

The surgeon's account also assumed that the operation was the main event. After surgery Jane told me: 'I expected to be in bed and to have pain. I didn't realise it would be all this effort and energy, all this hard work and exercising, and that I'd feel so ill'. Hours before her first operation, someone casually mentioned that she'd be staying in for a year, assuming that she knew. Her severe depression at this news was compounded by the unexpected pain, infection in the pin sites, sleepless nights partly owing to the noisy night staff (many other children said this), disliking the hospital school, missing her home, and hormone reactions. Jane was on steroids, because of the earlier tumour treatment, and the nurses took over administering them. 'It should be three weeks on and one week off, but they get them mixed up, and some days they forget to give them', which made Jane feel weepy and upset. The psychiatrist put her on tranquillizers, saying that 'even if the ward was perfect she'd still be unhappy and complaining'. Months later, Jane's parents were so concerned about her depression that they insisted on taking her home. Her father said, 'The psychiatrist said that it would be good for her to spend a year in hospital. I said, "Give me one good reason why she should stay in, and I'll give you 12 good reasons why she shouldn't".' The family felt they would have coped better if they had been warned far more clearly about the realities of treatment.

### To know the emotional costs

Jane felt that the costs of her treatment were understated or denied before and during her treatment. Twelve days after Jane's first operation, her mother said:

> *Mother*: I think they tried to tell her all the problems: it could go wrong, or she'd have a limp with one leg longer than the other. They took photos and showed us what she would look like with longer legs but still with short arms. She had a psychological assessment to see if she really wanted the treatment and could take it. After we came in we were told there is a slight risk of infection. But the *emotional* implications of the treatment weren't explained. They're very cagey about how long it will take, they won't even tell you if it will be six months or two years. We didn't know of the risk of breaking the new bone, and the terrible shock that she'd be hospitalized for a year.
>
> *Jane*: I wish they'd explained the risks and the emotional strain. I get nightmares about having to stay in here. I didn't expect to have the plates like this, hanging on. It feels as if they're going to snap off. It's a horrible thought that there's metal poking into your legs. I can't get up and wash myself. I feel like an invalid and I hate that. I hate the nurses and I hate myself.
>
> *Mother*: She's very embarrassed when the male nurses wash her. I asked

the sister, please could we stay in today so that we could see the doctor because Jane is upset. [Parents had to stay outside the ward during school hours]. But she seemed to take that as a criticism. She said, "We'd expect her to settle in better by now. She hasn't come to terms with it and she doesn't seem to be in the right frame of mind". Talking to the other mothers – a lot of their kids are tearful and a bit low. But it's the nurses' attitude. At times of stress they haven't been very understanding.

*Int.*: If a 15-year-old girl was waiting to have leg lengthening and asked you what it was like, what do you think it is most important to tell her?

*Jane*: Having to stay in hospital for a year. It's an effort and a strain. The metal plates are inside *and* outside. I'd tell her about the feel and experience of it. I think it's worth it in the end, but it's very hard at the beginning. I think I would tell her, it would help to prepare her.

### To avoid unnecessary distress

Unlike the other examples, of children knowing the effects on them of being informed or not informed, Sandra and her mother did not know that her treatment was controversial. Her consultant prescribed use of a spinal traction machine, to prepare for Sandra's seventh operation for congenital scoliosis. The metal frame had many leather straps and buckles to hold her head and feet while she lay down, pulling her feet up and down by bending her knees. Sandra, aged 10, was very small and shy and deformed. She dreaded walking all through the boys' ward to the exercise room at the far end. The interviewer wrote:

It took an enormous effort and I found it most distressing to see this frail little girl trying with all her will to do this as she thought it would help to make her back straighter. She was supposed to do it three or four times a day, for a few minutes as she got so exhausted, but it took a long time to cope with all the buckles. The nurses did not have time, and seemed reluctant. So Sandra's mother, who was not well, and knowing Sandra hated the exercise, would take her.

The machine hadn't been used for ages, because most doctors believed it was useless. One consultant had also stopped using other kinds of traction and halos for scoliosis children, saying that no research had proved their effectiveness. He claimed that his patients recovered as successfully, with much less discomfort.

Discussion of other surgeons' views would help patients to become more informed. Yet this can also increase their uncertainty and difficulty if surgeons do not offer a range of therapies.

## How much do children want to know?

It is perhaps impossible to discover whether children would prefer to be told about risk. Everyone who said that they had been told, and had worried, added that they would rather know. Yet they were either children whose treatment had gone well, and they were generally satisfied, or those whose treatment had been less effective and who appreciated warning of harms they experienced, or were upset about lack of warning. In retrospect, few people are likely to say that they would rather have been left in ignorance, and those who were ignorant were unlikely to know it.

Over two-thirds of the 120 parents said there was no topic they found 'hard to discuss' with their child. The others were reluctant to talk about certain risks, or aspects of the treatment or a gloomy prognosis. David's mother listened to his interview account of his treatment, and then said:

> He's got it right. We tried to tell him before, what it would be like. It was a strain on him and on the family. He knew they was going to build up the bone in his hip, but I didn't tell him where they'd get the bone graft from. He didn't see that other wound because it was under plaster for weeks. He's only ten, and he'd get all concerned, and his imagination would run riot, so I didn't go too deeply into it, but we told him more or less everything.

Some mothers were angry about what their children were told. 'The psychiatrist said to Eric, "I don't want you to think the [halo] screws go right into your brain".' They felt they had to 'pick up the pieces afterwards' left by insensitive informers, and to interpret and filter the consultant's information, feeling that 'Mr J wasn't on our wavelength', or 'I don't think Mr K belonged to our world'. Eric, aged 12, was very disturbed after being in halo traction, having nightmares for months afterwards. When asked what he would tell another boy about it, he replied, 'I don't know, I wouldn't want to frighten him, the thought is so awful'. Yet if it ever happened again he said that he would need more warning 'to get used to it first'. Mandy, who was unable to walk and was doubly incontinent for a time after her spinal fusion, praised her surgeon: 'He's been wonderful'. He had carefully warned her about the risks, and immediately came to talk with Mandy and her mother when the paralysis was known. Careful discussion generally seemed to increase children's confidence, but was not always easily achieved, as we found during our interviews.

## Ethical questions

Questions raised by our research methods illustrate difficulties in talking with children about pain and risk. Children's consent is a new area for empirical research needing to be approached cautiously. Orthopaedic surgery is seldom overshadowed by lifesaving and death-risking considerations, but it raises questions about how much children should be warned about harms and risks, or encouraged with the promise of benefits which may not be realized, so that they then feel doubly betrayed. Asking people questions about consent which they may not have thought of risks shifting them from certainty to doubt, from acceptance to questioning, and might increase stress or disrupt a precarious calm. Would our research raise frightening questions which everyone would rather avoid? How can honesty and reassurance best be combined? We asked general, open questions when possible, and saved several issues until after the operation.

After considering home visits before surgery, we decided to interview children in hospital the day or morning before their operation. Being on a waiting list was like playing roulette, with last minute cancellations, emergencies and list revisions. We could have spent weeks interviewing patients who did not then have surgery during the study period, and would miss many others. Some children were on waiting lists for more than one hospital. Details were often explained after admission, so interviewees might have little to say at home visits. Yet the chosen timing meant talking to particularly anxious people, which obviously affected the questioning and the replies. There are pros and cons for any interview timing. Interviews at the time of the experience evoke vivid, varied responses. Our home interviews after surgery tended to be much less detailed about hospital experiences and were highly coloured by gratitude, bitterness or uncertainty about the results of surgery.

Ethics guidelines distinguish between research associated with therapy and research which is not. Sociologists do not treat patients. Since their research offers no therapy, it should incur no risks, particularly research with children. 'Risks' are usually assumed to be the physical harms of invasive clinical research. Psychosocial research is quickly approved by some medical ethics committees as non-invasive, though it can be intrusive, mentally wounding, embarrassing and anxiety-raising. Researchers have to try to ensure that the wishes and feelings of each subject are respected. This is not easy, when patients may be too scared or embarrassed to show if the interview upsets them. If we sensed that this might be happening we tried to change the topic unobtrusively, and be ready to close the interview as soon as possible, without implying that the session was a failure.

Avoiding harm can be difficult. A probing question may wound or offer a welcome opening. People may enjoy a conversation at the time but later be unhappy about how much they revealed, or they may not enjoy it at the time but remember it gratefully. The research conversation tries to balance respect for privacy and anxiety with encouragement to people to reveal themselves. In this, it resembles patient–doctor discussions about consent, when patients question the surgeon's skill and knowledge, and surgeons try to give fair warning of harms yet also to safeguard patients' willingness to undergo treatment. Our research method was also our data. Interviews involve respecting people's willing consent to continue only as long as they choose. A main concern was to find ways of enabling children to talk about their anxieties, without undermining their confidence in their treatment or in the adults caring for them.

Denial complicated the interviews. Denial can help children to cope with fortitude, and was a major method of pain control in some wards. Questioning denial raises ethical problems. Eight-year-old Louise was often tearful about her leg lengthening, but was absorbed in her lessons, and then began her interview quite cheerfully. As we talked about her treatment she became quieter and sadder, and then pulled away the blanket covering her leg. She began to cry as she looked at her wounds, her father came to comfort her and we stopped the interview. Perhaps she needed to show her distress and ask for comfort more than was allowed in the ward where the policy was to distract children with firm optimism and 'normal' activities. Our research could be bland and misleading if all interviews stopped at the level of denial. Yet discussion can stir up feelings which children would prefer to hide or avoid.[13]

We did not want children to feel that we were part of the hospital hierarchy. Obviously we did not walk around in suits with clip boards and brief cases, and we aimed to be friendly and not pushy. Doctors would interrupt the interviews as if they thought we were other mothers chatting; children told us when they were busy and when we could come back later to suit them. Many people seemed to enjoy talking to us, and sometimes to find much needed relief in pouring out their thoughts. We hope that this was so, but research interviews are not intended to be therapeutic.[14] Research is about collecting data from people. They help us, and if we help them in return that is a bonus, but not the priority. The ethical responsibility is to remember this one-sidedness of research, and our obligations to the people helping us not to abuse them by taking more than they are willing to give.

### Combining protection and respect

Although protecting children by silence and respecting them by giving honest but alarming information are seen as opposites, they are also complementary. The idea that information inevitably frightens children, implies that they are empty vessels, without a thought unless it is introduced by an adult. It also implies that talking about harms is worse than experiencing them.[15] Yet young patients have misunderstandings and anxieties which information can protectively alleviate. Unless serious diagnoses and prognoses are, at least partly, discussed, the treatment can seem to the child much worse than the disease. Telling children about risk respectfully treats them as mature people, and protects them from the shock of unexpected harms. Yet telling them too suddenly can disrespectfully hurt them, and then protective silence can seem more respectful of their feelings. Patients having serious treatment can never be completely protected; the alternatives are unpleasant information, or unexpected unpleasant experiences. Respect and protection are combined when information is shared *with* children at their own pace, instead of being given *to* them.

Sharing information is then a process and an interaction, not just a standard transmission of messages. Children differ, and need adults to explore with them how much they want to know. This is hard to achieve without discussing more about harms than the child or the adults may wish to do. Yet giving too much information, too soon, can be avoided by using suggestion, following cues, asking what the child knows or believes will happen, and using other communication skills.[16] Through this two-way exchange, adults and the growing child can increase their understanding and ability to share knowledge. Avoiding discussion can be convenient for adults but less so for children, especially if it denies them a main reason for informing them, the chance to share in making decisions. Chapter 9 examines whether the children we met were able and willing to do this.

## Notes

1 Asking people if they think they have been 'told enough' implies that information is something they should have been given and understood. Although the question allocates responsibility to the professionals, it can be awkward for parents to reply honestly, 'I don't know' or 'I don't want to know'. Not wanting to make parents feel ignorant or negligent, we dealt briefly with these questions unless parents wanted to discuss them.

2 Another possibility is that children with chronic problems tend to be generally more compassionate.

3 The two-year examination course for 14- to 16-year-olds. GCSEs are much more practical that the old GCE exams. It is harder for students to read up the syllabus quickly on their own, and missing school during the course can very much lower continuous assessment marks. Many adolescents in hospital worry more about how their schooling is affected when GCSEs and core curriculum work penalize those who are absent from school.

4 Taylor, K. and Kelner, M. (1987) Informed consent: The physicians' perspective. *Social Science and Medicine*, 24(2), 135–43.

5 Maguire, P. (1985) Barriers to psychological care of the dying. *British Medical Journal*, 291, 178–83.

6 'Unemployed' means unpaid; the mothers were fully occupied in caring for their children. The mature adult-to-adult relationship which many children had with their single parent challenges the assumption that children from 'broken' homes are inevitably emotionally disadvantaged. Some seemed to benefit by, in a sense, growing into the space left by the absent adult.

7 British Scoliosis Society, *Advice for Those Consenting to Spinal Deformity Surgery*. Some surgeons also used this as an extra consent form warning of the risk of 'paralysis with loss of the use of the legs and loss of control of the bladder and bowels', which considerably alarmed families. The legal language and demand for a signature is an example of how not to give such information.

8 During the months of waiting for surgery, some parents felt they must keep reminding the child about the operation, yet some children firmly resisted this. They were perhaps the best judge of how much discussion they needed.

9 Which she did not have to wear, just as Kerry did not have full traction. Books of photographs of children having treatment are increasingly used, but may be better used selectively instead of routinely. Some pictures used by social workers, such as of the Milwaukee jacket, were out-of-date showing grotesque, obsolete or very rarely used equipment, which caused children severe, unnecessary anxiety.

10 Informed discussion about such bone grafting would include considering 'morbidity at the donor site, which includes postoperative pain, infection, wound scarring, anaesthesia of the buttock, herniation of muscle, meralgia parasthetica, subluxation [incomplete dislocation] of the hip, and prolongation of hospital stay [also that] the volume required often exceeds what is available, especially in children'. Nolan, P., Mollan, R. and Wilson, D. (1992) Living bone grafts. *British Medical Journal*, 304, 1520–21. Several of the medical terms express actual experiences which can be explained in plain English.

11 This example links the mothers' and daughters' need for information because their needs often overlapped.

12 *Slater* v. *Baker and Stapleton*, 1767/94 ER 60.

13 Psychotherapists at the Royal Free Hospital kindly allowed me to attend their discussions on whether denial helps children to cope or damagingly represses painful feelings.

14 Although there is evidence that sociological research interviews can be therapeutic. Oakley, A., Rajan, L. and Grant, A. (1990) The Social Support and Pregnancy Outcome Study. *British Journal of Obstetrics and Gynaecology*, 97, 155–62.

15 Part of the mind/body split in which the word counts for more than experience, and children who have little speech have little sense of experiences such as pain.

16 Cushing, A. (1992) Teaching communication skills in medical education. *Bulletin of Medical Ethics*, 79, 21–4.

# 9

## MAKING A WISE CHOICE: COMPETENCE TO CONSENT

*But are you going to lay on children the weight of their future? Perhaps let them make a decision that could lead to their death? These are impossible questions, but hospital staff have to find the answers. Am I big enough to say, "Whatever you choose will be valued, even if you decide against the tide; OK, you've made that decision, I'll do all I can to support you, and we'll go forward together"? It's such a big step for the adult to surrender power to the child.*

(Hospital chaplain, 1991)

Competence to consent to children's treatment involves three things: understanding the proposed treatment, being able to make a wise decision[1] and being free from coercion. This chapter mainly considers wisdom and coercion. It examines how competence can be defined and assessed, and reports adults' and children's views on when certain children are competent. Just as informing children raises tensions between respecting and protecting them, consent raises tensions between reason and coercion. If children disagree with adults, how far is it thought to be possible to reason with them, or necessary to coerce them? Views on this question will be discussed. Certain children such as Amy and her mother thought that she could decide competently about leg lengthening when she was 8 years old. At 12 she repeated her decision and began the second stage, but was her decision wise? Understanding and wisdom overlap but also differ.[2]

### Defining and assessing competence

Competence to consent is a complex and contentious topic.[3] There are basically three ways of testing competence.[4]

- *Status*: does the patient belong to a group usually assumed to be incompetent, such as being unconscious, senile or a young child?
- *Outcome*: is the decision competent in that it is likely to result in a desirable outcome?
- *Function*: can the patient pass tests of ability, either to decide about the particular operation, or to show general competence?[5]

**Table 14**   Views on when certain children can decide about proposed surgery

| Year group cited | Numbers of replies from: | | |
|---|---|---|---|
| | Patients (n = 120) | Parents (n = 120) | Health professionals (n = 70) |
| under 8 | 0 | 4 | 15 |
| 8–10 | 12 | 6 | 15 |
| 11–15 | 48 | 53 | 25 |
| 16+ | 36 | 37 | 10 |
| Don't know | 24 | 20 | 5 |
| Mean | 14.0 years | 13.9 years | 10.3 years |

Tests tend to set standards of abstract reasoning which many adults would fail.[6] 'Threshold' competence sets a definite boundary between 'competents and incompetents'. 'Degree' competence allows for an uncertain overlap between the two groups, realistically accepting that competence is usually assessed in doubtful, borderline cases.

There was much disagreement among our interviewees and in the literature about defining and assessing competence, as with understanding, so in our research we did not attempt to impose our own standards. Instead, we asked interviewees how they defined and assessed children's competence.[7] The 120 young patients were asked, 'How old do you think you were or will be when you're old enough to decide?' about proposed surgery. Their parents were asked: 'At what age do you think your child could make a wise choice?' about the proposed operation. When a mother and father were interviewed together, we took the younger age stated. Seventy health professionals were asked a different kind of question, to select from all their experience possibly exceptional cases: 'Children vary greatly, but what is around the youngest age when you think *some* of your patients could be trusted to make sensible, wise, mature decisions about proposed surgery?' Views on when certain children can decide are shown in Table 14, and ages given for boys and girls are shown in Table 15. The discussion in Chapter 7 on the complications within Table 9 applies to these tables.

As discussed in Chapter 3, 'competence' has complex, partly contradictory meanings: the wisdom to make a correct decision and the courage to stand by a best guess, to take responsibility as a moral agent. Interviews were complicated by these conflicting meanings which could not be disentangled, since each meaning is integral to modern meanings of competence. The shaky concept of competence in law and ethics has been criticized.[8] Competence is based on rationality, the linchpin of ethics. Rationality is promoted as the only means of resolving the conflict between what we *want* to do and what we *should* do within modern individualist ethics, when there is no longer common agreement on what is right or good and everyone has to work out a personal solution.

**Table 15**  Views of 120 parents on when their son or daughter could decide about surgery

| Child's actual age group | Mean age in years cited by parents | |
| --- | --- | --- |
| | Boys | Girls |
| 8–10 | 15.3 | 11.9 |
| 11–13 | 14.7 | 12.4 |
| 14–15 | 15.1 | 13.8 |
| Overall mean age | 14.9 | 12.8 |

Rationality has something to do with having consistent and coherent beliefs, but is far more clearly defined negatively by examples of irrationality. The clearest way for certain groups to claim competence is therefore to class other groups as incompetent. Constructing children as incompetent rescues adults from uncomfortable enquiry into their own ability and wisdom, which can be taken-for-granted through their adult status.[9] Some philosophers argue that almost all patients should be respected for their partial autonomy, since many are ill and anxious, instead of unrealistically assuming that some are highly competent, and dismissing the rest.[10]

The tables only indicate approximate ages when children begin to be considered competent, as a general guide to the wide range of views on how certain young children are respected. A fourth group questioned were the 983 school pupils (see Chapter 6, note 5) who were asked: 'At what age do you think someone is old enough to decide with their doctor about surgery, without their parents being involved?' The replies ranged from infancy to adulthood, and the mean age cited from each school was from 15 to 17 years. When the school and hospital studies are compared, the replies suggest that children who have experienced surgery are more likely to see themselves as competent to consent. The mean age of the girls we interviewed in hospital was 12.1 years, and that of the boys 12.4 years (Table 2). Yet the girls gave a mean age of competence of 13.1 years, and the boys a mean of 15.0 years. The parents' replies for boys and girls varied by over two years, as shown in Table 15.

Examples of some replies will be given, grouped by respondents who initially replied 16 years and over, or under 16 years. Children, parents, members of each profession, and staff within each ward gave widely varying replies. Obviously, professional relationships with children vary; teachers, for instance, have little to do with medical decisions. The range of professionals was interviewed to explore different understandings of children's competence, and the possibility of a ward team policy on competence. We did not find one, although professionals seemed unaware of differences among their colleagues, such as the sister who said, 'You'll find everyone here thinks children can consent when they're 13'.

### Competence at 16 years or over

The highest age, in effect 'never', was given initially by the surgeon, who said:

> Don't you think we're going in for over-kill with this consent business? Adults don't have the knowledge to make decisions. People should take their surgeon's instructions. I make it clear to them. "This is my opinion. If you don't like it then go elsewhere".

When asked about leg lengthening, he added:

> *Surgeon*: Oh, that's a massive undertaking, and it has major complications. Kids really have got to want it.
> *Int.*: How would you assess whether they want it?
> *Surgeon*: They would have to tell me themselves, spontaneously, with vigour.
> *Int.*: And you would say the decision is up to the child?
> *Surgeon*: Yes. It's important to find out whether the child wants it and not just the parents. The child must very vigorously *want* something done.
> *Int.*: At around what age would you expect them to be able to decide?
> *Surgeon*: Eight, nine.

A frequent reply was, 'Consent? I've never really thought about it', or 'Consent is not my responsibility'. There was uncertainty and confusion. A physiotherapist similarly modified her initial reply:

> *Physiotherapist*: With the children I've come across I would say consent begins at the age of 18.
> *Int.*: Before that, their parents have to decide for them?
> *Physio.*: Yes, I feel so.
> *Int.*: So it's nice if the child wants to have it, but if they don't want to, it's important that the adults override the child?
> *Physio.*: Oh, no, no, no. I see what you mean. No, I don't think parents should have the choice rather than the child. If it's something the child doesn't want to have, I think they should go by the child's decision.
> *Int.*: If it was a clinical decision, who should decide?
> *Physio.*: For a clinical decision, the parents should decide. For something cosmetic, or non-urgent or non-essential, the child should have the choice.
> *Int.*: Down to what sort of age?
> *Physio.*: Eighteen again.
> *Int.*: You said younger children?
> *Physio.*: Oh. I see. From the age when they can talk and understand, two or three if it's not essential.

Most people set the age of understanding proposed treatment as lower than the age of being able to make a choice about it. By stressing willingness but avoiding wisdom, and assuming that children could 'want' leg lengthening but could not understand it, these two interviewees were unusual in reversing the age order.[11]

Professionals who saw understanding as an academic matter usually gave high ages for competence. For example, a second surgeon said of understanding: 'They can't understand until they've seen tendons, learnt about them in biology, say for GCSE. I say to adult patients, "How on earth can I teach you in five minutes chat, when it takes doctors years to learn how to make informed decisions?" ' When asked about the youngest age when he thought some of his patients could make sensible decisions about proposed surgery, he replied: 'Help. [*Long pause.*] I suppose basically when the child becomes an adult. With my own children, when they're 16 I suppose, when legally they're allowed to make their own decisions'.

Yet the surgeon was interviewed after an out-patient clinic in which every child had unequal leg lengths. One 14-year-old's four-centimetre difference was on the borderline to be considered for surgery; he had advised her to consider the options and to write to him about her decision. The interviewer mentioned her, and asked:

*Int.*: You wouldn't operate if you thought just her parents wanted it?
*Surgeon*: No, certainly.
*Int.*: So you would leave the decision with her?
*Surgeon*: Oh yes. Unless they're very keen they're unlikely to carry it through to completion. The same with spinal fusion, or club foot. There are absolute indications, or almost, but there are grey areas, and then it's an awful lot what the patient wants. The treatment sometimes produces problems of its own. There's a lot of choice, and weighing up the pros and cons. Yes, children are allowed to refuse.
*Int.*: Do you think the child's willing acceptance of, or commitment to, treatment matters?
*Surgeon*: Yes, 100 per cent. There's no point in starting leg lengthening unless the child's willing to go through with it.

Several practitioners, who in theory assumed that children were incompetent, in practice treated some of them as competent. However, two SHOs, the most junior doctors who usually administered the consent forms,[12] asserted; 'Of course, I don't ask anyone under 16 for their consent. It's against the law' and 'The consultant has instructed us in the law'. Other doctors said, 'This is a children's hospital, it's always parents who give the consents'. A GP stated, 'I would never see a patient under 16 on his own. It would be too much responsibility for the doctor to make decisions without the parents'.

Several hospital teachers felt that 'understanding' meant GCSE or A level standard. They tended to be protective, as in one adolescent ward.

*Teacher 1*: I don't think they have any conception of what is involved, if they haven't already seen it happening. It's very important they understand as much as possible, but not to leave a decision to them. They won't realise that it's for their long-term good, and they'll be too frightened. So it would place a very unfair burden on them to leave the decision to them. Even adults and later teens take the doctors' advice and are not capable of taking decisions.

*Int.*: You seem to imply that if they're given the choice, children would refuse treatment, and it sort of has to be forced on them. But what actually happens here?

*Teacher 1*: I can't recall a child who said "no". They are all willing.

*Teacher 2*: It seems to me they expect to have their operation.

*Teacher 1*: If a child ever starts questioning, if we pick up any worries, we pass them straight on to the doctors or nurses and it's always ironed out.

*Teacher 2*: The little ones cry, but that's different. They're just frightened of going down to theatre.

*Teacher 1*: I think children should go along with it, but I think it's the parents' decision. Conflict between the parents and the child would be very undesirable. I think you should get them to agree. I think the age of consent to lots of things is far too young. Children aren't ready for them yet. But I've never seen disagreements.

*Teacher 2*: They do need to agree because they're all going to need each other during the getting-better process.

The teachers implied that harmony must mean the child's submission. Another teacher thought that routine decision making excluded children.

*Teacher*: Making a "decision" implies some alternative. But proposals are put in such a way here that there is no other alternative. Do you mean that what the child says should carry some weight? I'd like them to have a say, but I wouldn't want my own children to make a decision without me until they're at least 18. Then hopefully, they'll have the decision-making skills, and I'd probably trust their reasons. They probably could make decisions on a just basis earlier, and realise the full implications, but not solely on their own. If my 15-year-old went for family planning I wouldn't be pleased, but I'd accept that. But not for life-threatening surgery. She wouldn't have the breadth of experience to draw on to know all the pros and cons.

*Int.*: Yet contraception involves all kinds of implications – personal relationships, the possibility of pregnancy, STD, AIDS.

*Teacher*: Yes, but they will have learnt something about all that at school. But life-threatening surgery is different.

One hospital teacher, the mother of teenage children, said that she had spent a sleepless night worrying after her interview: 'I'd never thought about these difficult things and it really upset me. I like to think of a caring family, where the parents make all the decisions and protect the child from such things'.

Some people gave very young ages for understanding but high ages for competence. A play specialist, who thought that 1- and 2-year-olds could understand much through play preparation, said for competence; 'Possibly at 16, but before then, they don't think of the long-term effects, and they all regress to an earlier stage when they're in hospital'.[13] A psychologist from an oncology ward who was concerned that 'the end-stage sometimes goes on being hopelessly treated', referred to her training decades earlier. She said, 'My developmental training tells me that it isn't right to expect children to have to consent, to load them with that responsibility and that potential for guilt'.

A psychiatrist thought that discussing children's competence was 'impossible', and 'extraordinarily difficult outside a developmental context'. It could only be understood by expert doctors, trained to test children's reading and mathematical ability. (Hospital teachers thought a maths test was irrelevant: 'It would only tell you whether the child understood that maths problem'.) Most hospital staff, the psychiatrist felt, were 'naive assessors', not trained to judge 'intellectual development' or determine the 'relevance' of information:

> *Psychiatrist*: What children consent to may be a lot more or a lot less than they understand.
> *Int.*: Can it be called consent if they don't know what they're agreeing to?
> *Psych.*: That's the whole problem about consent. Of course they can consent, but if you're talking about a legal framework, what does consent mean? Does it carry the implication that if they don't consent they don't get it? Is consent purely a subjective experience, or does it in some way influence the other person?

The psychiatrist felt that young children could not grasp abstract concepts of preventative treatment and, 'By and large, naive children don't have a concept of death till they're about ten. There are stages of death concepts – a book by a girl called Sylvia Anthony'.[14] He saw children as passive.

> Informed consent means that you explain to them what is going on, and you say, "Do you understand?" And they can say "Yes" or "No", so they can give consent in that way. There is a difference between what a child says they understand and what an adult actually decides to do. I do think there are definitely occasions when children do not want a procedure to be undertaken. It should still be done . . . in the developmental interests of the child. I think children absolutely have that right to know exactly what is going to happen, why they are having it, the benefits of having it, and the risks of not having it.

Treatment is here implicitly benign, without risks or harms. The psychiatrist gave examples of children's 'non-compliance' with dentists', teachers' and surgeons' decisions. He attributed these to 'psychiatric disturbance, neurotic disorder, always in relation to family disturbance of some sort', and insisted that if refusal was 'only due to fear' it must be overcome. Eventually, when asked whether he thought that operations could ever be unnecessary or unhelpful, he looked very surprised:

Psych.: An operation unnecessary?

Int.: Do you think children can't refuse? You seem to imply that children can't make rational choices. If a surgeon says, "You need this done", and the child says "no", the surgeon is always right and the child is always wrong.

Psych.: You mean the surgeon is wrong about recommending the need for surgery? [Long pause.] Well. That's an interesting idea. Rather than that the child doesn't like the surgeon?

The psychiatrist appeared to be unaware of 'grey areas' when, surgeons told us, they preferred children to decide. Asked whether he would actually enforce treatment, the summary of his long reply is: '[No, but] we go on and on until we get what we think is right . . . It would be irresponsible not to make them have it . . . Otherwise one is colluding with the self-destructive behaviour on the part of the child'. The psychiatrist was called in if a child refused surgery. He seemed to see refusal as a form of mental pathology which he should cure.

Parents and children, who gave an age of competence of 16, 18 or 21, tended to believe 'you're not allowed to before then' by law. They identified competence with 'being grown-up'; 'you can decide an operation when you're old enough to go out to work, or leave home'. Replies were affected by experience. For example, 11-year-old Kevin may have been influenced by guilt and bad luck. His leg was injured in a traffic accident when he was 7 years old. After three operations, including a skin graft when his leg became severely infected, he was critical of his local hospital which eventually referred him to a specialist centre: 'They knew they done it all wrong, so they sent me here to the professionals'. His operation date was brought forward because his leg was so painful.

Int.: Who do you think the doctors should talk to, your parents, or you or all of you?

Kevin: They should talk to my Mum, 'cos she understands more and she'll tell me.

Int.: Who decided that your operation should be done now? Doctors, or parents, or you, or all of you together?

Kevin: Me.

Int.: Who do you think should decide?

Kevin: Me, 'cos the pain in my leg might be getting worse all the time, and if they leave it, it might get really bad. But, well, maybe it should be decided all together. I don't know. It's up to me, but if my mum

and dad wanted it left until later, then I'd have to go with them, 'cos
they have to sign 'cos I'm their son. And if I decide and then it goes
wrong, then I'd get the blame.

*Int.*: How old do you think you'd be when you were or will be old
enough to decide?

*Kevin*: 18, 16. At seven, the parents can decide without the child, and
after eight, they start talking with him.

*Mother*: I think Kevin is right. About eight you can start, and he could
understand as well as I could at about eight or nine, and decide for
himself when he's seventeen.

Moira's mother was unhappy that the surgeon had accepted Moira's refusal
to have a toe amputated and one arm slightly altered, as advised by her physiotherapist. Moira, aged 14, walked very slowly in callipers; with her rigid limbs
she was unable to protect herself if she fell. She believed that she could decide
about surgery 'when I was 12'.

*Moira's mother*: Especially in your teens, you battle with your parents
because you think you know. You've been unreasonable, ever since
you were a tiny baby. I don't feel you can make the correct decisions.
[She quoted people who had refused surgery in adolescence and, "when
it was too late", in bitter regret blamed their parents.] It would be
easier to lift her if she had her foot done. It kills my back trying to
lift her. The school physio was really disappointed, she couldn't believe
it hadn't been done. Moira pretends everything's all right. Perhaps
I and all my friends are old-fashioned. I think there's a difference
between a child understanding what's going to be done, and looking
to the future.

*Int.*: Do you think you can look ahead to the future, Moira?

*Moira*: Yep.

*Int.*: Such as when you're 30? What will it be like?

*Moira*: I'll have an electric chair.

*Mother*: Yes, right. You need to think of other people, not yourself, but
I don't think that is something a child can. It probably comes with
maturity.

*Int.*: Do you see yourself as being more independent because you'll have
more aids?

*Moira*: Yes [laughs rather bitterly].

Moira's mother described the long battle between Moira, who wanted to live
as much like her disabled friends as possible by using aids, and her mother and
physiotherapist, who insisted that she walk and use her limbs as much as possible as a 'normal' girl would do. The dispute between Moira's idea of social
normality, and the adults' idea of physical normality, related to whether the
surgery decision was considered wise.[15]

Adults who gave high ages for competence tended to value textbook knowledge over learning through experience, both in themselves (by quoting books or training rather than their own experience) and in children (by linking competence with academic knowledge). They tended to discuss children in abstract terms. The psychiatrist spent two hours insisting that it was impossible to generalize, but refusing to discuss individual cases (although children's decisions, such as Amy's choice of leg lengthening, easily look bizarre, unless seen in the context of their personal experiences and values). These respondents stressed the need for wise adults to protect immature children. They avoided considering the problems of coercion if children resist adults' decisions, such as by seeing any coercion as rightful law-enforcement, or necessary firmness. They tended to be functionalists,[16] assuming that the correct solution chosen by those in authority fits everyone's best interests. They advised formal testing of competence, but mainly identified competence with the status of adulthood; 'developing' children were seen as incompetent and *tabula rasa*.[17]

### Competence before 16 years

Adults who replied that children under 16 years could be competent tended to discuss their experience of individual children, stressing the need to avoid generalizing and assess carefully.

> *Paediatrician*: You'd look at how articulate the child is, whether they've normal personality and general development, whether their background will allow them to understand quite readily what we're talking about – educational, social, ethnic. Sometimes language difficulties are quite a problem. I think anyone over the age of 9 or 10 who positively refuses to have blood taken, or have an IV cannula put in to be given sedation, then I'd be extremely unhappy to proceed.
>
> *Int.*: What would you do then?
>
> *Paed.*: Well I usually get the play ladies involved, or a psychologist, or give oral sedation first. The child may later be sufficiently happy with life, provided the parents are happy of course, to allow the cannula to be sited.
>
> *Int.*: So it's mainly a question of overcoming their opposition as kindly and gently as you can?
>
> *Paed.*: Yes.
>
> *Int.*: We're talking of irrational refusal?
>
> *Paed.*: My experience of spectacular refusals are to do with the child's previous experience of procedures. They've obviously been so disturbed by some procedures that they freak out. If you haven't got compliance in recurrent interventions, then of course you get poor take-up later – with cystic fibrosis or diabetes. You often run into trouble in

the teenage years because they haven't been entirely happy with the previous treatment.

This consultant thought that children's requests for unnecessary surgery 'for some cosmetic problem they're terribly worried about' were more likely to occur than their refusal of necessary surgery.

Professionals discussed how competence was affected by children's temperament and experience, their independence and optimism, caution or courage, and relations between parents and child. A chaplain said:

> You can't suddenly give rights to children when they may not have the experience to equip them to cope. If you accept that children have rights, you bring them up as a valued person, you ask your child to make decisions almost from the word go.

Three hospital teachers agreed that children of around nine could be competent. They would assess children by 'whether they ask what's going to happen, and how it might affect them and its implications':

> *Int.*: Do you think the child's willing acceptance of, or commitment to, treatment matters?
> *Teacher 1*: Yes, and the parents' acceptance matters too. [She gave examples of non-cooperation with treatment.]
> *Teacher 2*: If the child and parents and nurses are all willing, then they are all pulling the same way, it's a shared response.

One surgeon thought, 'The variation is absolutely enormous. I know lots of adults who can't make decisions'. He had 'come across a couple of children who are able to make decisions remarkably well' at 8 years, and thought some 13-year-olds were 'much more sensible than their parents'. He repeated the terms 'manage' and 'deal with', referring to the child's emotional maturity to cope with hard concepts: 'If they ask an appropriate question leading on from the information, I think you can assume that you are able to communicate something they've taken in, and understood, and can deal with'.

A social worker in a bone marrow transplant unit thought that 'the oldest survivor in our unit is 14 and he could probably make very informed decisions, because of what he's been through'. However, she felt that few patients could understand. The treatment was not for leukaemia, but to prevent genetic diseases from progressing; the children were still healthy and usually very young. It is far harder to explain severe preventative treatment than to explain treatment intended to alleviate or cure problems which the child is already experiencing. The social worker suggested how understanding shades into wisdom:

> Some children understand practically, but maybe not emotionally. They may be told that, "Your hair will fall out, and steroids will make you swollen and you'll get lots of pain and tummy ache", but they can't know

until they experience it, and then there's no turning back. How can you explain that they totally degenerate without treatment? Or that if they survive they'll be sterile? Should we be doing very, very intrusive, invasive treatment to children when you don't know what the results are going to be?

How can you explain to a 3-year-old donor why you are causing pain? And if the other child dies – whether the donors perceive that as actually killing the child? And once you've been transplanted you have no say, it's not as if you can undo it all, it just carries on like a rolling stone on a hill. They can have relapses much later and die. One 7-year-old went through the transplant very smoothly, but now he's returned with an ulcerated mouth. He's extremely depressed and he speaks very little English. His parents are at his home in the Mediterranean.

They may tell you they understand the treatment, but their behaviour tells you they don't like it. They spit out the drugs. It's a way of maintaining control over their own body, when they've lost almost all other control.

Besides inner qualities such as age and maturity, competence is affected by external influences, such as the doctors' approach. An SHO said:

I think the doctor needs to make an effort to get them to like you as a person. This way they feel relaxed and more likely to chat. If problems arise it's easier for them to be open about it, than if the doctor is up on a pedestal. I think then the idea of blame can arise, instead of all being in it together, sharing the fact that we are doing what we think is best, but realizing that nothing can be certain and sometimes there are disappointments for the doctor and the family.

A chaplain supported sharing decision making more fairly:

We need to break down professional images that isolate people and show doctors as gods. For someone to oppose the collective will of the medical staff takes a lot of courage. To live with the result, it's much easier to blame the doctors. We all hide behind someone else, give ourselves let-out clauses, look for someone to blame if it goes wrong. Many people are uneasy in schools and hospitals, because of past failures. And they're afraid of losing the goodwill of nursing staff if they refuse treatment for their child. We want people to respond out of honesty, not out of fear.

The SHO felt that parents' attitudes influenced children's consent:

Many "average" or "blue-collar" parents are intimidated. The working class scouser [Liverpudlian] has a very sensible disrespect for doctors. And also the professional classes, they'll be sensibly probing and asking difficult questions. I wish more people would do that.

The theme of competence assessed and expressed through relationships rather than through impersonal skills was emphasized by adults who believed that very young children could be competent. Enlightened cooperation is perhaps more essential for on-going therapy and medical treatment than for surgery. A speech therapist felt that from 2 years onwards, she could 'only work with their cooperation. They want to have therapy because they want to improve their speech and they know it will help them'. A community paediatrician described competence as a relationship of trust: 'From 3 years upwards, I would trust 90 per cent of children, I think they are sensible. Though it does depend on their cognitive development, and how they've been treated'. A hospital paediatrician remarked:

> *Paediatrician*: Some children have really learned to suffer, and some are incredibly aware and wise. It's a growing process with chronic conditions. I've been adult-trained and I'm not good at ageing children. The most important thing to me is relating to that child. I go for a rapport between the child and me. When they're very disabled and have lots of horrible treatment, I know we don't do it, but I think it is possible to extract informed consent from them.
>
> *Int.*: So if they think they have had enough [treatment], what would you do?
>
> *Paed.*: I would be very influenced by what they expressed. I would try and do what they want.

A hospital chaplain and former headmaster thought that:

> With some severely ill children, it's not scorable, that kind of wisdom, there are no measures. Some people know through intuition the response which they know they can live with, though maybe they can't reason it out. Consent is a legalistic term, giving your OK to have the operation. I find consent is much more an acceptance gradually by the person that they'll be willing for it to happen – or not even willing but that it's inevitable. It's growing into something.

Faced with a mystery, which cannot be objectively defined or assessed, adults described their intimations of competence: 'You look them in the eye and watch their responses'; 'You try to get to know them in the context of their family, away from the false setting of the hospital'.

A psychologist mentioned a therapeutic advantage of obtaining the child's reasoned agreement:

> I think 5- and 6-year-olds can evaluate things like leg lengthening, and they think about what's fair and not fair. It's always multifactorial, but if they don't get an explanation, then they're angry, or they disagree, then that could produce a physiological response. Resentment, and if you're trying to escape from a situation, and it's going on chronically, that will produce certain endocrinal responses.

Research with adults, showing that patients having their treatment of choice are likely to have improved outcome, may apply to children.[18] Some clinicians are convinced that adolescents only recover from anorexia when they learn to control their own life, and the more coercive the treatment, the poorer the outcome.[19] Nurses report that treatment for enuresis will only work for young children 'who want it to work'.[20] An expert in treating diabetes reported that his successful career was interrupted by an 11-year-old, whose 'brittle diabetic control' and frequent comas he was unable to remedy despite every effort. She stopped attending his clinics for a few months, and when she returned she reported a sudden and lasting improvement which appeared to be linked to being given a kitten and starting to care for a 3-year-old neighbour (becoming the agent instead of the object of care). The doctor concluded:

> She taught me volumes: to look for those things we cannot measure in
> a test tube; to know that the manifestations of disease are often the result
> of strange combinations, and interactions of people, moods, beliefs,
> objects and places do affect our physiology and biochemistry; to realize
> that the severity and course of a disease is sometimes unique to the life
> events of a single patient.[21]

A family care worker working with children with dystrophies and atrophies knew them for years and visited them at home. She discussed the policy of encouraging children to continue to walk for as long as possible, for the sake of their physical health:

> Around six, seven, eight, we have some children who want to go into
> wheelchairs and who don't want to have callipers and surgery to help
> them to go on walking. That is very minor surgery, but it's a lot of
> physio and motivation and hard work afterwards, and it probably isn't
> right to do it unless the child wants it.

The care worker thought that even if hospital staff pressed children to delay using a wheelchair, back at home each mother 'would end up with a huge fight every day of her life'. Despite the physical benefits, she was against enforcing treatment on resisting children. She would assess competence 'on the strength and conviction with which they talk to you, or that their parents say they feel. It's a kind of feeling you get. I suppose I just judge by knowing the family and child, but you might be wrong, it's tricky'.

Parents gave a range of reasons for respecting younger children. For example, Valerie's mother said, 'I trust her judgement now, at ten. We've always treated her as a small adult. She's emotionally grown up a lot. She has started her periods, and now we talk woman to woman'. Valerie said, 'I preferred not to talk about operations, because it worried me, but I wanted to talk about this one, because I'm older'. Some parents who gave high ages for competence were nevertheless influenced by young children. The parents of Ruth, aged 8, said that they were hesitating over whether she should have more surgery: 'It changed our lives. We heard Ruth say to a friend, "I know Mummy and Daddy will make the right decision for me". We knew then that we *had* to decide'.

Children's willingness to accept their parents' decision is itself a form of consent. Young children also worked on their parents' authority.[22] For example, Louise said, 'Well I suppose I usually do what my mum says, but I go upstairs and have a big sulk'. Alan, also aged 8, said, 'My dad is the softy, he lets me do what I like. But my mum is the fierce one. She bosses me about all right'.

Our interviewees illustrated how parents' perceptions of a child's competence affected the child's confidence.[23] Intense disputes, besides splitting families apart, united some, when they realized that a dilemma had no perfect solution. Amy's mother gave up her career to nurse Amy through the disruptive years of leg lengthening. Another mother said, 'I cried buckets over my daughter's decision, but in the end, your children have to live their own lives, and you have to let them make their mistakes and help them to make the best of it'. Many interviewees identified maturity with more equal, detailed discussion, instead of deciding in lonely autonomy. Mothers would say, 'If I needed an operation, I'd always want to talk it over with my family first, and we'd come to some kind of decision. I wouldn't just decide on my own'.

Parent and child often gave different ages of competence. The extreme examples were Alison (aged 14) and Sally (aged 12). Their parents gave the youngest ages for competence, yet both girls said they could not envisage a time when they 'would be old enough to decide'. Sally repeated 'it depends', although at about 8 years, she had insisted on having a wheelchair, despite being able to run in callipers. She was listening when her mother said:

> *Mother*: It took me about a month to get over the terrible shock to be told she needed a spinal fusion. I think Sally accepted it almost at once. It was me that needed time. She's grown-up enough to make decisions. It's her life, and she knows her condition gets worse and worse, and without this operation she'd die anyway.
> *Int.*: At what age do you think Sally can make a wise choice?
> *Mother*: She's always been fully informed and involved. We talk and share everything together. We've always spoken to our children as adults. They're always very sensible. I couldn't give an age like ten or six. Knowing at two she's got SMA, you've had to be open about everything with her.

Alison and her father had separate interviews. Her father said:

> I have always trusted my children. I have never forced either of them to do anything, I have never hit them, and they make all their own decisions. From the time that they can walk, they can make wise choices. If you wait until they are 18, you have failed them as a parent. I can't see any decision, unless it was life-threatening, that I would have to override.

Alison said:

> My dad and I are the same. We're not father and daughter, we're friends.
> He stands up for me if I want something, within reason. I ask him what
> he thinks, though I might not take it, but then he wouldn't really mind.
> But I would always decide about something like an operation with him,
> because he is a doctor.

When there is mutual respect between parents and child, an age of consent
is hardly an issue.

People who believe young children can be competent tend to emphasize
personal wisdom gained through experience. They acknowledge how intuitive
assessments of competence are; it is often developed through relationships of
mutual trust and respect, although Moira's determination seemed to develop
through resistance. Competence is more influenced by the social context and
the child's experience than by innate ability.[24] These adults try to avoid the
dangers of coercion, preferring reasoned discussion which they take seriously
because they are ready to respect young children's views. They are less likely
to see wisdom, competence and medical information as factual matters, instead
regarding them as possibly tentative and questionable, open to faith rather than
proof. They tend not to think in sharp dichotomies of wise adult/immature
child, infallible doctor/ignorant patient, but to see wisdom and uncertainty
shared among people of varying ages and experience.

### Life-improving decisions

Competence is affected by how complex, serious and irrevocable is the decision
concerned. Most orthopaedic surgery is intended to improve the quality of a
child's life, and in these decisions adults usually felt there was less harm and
greater benefit in involving children. Recognizing that adults can be uncertain
or misguided increases the importance of respecting children's views and
restricting adults' powers of control.[25] A chaplain said:

> A free decision is always loaded. What's the baseline of the freedom an
> individual is working from? What brought them to want or need this
> operation? You're discounting their experience if you say they're making
> a "free decision". It's a joke, a copout. You make the best decision you
> can in the circumstances you find yourself in. In a real world, people are
> damaged and frightened. We are free to make decisions, but we are a
> product of our past, and the future is framed by what we are.[26]

Listening to children can help to avoid harmful decisions, and contribute
towards informed decisions, if wisdom is seen as part of one's individuality
rather than as learning 'a certain body of information'. There are no general
answers (based on 1992 knowledge of outcomes) as to whether Amy should

accept treatment for short stature or Tina should refuse it, because the salient questions concern each girl's unique identity. A decision could be right for one girl and wrong for the other. There is no standard formula for making such personal decisions, as some surgeons acknowledged:

> Kids are all different. Some can't stand their deformity and can't wait to have an operation. The next one says, "I'm happy with my body. It doesn't worry me". Then good luck to them.
>
> From 7 or 8 years upwards they will certainly have an opinion as to whether they want something doing, an emotional feeling that's very important. I think any child facing surgery needs to be happy in their own mind that they actually want something doing, not just that their parents want it. You certainly should never, ever coerce a child into anything unless it's life-threatening. If something gets a little bit worse because you've waited a few months for them to get used to the idea, that's probably better than any coercion. You can destroy lives if you don't operate [on severe scoliosis]. It's only rarely that it causes major physical disability, but in later life, far fewer get married or are employed. I think that makes it even more important to listen to children's views.

In quality of life decisions about surgery, the child is here seen as expert. One SHO said:

> They obviously want to know how the operation will affect them, and they are the ones who will have to bear any consequences or complications. If they are persuaded against their wishes, or forced before they are ready, they'll hold their parents responsible, which isn't a good situation.

Parents who respected most of their children's decisions, usually wanted control over a few issues. The father of Krishna, aged 13, said:

> Krishna can understand sometimes more than I do, because he goes to school which I did not do. At 12 to 14 children change. He used to accept things. Now he won't listen and respect. In olden times in India, people say that a child needs direction up to 16. Our religion says that too. After that children can take a decision. But we discuss everything. I treat him like a friend. I don't force him. Only if he's completely wrong. Once or twice a year, you insist on your standards, and then he knows how far he can go.

### Life-extending decisions

Most parents wanted ultimate control over life-extending decisions.[27] 'How can you stick an age on it?' demanded Niki's mother, refusing to give an age of competence, and Niki preferred to be vague but eventually said, 'around 14 or 15 maybe'.

*Niki's mother*: Like, the doctors said to me, it was my decision, they could only advise, not tell me what to do. But what else can you do when . . .? [She shrugged, implying that the risks of refusing this operation were too high.] If your ears stick out, or your teeth are crooked – if the child says, "No, I don't care how I look," OK. But if it's a life and death decision, yes, involve the child, but it's up to you. Which is a terrible thing to say.

*Niki*: You did say before I had it that it was up to me to decide, and I needn't have it if I didn't want it.

*Mother*: No I didn't.

*Niki*: You did.

The interview illustrated the ambiguous mixture of guiding, controlling and respecting a child's decision. If there is agreement, the parents' control need not be made explicit. Traditional views about wise adults and foolish children set a catch 22: a child's wise decision can look like dependence or compliance; during disputes the child can appear foolishly incompetent. Then parents' irritated anxiety and children's resentment can force young patients into seemingly helpless incompetence.[28]

All the children who discussed life-extending surgery with us said they would agree to it. A senior psychologist said that it was very rare for a terminally ill child to refuse such treatment, and that he would take such a response very seriously.[29] Psychologists wished to assess whether 'memory and ability are affected by drugs, or progressive disease, or being very ill'. Although they affected few children in our orthopaedic study, life-extending decisions are the most serious issue for children's consent. An interview with a sister experienced in decisions about children's life-extending treatment is therefore quoted at some length. The sister in a heart–lung transplant unit thought that very ill children, such as those with cystic fibrosis (CF), could understand curative attempts (unlike preventative transplants discussed earlier). She felt that children with severe heart disease, who often feel well, had less understanding.

I feel that when transplantation is being considered, it is the *only* time parents have the opportunity of true informed consent. With more conventional surgery, parents are given enough information to sign the consent form, but I do not believe that they are aware that they have the option to refuse. Transplantation is about choice, therefore you feel able to give families 100 per cent information on which to *make* their decision. You include all the risks, complications and long-term difficulties, you spare nothing.

Naturally you have to tailor your information to the individual child's age and cognitive development. You'd probably say, "Do you know why you're here? Do you know what's wrong with you? Are you taking any medicines? What are they for?" You would talk about the treatments they will need after they have a transplant and that some may be unpleasant and that you wish they weren't necessary. You talk about body changes, including the puffiness and possible hairiness.

Following that type of discussion, I remember one 10-year-old who said, "I don't want it". These children are given that right of choice. It's not a question are they capable of making a decision? If a child truly understands what is involved and the alternative outcome, then they are not forced into agreeing to a transplant. That causes a lot of problems for nursing staff when the age of consent is now what, 16? Certainly that is an age we are comfortable with. Because transplantation is a limited resource, it is important to select the children most likely to benefit from it, and we have time to do this . . .

The children we see are often very depressed and demotivated. Are they capable of taking in the information? How easy is it for them even to remember what it was like to be well? Often they've always had to go along with having lots of treatment to keep well, but they haven't *felt* better. I think it's very hard for them to believe that any treatment is going to make them feel better.

We try to be neutral. I think that's made easier because none of us know whether transplantation is an appropriate treatment. There's only what is right or wrong for individuals. We don't have the right to assume we know what's appropriate for a particular family.

Families stay in the unit for four days of assessment and 'pretty horrendous' discussion. Yet do the pressures of very serious illness lessen children's rationality and autonomy?

All the children we see have demonstrated an ability to make their own decisions. Whether they do it or not is another matter. Many aren't autonomous enough. One mother said to her son after his brother had died, "We owe it to your brother for you to have a transplant". He was very distressed. I said to him, "If you didn't want that operation would you tell us?" He said, "No, because my mother would be so sad if I said that".

I would say that often as young as four or five they can understand a lot about a transplant. Of course, it varies very much, and you can't generalize. I believe the child *always* has to be involved. We know that they literally have their life in their hands afterwards. If they stop taking their medications, for example, they will die. Children may find a way of keeping control. One, previously very active, little 7-year-old girl with CF became desperately ill. The family had been denying how ill she was. Our assessment indicated that she only had a few months to live. She cried desperately when she was told she needed a transplant. She died two weeks later. She had developed an infection, but medically there was no reason for her to deteriorate quite so dramatically. I think that if children don't want something, then they can give up, and I believe she gave up.

A girl in another hospital on the transplant waiting list died and they found a bag of food in her locker. She hadn't been eating.

Very young children are often thought not to have informed, constant values based in a firm sense of identity, the moral and rational basis of wise decisions.[30] The sister discussed whether young children can evaluate risk and benefit:

> *Sister*: A little girl of about seven with CF ended up by summing up what I had said beautifully. She said, "You're telling me that with CF you can get very ill and die". I said, "We hope very much that won't happen, but that's why the doctors are thinking about *whether*, and it is only whether, a transplant might help you". "And you said that even if I say I want it, I might not live long enough to get one". I said, "Well not everyone does. We think you probably will because you're fairly well at the moment but people do die waiting". "And you're telling me that I could *die* when I have the operation". "We haven't had anyone die in the operating theatre, but yes it could happen". Then she said, "Even if I survive, you're not promising me that everything's going to be good, or that I will be able to do all the things I want to". So I said, "When we put new lungs inside somebody, you *should* be able to do a lot more, but it's not a promise that anyone's going to be able to give you". She said, "But, there is a chance that I could feel really good and I could come first in a race on my pony". And I said, "Yes". Then she continued, "All those other things are going to happen to me anyway, so please ask them to give me some new lungs".
>
> I think for someone of seven or eight to say that illustrates how she had totally taken on board as well as I could, the consequences of transplantation. She had managed to set it all out and look at it very clearly. She had understood the uncertainties. OK, on a child's level, but who could better it? I couldn't.
>
> I think it's very different when they have CF. Children who have been perfectly healthy don't have that perception of the value of life. Whereas these children were looking at certain death and exchanging that with the uncertainty of transplantation.
>
> *Int.*: So you think their suffering, rather than retarding their understanding, heightens it?
>
> *Sister*: They are the most sure, mature children. They're physically immature, but their understanding of life and death knocks spots off us. I think they're immature in some of their attitudes, but their understanding of their own well-being and what life is all about is mature. Of course they have temper tantrums. They've got this debilitating illness. They've done nothing to justify being sick day in, day out. It's awful for them. But they tell you it all. Why they have this

nebulizer, what this tablet does, et cetera. They're very manipulative children. Knowing that food is a major issue, they'll have steak at 2 o'clock in the morning. But that's very different to their actually understanding.

*Int.*: It seems that suffering and difficulty help some children to grow. The usual convention is that this holds them back.

*Sister*: I think it often holds them back in some of the academic things because of missing school. They often have a poor concentration span, and their IQ may be lower.

*Int.*: Some people have related IQ to wisdom.

*Sister*: I think it's totally, totally different. If I'd had this conversation with you three years ago, it would have been very different. Working with these children is a real eye opener. Previously I'd have said that some level of understanding might be possible, say, for an 8-year-old, but I would not have felt comfortable involving a child in actual decision-making unless they were at least 12 years or 13 years old.

Protective adults who want to spare children the risk of making harmful decisions with ensuing blame and guilt, themselves risk making harmful decisions and being resentfully blamed by the child. Yet sincere attempts to listen can sometimes resolve deadlock. A girl aged 10 years whose brother had died of CF refused to consider having a transplant. The sister respected her refusal, but added:

The next day she asked to go on the waiting list, because, "You listened. I don't like physio but I'm told, 'sorry you have to have it'. It's the same with medication. I just wanted to see what would happen if I said 'no'. If you would take any notice".

The girl's change of decision meant that treatment could be given with her fairly willing cooperation, instead of being withheld or enforced.


**Wanting to choose**

So far, views on children's ability to give or withhold consent have been reported. A separate question is whether children want to take on the burden of choosing. Parents and young patients were asked who they thought *made* the decision whether to accept proposed surgery (Table 16) and who *should* be the 'main decider' (Table 17). The ages of the 13 'main deciders' ranged from 8 to 15 years. The figures represent widely ranging comments, such as Julie aged 11, who said, 'I think everyone should give an opinion, and maybe the doctor put them together'.

The children showed more confidence in their doctors' than in their parents' judgement. The figures suggest that parents are seen as mediators rather than

**Table 16**   Views about who was the 'main decider'

| Main decider | Views of what did happen | |
|---|---|---|
| | Parent's view (n = 120) | Child's view (n = 120) |
| Child | 13 | 13 |
| Child + adults | 62 | 44 |
| Adults | 32 | 60 |
| Child accepted after persuasion | 9 | – |
| Don't know | 4 | 3 |

**Table 17**   Children's views about who should be the 'main decider' (n = 120)

| Main decider | Views of what should happen | |
|---|---|---|
| | Before op. | After op. |
| Child | 18 | 21 |
| Child + parents | 3 | 5 |
| Child + doctors | 3 | 1 |
| All together | 49 | 41 |
| Parents + doctors | 19 | 13 |
| Doctors | 25 | 25 |
| Parents | 2 | 7 |
| Don't know | 1 | 7 |

'main deciders', and that joint decision making is a major preference. Some children were unaware of the possibility of choice and consent: 'What form?' asked 9-year-old Andy, when his parents were discussing the consent form. Kazim, aged 15, who felt hopeless and excluded said, 'It's not the doctors' fault if something goes wrong. Your parents are to blame, because they've signed the form, it would be their fault'. However, three other Muslim children, all girls, were much respected by their parents: 'She is the second woman in our house', said the father of one 12-year-old, and another praised his 'astute' 10-year-old daughter. Formally signifying consent is a step beyond consenting in principle. Several young patients said they were pleased to consent to surgery, but not to sign a form.

The young patients were asked what they might do if they disagreed with their parents over the decision about surgery (Table 18). Boys were twice as likely as girls to say that they would try to get their own way.

**Table 18**  Boys' and girls' responses if they disagree with their parents (%)

| Response | Boys (n = 54) | Girls (n = 66) |
|---|---|---|
| Would not disagree | 9 | 11 |
| Negotiate | 22 | 27 |
| Try to get own way | 22 | 11 |
| Accept parents' view | 32 | 33 |
| Other | 2 | 4 |
| Don't know | 13 | 14 |

### Reason and coercion

Professionals who thought that younger children could be competent tended to be concerned about coercion:

> *Senior sister*: A 13-year-old boy came in to have an arthroscopy for a painful knee. He refused to get on the trolley. The other nurses were trying to persuade him and his mother was very cross with him. I just said, "Leave him alone", and he was sent home. We've made further dates but each time he refuses to come in. I've been on the 'phone for ages to his mother, she wants it done, and wants us to sedate him so he has no option. I've explained if he doesn't want it doing, there's no way we can go ahead. The anaesthetist and the surgeon agree. Some other nurses think it's a nonsense and he should be "made" to have it. He is obviously terrified of something.
>
> *Int.*: Have you had any other children refuse surgery?
>
> *Sister*: In the past it just never happened. The whole atmosphere was much stricter, the nurses much firmer, we'd never have allowed it to happen. The doctors used to have much more power and the nurses never questioned anything. Gradually, particularly senior nurses have gained more power, and over the last few years I have changed my practice. As nurses we must act as patient advocates. Nurses now have the right to say no. Three years ago, we just refused to give intramuscular injections. Caused quite a stir. We were helped by the arrival of EMLA cream – it's nonsense to put that on the hands and then give an IM in the thigh. Also a new woman anaesthetist arrived who stood up for patients and made a big difference. She came from Sheffield where they never give IMs. Nurses must have the courage of their convictions, be confident and remember they are professionals in their own right. If a junior doctor is setting up a drip and causing distress to the child by not finding the vein, I will suggest firmly but sympathetically that someone more experienced should do it. We must always put the needs of the child first.[31]

One SHO described a 12-year-old with a slipped vertebra:

He was well prepared and it really needed doing, but at the last moment he couldn't face it. The ward staff 'phoned theatre, and there was no problem, immediate agreement to cancel. He stayed in for a week, and then agreed and it went ahead. Choices are being made, and discussions are going on all the time, when some children keep coming back to clinics for years. It is very important to allow them breathing space and thinking time and to discuss it calmly, not leave it to the last minute when there's a panic over wasting theatre time.

A play specialist said:

From about seven, you'd begin to expect a child to make a decision based on their experience. If the child is unhappy about the treatment, you should find out why, and not just bulldoze your way through it, and presume that you know better and they will accept it later. Building up a relationship with the child before treatment, working it out with them, giving them space to be able to make an informed choice can reap huge rewards, but unfortunately there is often not time.

Without consent, surgery and any touching of the patient is battery. Professional skill and good intentions do not transform surgery into a legal activity (except in an emergency or to save life); only consent can do that, freely given by the patient or, for incompetent minors, by the parent or guardian. Consent enshrines the basic legal right of autonomy, and physical and mental integrity. The crucial difference between adults and incompetent children is that treatment can legally be enforced on the latter. The law appears to be based on the assumption that the non-competent child has no understanding worth considering. However, very young children do reason and can perceive unexplained treatment as assault which opens a credibility gap between the child's perception of harm, and the adults' intention to benefit.

Severe or prolonged treatment can induce terror and despair in the child. Professionals are concerned about general harms to children, from disease and disasters, and abuse by parents; they rarely consider the third major harm, abuse by professionals.[32] Children who perceive treatment as worse than the disease risk having similar reactions to those of torture victims.[33] The more severe the treatment, the more severe the disease or defect is likely to be, so that the children affected tend already to be the most vulnerable ones with a fragile sense of identity and difficulties in sustaining self-esteem and rewarding relationships. Long and frequent episodes in hospital do not help children to develop relationships at home and at school.[34] From early infancy, children begin to reason and to suffer mentally. Acceptance of a general licence to enforce treatment on 'non-competent' children, as if they are unthinking beings, is therefore misguided. It is preferable to defer any treatment which is not urgent until the child can accept overall (allowing for periods of doubt) that the disease is worse than the treatment.

It can be argued that all treatment decisions are either reasoned with patients or forced on them, and that reason and force are at opposite ends of a spectrum, with persuasion in the centre.

| reason | persuasion | force |
| --- | --- | --- |
| impartial discussion | over-optimism | ulterior constraint |
| negotiation | deceit | duress |
| informed choice | fraud | violence |

Impartial discussion is inevitably qualified by medical uncertainty, choice of words, pressures of the illness or disability being treated, and attempts to respect but also protect anxious children. So persuasion overlaps broadly with reason at one end and force at the other. Yet at some point persuasion moves from informed optimism to deliberate distortion. Adults who gave high ages for competence tended to dismiss coercion as necessary firmness – Kids only play up'; 'They're only frightened', – as if fear is irrational and therefore unimportant: 'They've got to learn to put up with it for their own good'; 'There isn't time to hang about until they're ready'. The most powerful way to justify coercion is to deny that children can reason, and to align reason with force; children's resistance is then seen as mindless 'self-destruction', to be overridden by rational adults.

Adults who respected consent at a younger age worried about the reason–force divide. A sister said, 'I would always try to get a compromise'. A surgeon said, 'I don't try and persuade people. If someone isn't happy with the idea of surgery, we'll talk again in a few months' time, or a few years, and very often they've changed their mind'.

Consent to surgery entails consent to bodily invasion and loss of control. Sometimes urgent force was required, and parents could help children towards accepting this.

> *Kerry*: I wanted my Mum to stay with me all the time. I didn't want them to do anything without her there. [She described attempts to insert a catheter.] It took them an hour to get it in, and then they took it out again, and they gave me an infection doing that. I get stomach ache a lot now.
>
> *Int.*: Did you ask them to stop?
>
> *Kerry*: Yes, but it just took more of them to hold my legs open. [She had very stiff hip muscles and had been going to have surgery to release them.] My mum thought I had to have it, otherwise I would get ill.

Another surgeon commented:

I regard the issue of consent as a partnership between parents, the patient and the doctor – none of these can work independently. The success of this depends on a lot of things, including the age and understanding of the child. Because of the risk that children will refuse necessary treatment, it is so important that the atmosphere is right, so that the child can voice their fears.

Forcing information onto patients who would rather not know can be a form of coercion, but was usually seen as the lesser evil to forcing treatment on unprepared, resisting children.

Parents were much involved in all forms of persuasion and pressure. A social worker said:

One person here feels that parents ought to show that they are authoritative and strong and are able to take charge of their children, then their child can trust them. Other people feel that if the child is so frightened, then the parents shouldn't coerce him. And I feel half way between. We had one girl, long ago, with a bad [spine] curve who was 12. The girl screamed an awful lot, and we just pulled the curtains round and let her sit on her mother's knee and do a lot of crying. She took surgery very well in the end.

The extent to which parents contain children's anxiety was shown by one unusual child who cried for weeks, sounding like a wild animal. He was alert and intelligent, and attended a boarding school for physically handicapped pupils and his parents were abroad. The nurses could not relieve his misery and terror about each procedure. His reactions suggested the levels of distress and anxiety which the parents helped to prevent and relieve in their children, by their support or control.[35] Parents' support possibly helped children to feel valued and loved, nurturing their sense of self-worth which could make the distressing treatment seem worthwhile. Children's refusal was sometimes blamed on parents' 'ambivalence'. It was not clear whether parents were ambivalent about agreeing to treatment, or about enforcing treatment on a strongly resisting child. In either case, especially in the latter, ambivalence is surely preferable to unthinking agreement or coercion.

Consultants who ordered tests and treatment seldom witnessed how these might be enforced by rushed junior doctors and nurses. A charge nurse read a sentence from the leaflet about our project:

"How are young patients involved when decisions are made?" In this ward? Nil. The kids and parents just don't get informed. Some of these doctors treat children as pieces of meat. I don't mind you quoting me on that, it makes me so angry. They have no consideration for how they feel. I'm used to working in a medical ward where it was completely different, communication was good.

Force was not unusual. Niki was the most assertive young patient we met. Lying on her back doing origami, she described her first spinal fusion nonchalantly. Then a doctor came to take some blood, and Niki began a terrified protest. Her mother, frightened that her writhing would damage her spine, tried to reason with her as the doctor and nurse held her down. All the pain and humiliation that Niki had coped with well until then seemed to be symbolized by the needle, the most major procedure to her, but a 'minor' one to the staff. Jim's anxiety about his operation was not helped by not having eaten all day, and waiting until 5.30 p.m. As one parent described, 'When the porter arrived with the trolley, Jim was hysterical with fear, going mad. Sister stormed up the ward shouting at him. He shouted back, crying and terrified'. Yet allowing time and offering the child responsibility could work well. A sister described a boy of 13 who 'argued and fought' until his operation was postponed: 'When the second operation day came, to our surprise he was as meek as a lamb, no problem. It wasn't a case of gradual persuasion, he protested right up to the day before, but he was old enough to realize it had to be done'.

### Children with learning disabilities

Some parents of children with learning disabilities thought their child would 'never' be competent; others, like Sue's mother, thought that their child's willing agreement was essential:

It's just as important to listen to them, perhaps even more so. Sue is 12 but she has a mental age of about six, but she's older in some ways. She needs me with her all the time. That's her way of coping. For example, the nurses kept saying, "Do you have any pain?" Sue obviously did, but she kept saying, "No". At last she asked me, "Does pain mean it hurts?" and then I was able to explain and arrange for her to have pain relief.

No-one understands these children like the parents do. She can't read and she needs me to entertain her. The other children don't make friends with her. Her answers sound all right but she doesn't know what she's saying. People with hydrocephalus often sound a lot better than they are. She gets it almost right.

Sue's had spinal jackets since she was four which she hated. It's taken a year to persuade her to have the surgery. The extra maturity has helped her tremendously, and we worked on her to change her attitude. Her spine was in two "S" bends. I was worried she wouldn't survive, it took us so long to persuade her. Mr Y is brilliant. He said things the way she needed and understood. He knew she wouldn't have taken it earlier. You have to explain everything very carefully. When she heard she was having a plate in, she imagined that it would be as big as a dinner plate and was very frightened. She'll always need guidance.

Sue spoke confidently and fluently. She was extremely determined. During her previous stay in another hospital she went on hunger strike.

> Her way of saying "I want to go home" was to say that she wanted to go to a café near our home. She went into a coma, with hunger, and had to be put on a drip. In the end they had to take her by ambulance and stop outside the café and give her a plate of food – which she ate.

Eventually, Sue tolerated three spine operations fairly calmly, and was proud to be so brave:

> *Sue's mother*: You are coping beautifully aren't you. It's becoming a routine going for your operation. You know what to expect and you are *coping*.
> *Sue*: No, I'm not sure I can cope.
> *Mother*: [*firmly*] Yes, you are coping. And now there's only one more operation.

## Competence tests

One way to assess competence is to test children. During interviews they usually told us about their treatment willingly, but Sally was vague when asked about her spinal fusion, saying, 'don't know, I've forgotten'. Yet a therapist said, 'Like many SMA children Sally is very bright, and is top of her class'. She would have scored low in a formal test, yet from observations and indirect comments she was obviously well informed, and any failure would be due to the method of questioning. Her reluctance could be seen as a sign of competence in controlling how much she wanted to say. Similarly, she agreed to surgery but was unusual in refusing to do any physiotherapy, and in hardly speaking to anyone during her five weeks in the ward. She seemed to have decided firmly how far she would accept adults' interventions. Attempts to test competence can anger or humiliate some people. Like understanding, competence is more than a skill; it grows or withers within relationships, and is perceived subjectively. Each adult's views about competence seemed determined less by training or logic, than by a disposition to trust or control children.

## A right to decide?

Some people believe that it is unwise and unkind to expect children to share in making major decisions; they are concerned about the neglect or abuse (through under- or over-treatment) which young people are exposed to if they take responsibility for their life. Other people believe that children should be involved and that, given information, support and time, they will usually arrive at an enlightened decision. These adults are concerned about the neglect or abuse which young people are exposed to if they are prevented from taking some responsibility for their life.

Children's ability and desire to be involved varies; respecting them means supporting them as far as they want to go, trying not to impose on them either over-involvement or exclusion. Many young patients choose to accept their doctors' or parents' decision, others wish to share in deciding, a few want to be 'the main decider'. No-one has the unqualified right to decide. The adults have responsibilities but not rights; the child does not have unrestricted choice, but has to choose 'wisely'. In our study, children and parents usually agreed. In cases of disagreement, a middle way can often be found of reasoning and compromise, until informed and willing consent is agreed.

## Notes

1 'Sufficient understanding and intelligence to understand fully what is proposed', having 'sufficient discretion' to be able 'to make a wise choice' in one's own interests' are required in *Gillick* v. *West Norfolk & Wisbech AHA* [1985] 3 All ER 410.

2 The overlap involves some repetition of earlier chapters, which has been avoided as much as possible. 'The distinction between knowing what is involved and having the capacity to make a wise decision is an important one. In the case of an adult, it is axiomatic that understanding, not wisdom, is all that is required for a man may go to the devil if he chooses'. However, the 'first and paramount consideration' throughout the law is the welfare of the child herself, decisions must 'promote her welfare'. Hoggett, B. (1986) Parents, children and medical treatment, the legal issues. In Byrne, P. (ed), *Rights and Wrongs in Medicine*, p. 165. London, King's Fund. This opinion is criticized by lawyers who cite laws prohibiting, for example, self-multilation, and say that adults' autonomy is also limited in law.

3 As shown by the lengthy, inconclusive literature. I use the US term 'competence', rather than the British term 'capacity'. See: National Commission for the Protection of Human Subjects of Biomedical and Behavioral Research (1977) *Research Involving Children*. Washington, DC, DHEW; Gaylin, W. and Macklin, R. (eds) (1982) *Who Speaks for the Child?* New York, Plenum Press; Melton, G., Koocher, G. and Saks, M. (eds) (1983) *Children's Competence to Consent*. New York, Plenum Press; Nicholson, R. (1986) *Medical Research with Children: Ethics, Law and Practice*. Oxford, Oxford University Press; Kopelman, L. and Moskop, J. (eds) (1989) *Children and Health Care: Moral and Social Issues*. Dordecht, Kluwer; Buchanan, A. and Brock, D. (1989) *Deciding for Others: The Ethics of Surrogate Decision Making*. New York, Cambridge University Press; Cutter, M. and Shelp, E. (eds) (1991) *Competency: A Study of Informal Competency Determinations in Primary Care*. Dordecht, Kluwer.

4 The three ways cut across three main approaches to ethics – deontology, utilitarianism and rights; also three approaches to children's rights – paternalist, interventionist and libertarian (Chapter 3).

5 Three methods are disputed. Pyschologists set complicated function tests of abilities

such as 'communication', but lawyers argue that setting very high standards of competence threatens civil liberties. They also point out the difference between being able to decide and to communicate a decision; Department of Health (1989) *Code of Practice Pursuant to Section 118(4) of the Mental Health Act 1983.* London, HMSO.

6 Grisso, T. and Vierling, L. (1978) Minors' consent to treatment: A developmental perspective. *Professional Psychology,* 9, 412–27. This paper dominates American debates about children's competence.

7 A more 'scientific' method would be to break competence down into a set of questions on children: being able to be consulted; wanting to be consulted; evaluating medical information; evaluating the personal context; wanting adults to decide; wanting to influence the decision; wanting to be responsible for the decision; making a range of small to major decisions; negotiating disagreement with adults; and so on. Yet separated replies may well have been stilted and hypothetical. Competence does not necessarily develop systematically, because major decisions do not arise in a child's life in any orderly sequence. Our open-response questions evoked much discussion which highly structured interviews would miss. Some people criticized the vagueness of our questions. However, people from every age and background were bored and impatient if we tried seemingly repetitive, academic abstractions, whereas they were happy to tell detailed stories. An analogy would be to ask parents how their child learned to talk by questioning the development of pronunciation, syntax, vocabulary, and so on, instead of asking for the story of how a particular child started to talk.

8 Young, A. (1990) Moral conflicts in a psychiatric hospital. In Weisz, G. (ed.), *Social Science Perspectives on Medical Ethics,* pp. 65–82. Kluwer, Dordrecht.

9 The philosophy has powerful psychic elements appealing to adults' longing to escape vulnerability and to attain the myth of inviolable adult autonomy. Emotions are then associated with 'childishness', 'regression', 'the child within', instead of being recognized as a valid, integral part of humanity at any age. Ageism usually describes discrimination against older people. We do not even have a term for 'childism', the endemic prejudice against children. Adults who fear and despise 'childlike' aspects of themselves are unlikely to be able to trust children. See, for example, Midgely, M. (1989) *Wisdom, Information and Wonder: What is Knowledge For?* London, Routledge.

10 O'Neill, O. (1984) Paternalism and partial autonomy. *Journal of Medical Ethics,* 10, 173–8.

11 An example of the reason/emotion split pervading medicine and ethics, when consent is usually confined to rational choice. Here it is one-sidedly seen as emotional choice. However, informed and voluntary consent balances reason and emotion.

12 The problems of the most inexperienced doctors usually administering the forms are discussed in Alderson, P. (1992) Consent to surgery. *Hospital Update,* July, 529–32.

13 The nursery approach of informing children very well through play, but with the risk of infantalizing them, is dicussed in Alderson, P. (1992) Children's consent to surgery. *Paediatric Nursing,* 3(10), 10–13.

14 Sylvia Anthony's work was published in 1940 and 1968. Later work mentioned in Chapter 5 shows how her ideas, and Piagetian notions that children cannot think abstractly, have long been superseded.

15 Social and physical normality are discussed in Chapter 3.

16 The theory that the whole community/family/hospital functions as a single organism, each part benefiting from that which benefits the whole. The theory dismisses conflicts of interests, ignores the way the powerful tend to benefit at the expense of other groups and, if the latter resist, labels them as deviant minorities. This conservative approach flourishes as parentalism in families and interventionism in hospitals, schools and law courts. Benton, T. (1977) *Philosophical Foundations of the Three Sociologies*. London, Routledge, links functionalism with conservatism and positivism, the tendency to see data as absolute facts, and in this way to accept the *status quo*. These interviewees tended to believe in the factual certainty of medical knowledge and adult wisdom.

17 'Empty or effaced tablet', the idea that children were empty slates for adults to write on, originally from Hooker, J. (1596) *Of the Laws of Ecclesiastical Politie, Book 1*. Quoted in Locke, J. (1690) *An Essay Concerning Human Understanding*, Vol. I, p. 48, edited by Clarendon, A. (1894), London, to show why minors cannot be citizens; and see Chapters 3–5 on rights and research.

18 Chadwick, D., Gillat, D. and Gingell, J. (1991) Medical or surgical orchidectomy: The patient's choice. *British Medical Journal*, 302, 572; Fallowfield, L., Hall, A., Maguire, G. and Baum, M. (1990) Psychological outcomes of different treatment policies in women with early breast cancer outside a clinical trial. *British Medical Journal*, 301, 573–80.

19 Gowers, S. (1992) Eating disorders. Paper presented to *Paediatrics: Modern Problems, New Ideals*, Paediatric Study Day, Burnley Health Care NHS Trust, 7 October.

20 Webb, A. (1992) Enuresis. Paper presented to *Paediatrics: Modern Problems, New Ideals*, Paediatric Study Day, Burnley Health Care NHS Trust, 7 October.

21 Meador, C. (1992) The person with the disease. *Journal of the American Medical Association*, 268(1), 35.

22 We discussed with families how they negotiate decision making. There is not space in this book to report this material.

23 It could be argued that children become competent by first being treated as if they are competent; a baby learns to talk through being treated as if she already can talk.

24 Social influences on competence are discussed in Alderson, P. (1992) In the genes or in the stars? Children's competence to consent. *Journal of Medical Ethics*, 18, 119–24.

25 Abramovitch, R. *et al.* (1991) Children's capacity to consent to participation in psychological research. *Child Development*, 62, 1100–9, reports parents enroling resisting children into research projects, and questions the benefits of parents' proxy consent.

26 The philosophical split between behaviourism (the person as passive, infinitely plastic and shaped by society) and existentialism (the person as pure, abstract will) is simplistic. Freedom is not choice in a vacuum; before choosing between two things, you have to want them in your own personal physical and emotional nature and capacities. J.S. Mill's concept of liberty as people like trees having full, natural shapes, not pollarded, allows for this when there is no single stereotype, but a 'rich, varied, hospitable enterprising society'. Midgely, M. (1981) *Heart and Mind: The Varieties of Moral Experience*, p. 40f. Brighton, Harvester. Lagerspetz, O. (1992) Dorothea and Casaubon. *Philosophy*, 67: 211–232, quoting Gaita, R. (1989) The

personal in ethics. In Phillips, D. and Winch, P. (eds), *Wittgenstein*, pp. 124–50. New York, St. Martin's Press: 'Who we are, is in a certain way shown in the moral problems we are capable of having and a personal decision depends on the spirit in which it is undertaken'.

27 In the tables, parents' replies are mainly listed in the age group they would respect for the operation their child was having. Niki's lungs were affected by scoliosis and spinal muscular atrophy.

28 Such as with Moira and Jenni.

29 As the means of prolonging dying increase, so does concern for those who wish to end treatment, as shown by numerous ethics book and papers.

30 See the work of Grisso and Vierling, quoted in Chapter 5. See note 6.

31 This book does not attempt to review the growing literature on nurses as hand-maidens or independent practitioners, yet this debate has strong effects on whether nurses enforce medical decisions, or support child-patients' decisions. Most people are lower-middle or working class, so respect for child patients and their closest advocates often means reversing the usual hierarchy in class, gender, age, education and race. It challenges many deep prejudices (which complicate child advocacy); see Stacey, M. (1988) *The Sociology of Health and Healing*. London, Unwin Hyman.

32 The history of medicine, education, religion, pedagogic child-rearing, psychology, social work, politics, industry and the armed services records the high incidence of severe harm to children and unevaluated benefit. Ironically, the main criticisms of hospitals stress 'maternal-deprivation', a form of parent-blaming (Bowlby, Kennel and Klaus), rather than addressing professional power.

33 Torture is defined as 'breaking down a person's sense of identity'. It is exacerbated when people are in a strange culture (such as a hospital ward). It arouses feelings of utter helplessness, being out of control of events and one's own body (inability to sleep, or concentrate, irritability), confusion between feeling bad and being bad, the disintegration of mind and body. 'A perfect way to cope with torture and prison is to disassociate your feelings from your experience; this is not the perfect way to cope with a love affair' or any intimate relationship. If it becomes a habit, children become emotionally crippled. Melzak, S. (1992) Secrecy, privacy, survival, repressive regimes, and growing up. *Bulletin of Anna Freud Centre*, 15, 205–24. Children as young as 2 years suffer such stress after disasters. They know why they have come for therapy: 'I was on the ferry and saw lots of dead bodies'. We formerly thought they did not understand, because we did not ask them. A 6-year-old attempted suicide after a ferry disaster: 'I couldn't stand the bad pictures of the ferry in my mind any more'. Yule, W. (1992) Lecture at Medact seminar, 4 July, London: Post traumatic stress disorders in children. *Current Opinion in Paediatrics*, 4, 4.

34 Douglas, J. (1968) *All Our Futures*. London, Peter Davies.

35 The effects on their decisions of children's motives, from hope to fear, need further research.

# 10

# THE MANY STAGES OF SURGERY

*Young people should be kept as fully informed as possible about their condition and treatment to enable them to exercise their rights. Even where younger children do not have the required understanding they should be provided with as much information as possible and their wishes ascertained and taken into account.*[1]

*I'd like people to accept that information and consent go on all the time. I'd like to see more effort put into that, and I'd like more honesty ... I would like to see the children given more respect. They are individuals and many are capable of making all sorts of decisions for themselves, what food to eat, when to go to bed and get up, certainly when to have a bath.*

*(Two ward sisters, 1991)*

Consent to surgery is often assumed to mean signing the operation consent form as part of a three-stage process: one, exchanging information; two, signing the form; three, giving treatment. Yet in reality, information, consent, treating and touching patients are part of the many stages of treatment surrounding each operation. As one surgeon said, 'Consent enters into every discussion from the very first clinic', right through to the examination at the final out-patient visit. Consent pervades all health professional–patient encounters, whether it is openly discussed, assumed, ignored or overridden.[2]

So far, this book has mainly examined the traditional idea of consent as a major overall blanket decision about *whether* to have treatment, implying agreement to every interim step. This chapter considers the important but neglected issue of consent to 'minor' procedures. It is about consent to *how* treatment is provided, an especially important issue for children. Although they may not be able to share in major overall decisions, they still have strong views on minor ones. Through sharing in minor decisions, children gain the skill and courage to learn to share in major ones. When children's views on all aspects of treatment are respected, standards of hospital care can greatly improve. From many possible aspects of care, the stages of surgery, pain relief, parents' involvement, schooling and diet will be reviewed to show how children's consent can be respected.

### The stages of surgery

Orthopaedic surgery entails far more than a few hours of the surgeon's work. It usually involves many stages from the first out-patient appointment to the final discharge and can include weeks of demanding nursing and physiotherapy mainly provided by children and parents, frequently at home. When this reality is appreciated, the overall planning improves. Some hospitals still act as black holes absorbing in-patients. Others, like stars, radiate outwards, treating in-patients as briefly as possible, supporting further treatment at home, and recognizing that 'real' nursing is not done only in hospital. A paediatrician said that medicine is best practised in the home, and being a hospital doctor is 'rather like being an ornithologist who only looks at birds in cages'.[3] Some children stay in hospital for spinal fusion for only six days,[4] whereas some lie in bed for six weeks between two operations. In the words of one paediatric neurologist, this 'can be tragic' for those with dystrophies and atrophies. Their muscles can only be loosened afterwards through agonizing physiotherapy which is not always effective. Policies are changing. With the help of community paediatric nurses, children and parents manage intravenous drips, nasogastric tubes, dialysis, and ventilators at home.[5]

Early discharge requires child-centred methods of nursing. One example is the use of methods for cleaning leg-lengthening pin sites which are not necessarily those by which nurses obtain the lowest infection rates, possibly by surgical spirit. Instead, the chosen methods are simple and less painful, the ones which children can use most effectively.[6] Each method is assessed for its clinical and its practical merits. Some of our interviewees arrived home in large plasters without even a bedpan. Their parents had to improvise and get help and advice wherever they could find it. A few children stayed unnecessarily for weeks in hospital waiting for hoists to be found, or wheelchairs to be adapted. Well-planned continuing care, from before admission until recovery, can prevent much anxiety, distress and wasted bed space.

Whereas some orthopaedic surgeons believe that early discharge cuts infection rates and promotes recovery,[7] a few keep children in hospital for months as the best way to provide physiotherapy and schooling. With purchasers' and providers' budgets[8] being more tightly controlled, it becomes more obviously economic to purchasers to have patients sent home early, to use local community physiotherapists, and to urge local authorities to provide better tuition for children who are unfit to attend school. At first, John was alarmed to learn that he would not stay in hospital during the months of leg lengthening. Later, he was very pleased that during those months he had managed to study for GCSEs at his local school, play in a brass band and keep his allotment garden flourishing.[9]

Treating children as in-patients for months perpetuates the tradition of the hospital as a centre of healing. 'Where mercy, peace and pity dwell' was inscribed on the gate of one hospital. A psychiatrist expressed this view:

> I should like more training of staff in how to ask children how they think and feel about what is happening to them. It would be healthy if they did that. Studies show improved wellbeing after discharge where there

has been particular attention to enabling children to talk about their whole experience in hospital. It's beneficial to vulnerable children and those whose relations with their parents have been compromised before admission. If more professional time was dedicated to it, then the morbidity that follows hospitalization would almost certainly be reduced.

Talking therapy is seen here as a healing way of reducing morbidity after discharge. Morbidity is attributed to the child's vulnerability or poor relationships with parents, but not to the hospital. Sympathetic listening is important, but is only a partial solution. The greatest cause of distress our young interviewees told us is hospital practices, the 'mortification rituals',[10] such as: spending weeks in some wards in large crowded rooms with never any private time alone; 'always being poked and prodded and stared at by strangers'; 'the needles'; 'having to go into the doctors' meeting and be talked about'; 'they jerk you about and don't even know your name'; 'only having food that makes you feel sick'. Increasingly, hospitals are centres for rapid, impersonal, mass treatment, the traumatic stage of therapy; healing occurs mainly after discharge. Hospitals are also harmful places where, routinely, patients endure fear, boredom, frustration, loneliness, humiliation, distress and the longing 'to get out of here', as well as the documented risks of infection. 'Morbidity' is very often not in children's reactions but in professionals' activity. Really listening would include taking children's complaints seriously and acting on them, in order to remove or reduce distressing incidents. The psychiatrist quoted above implies that the hospital is therapeutic, and he mentions parents only pejoratively. Yet respecting children often means respecting parents as children's best advocates. Paradoxically, mothers who tried hardest to improve care for their child and others were, in some wards, dismissed as trouble-makers.

Being unwell and needing to grumble do not wholly account for the high levels of expressed unhappiness we encountered. The emotional costs of long treatment, such as disruption to friendships and loss of self-esteem, must be considered when planning treatment. Friendships are known to increase adults' sense of well-being and self-esteem and health.[11] Friendships are also very important to children.[12] Even a few days off school have been shown to affect boys' friendships adversely.[13] Although friendships are made in hospital, these are only temporary. Some children in follow-up interviews reported difficulty in reintegrating into home and school life. Integration links to integrity, in that each person feels accepted for himself or herself. This delicate meshing takes time to develop and sustain, especially for children with chronic defects whose self-esteem may be tenuous.

Four elements of self-esteem in children have been identified: security in being loved by significant others; a sense of competence; a positive regard for their own ethics; the extent to which children see themselves as influencing their own lives and other people. Self-esteem is encouraged when parents supportively respect their child's independence.[14] Life in hospital can threaten all four elements when children are treated as helpless and powerless, are regimented, and denied personal time and space away from the public gaze. Robin spoke for many others when he said, 'I miss my bedroom, it's my castle'. When professionals consider that their responsibility is to make expert decisions, they may feel that it is wrong to share choices with patients. However, patients can then be left feeling powerless to affect medical decisions and fall into a position of learned helplessness[15] and despair. 'I hate myself', was said (in earlier chapters) by Jane and Kerry when they felt most powerless. Successful surgery can help to raise self-esteem, such as through improving appearance or mobility. Yet prolonged, distressing hospital experiences may counteract benefits gained from the surgery. It is therefore vital to recognize surgery as a series of stages and to take account of children's wishes during each stage.

## Pain

*Treatment of pain after surgery is central to the care of postoperative patients. Failure to relieve pain is morally and ethically unacceptable.* For decades, however, research has continued to show a high incidence of postoperative pain. Paradoxically, the same research often shows a high level of patient satisfaction suggesting that postoperative pain is commonly seen as inevitable (emphasis in original).[16]

The report just quoted also states that even 'fewer and relatively smaller doses' of pain relief are given to children than to adults, and that little has changed since the 1950s. One study showed that, after the same types of surgery, whereas the 18 adults had 671 doses, the 25 children had a total of 24 doses of analgesics.[17] Of the 120 young patients we interviewed, 13 said they had 'no pain'. Heidi, aged 12, said: 'I was very surprised that it didn't hurt. I had an epidural for a few days after my spinal fusion and I didn't feel any pain. It was a bit uncomfortable after that but not painful. I'd been expecting it to be agony'.

Forty-five said they had 'middling pain' and 62 had 'severe pain'. This may be an underestimate, since some young people seemed to be embarrassed to admit to apparent weakness. Whereas some mothers reported severe pain in their child, others tended to discourage complaints. Tim was aged 10, and his mother said:

> They've got to find out first how bad the pain is. You can't keep doling out tablets. Tim would say he was in pain and they'd say, "Is it bad enough for an injection?" He hates injections so he'd hardly ever say "yes", and if he did they'd give him some medicine. I don't think he ever cottoned on that it wouldn't be an injection.
>
> There was a lovely atmosphere in there. They'd say, "Don't worry, cheer up". One nurse said "Don't you feel well?" and Tim said, "No,

I don't". She said, "You're not allowed to be ill in here". That keeps the child's morale up, to tell them there's nothing really wrong. I don't know whether it's a front or really him, but he doesn't worry. So much has happened to him for years that he just accepts what comes. His favourite word is "tough".

When asked what they were least looking forward to in hospital, of the 120 young patients, 62 said 'injections!' (50 per cent of under-11s, and 52 per cent of 11- to 15-year-olds); 35 mentioned two or more things, often including injections, blood tests or having stitches or drains removed. Only 12 said 'the operation'. Puncturing the skin was by far the most common fear. When John was 17 years old, he said, 'I don't know why it is, but I break out into a cold sweat and I shake all over if I have a blood test. And then it's over, it wasn't so bad yet I'm always terrified'. Needles were often used unnecessarily, to give pain relief or to collect blood routinely in case children would have surgery next day. Kerry described how she argued with a phlebotomist. 'I was right. I didn't need the blood test, but if I hadn't argued with her I would have gone through all that pain. It's silly, I don't mind the operation, but I don't like having the needle go through you'.

Apart from pain, children describe their horror of injected substances as cold, icy, invasive poison, and their fear of blood being removed or 'stolen' saying, 'I need it, I want it back'.[18] One boy told me, 'You can still feel the stuff going up your arm, horrible'. Many children said, 'I don't know why, but I just hate needles so much'. A minor procedure becomes for many young people a major symbol of everything they fear about hospitals.[19] In fact and fiction, the skin is usually penetrated either for medical reasons or to harm or kill, the latter purpose being so frequently and vividly flashed across television screens that it may be hard not to see menace in the approaching needle. The skin is the only fragile barrier between the tiny self and the otherwise infinite not-self. Patients' sense of self is threatened and constrained in hospital; they have left at home their possessions, friends, familiar life, freedoms and everyday social identity. Those without a secure sense of self are liable to feel lost and overwhelmed; the needle reinforces these feelings when it breaks through the division between self and not-self. If forced onto resisting patients, the needle combines pain with fearful invasiveness. To small children, the syringe is proportionately larger. Several of them said, 'I don't mind the operation, that's the easy part because you're asleep for that'. Needles are often inserted in view of other patients, which can increase children's stress and embarrassment, although they dreaded going into treatment rooms.

Ten-year-old Katy described having her stitches removed:

I was fine up till then. Then I had two stitches taken out and I screamed the place down because I didn't want it done. But they said I'd be in absolute pain if they were left in, so next day I decided to have it done. It took 35 minutes. Well, it could have took less than that but they had

to keep stopping for me to have a drink. It made them frustrated a bit.
They were so good. It didn't hurt at all. I just wonder why I was so
upset before. I thought it was going to be so horrible. I was saying if
I had to have it done I was going to kill myself, and I wanted it done
in the anaesthetic. So I decided to have it done in the end. It was lovely.
Mum said I was very good. Next time will be OK, because I know
what's going to happen. They made a deal with me, if it hurted too much
they'd wait a few days, but I decided to have it done. They gave me
a bit of a push, just to tell me to have it done, but they said they weren't
going to mess about. They'd do it later if I screamed again, so I said
I wouldn't scream. And I got through it perfectly well, otherwise the
stitches would be pulling and dropping out and they would be very sore.
It was the best thing to do. Other people said the stitches don't hurt
a single bit.

Katy's response suggests that needles and removing stitches are potent symbols
of other people being in control. Screaming is the child's attempt to assert some
control. Children are respected when a 'deal' is agreed, and the child gives consent – as Katy said three times, 'I decided'.

A research study purported to show that children do not mind needles. A
psychologist interviewed parents 18 months after their child, then aged 4 years,
had visited a clinic for a single blood test. Hardly surprisingly, the parents
reported that most children had behaved and recovered well. Observations and
interviews with the child near the time of the event are likely to give more
accurate reports, and a short visit to a community clinic does not compare with
admission to hospital for surgery.

Words cannot express raw pain. In her eloquent book on physical, mental
and spiritual pain,[20] Margaret Spufford writes of her difficulty in breaking
through taboos to write of her own pain, from osteoporosis. The most painful
moment of her life was when two ambulance men carrying her both stumbled,
and dropped her stretcher a couple of inches before recovering their balance:

> The effect was terrifying. All my reflexes seemed to go berserk with pain.
> I, who so much valued control, was completely out of control . . . the
> world ran amok, and my husband who was there, was utterly irrelevant
> through the pain. He could not reach me. Nor could anyone.

The pain began through the sudden jolt, but also through fear of hitting the
ground, which did not actually happen. The incident shows how powerfully
terror increases pain, and then how fear and pain can block out relief. Margaret
Spufford's complete dependence on the men carrying her is similar to children's
complete vulnerability to the adults caring for them. As she says, 'small children
suffer very acutely, and worse because no explanation is possible to them'.
After long periods spent in intensive care children's wards with her daughter,
she wrote that a child could be 'emotionally deformed by experiences which

impaired her ability to love and to trust'.[21] Far more needs to be known about the effects of painful treatment on children and how to alleviate them.

Denial and injections are being replaced by more effective methods of relieving pain. Many anaesthetists aim to prevent postoperative pain with nerve blocks or epidurals which take effect before children regain consciousness. In our study, pain after spinal surgery tended to be far better controlled than after leg and hip surgery. Yet after the first few days on a morphine drip, in some wards children were suddenly expected to manage on infrequent doses of paracetamol, a policy that was criticized in wards where patients were carefully weaned off pain relief. When patients control their own pain, overall they are found to take less analgesia. Picture and number charts are used with very young children to discover and then treat their level of pain.[22] Pain is coming to be defined as 'what the patient says it is' though, for instance, an 11-year-old told us, 'They say I can't have EMLA any more, now I'm 11, but the needle still hurts just as much'. One method which relies on the patients' own knowledge is the patient controlled analgesia pump (PCA), a drip timed to give a continuous, safe dose. Children as young as 3 years can press the pump when they need an extra amount.[23] Psychological pain control is now used in children's wards as hypnotherapy, in which children and parents use visualization techniques to relieve pain.[24] These methods literally put control into the child's hands. A sister commented that a few years ago, young children were thought to be unable to realize clearly what pain is. Now they control powerful narcotics competently.[25] An example of the importance of listening to the patients as the experts in pain is shown in new policies to administer rapid pain relief, to discuss anxieties and to support people with sickle cell disease crises.[26]

## Parents' involvement

Child–parent relationships are complex, changeable and highly individual, but some children are still treated according to age stereotypes based on outdated theories.[27] Children's partly conflicting needs for protection and for respect[28] are often split in hospital practice: young children's need for protective parenting care is now widely understood but their privacy is less respected; adolescents' need for independence is stressed (especially in adult wards where most adolescents are nursed), but their parents' protective care is sometimes discouraged. Many young patients' wishes are more complex than the stereotypes allow.

Young children were described in some professionals' interviews as unselfconscious. They are 'not worried by their disability' or 'privacy does not matter to them'. However, parents described the anger and depression of children aged 3–5 years, who mourned their differences from other children, as well as cruel teasing at school from around age 7 years. Early self-consciousness is recognized by many other professionals, such as the burns sister who said that even babies hate their own body when it has been burnt, and they have to learn to love their body that has been so deformed.[29] Surgery can also scar and deform. Young children were very embarrassed to use bedpans when skimpy screens half hid them from view. They lay on soaking sheets rather than confess their incontinence to the nurses. They were ashamed if they cried in front of other children.

Nurses who stress adolescents' need for independence from their parents respect young people's autonomy in principle,[30] but often deny it in practice. Most adolescents we interviewed preferred, at times, to be nursed by their mothers. Whereas 68 of the 120 children wanted a parent to stay with them in the ward at night, including 15-year-olds, this was arranged for 30. In spacious but unwelcoming wards, parents tended to say they did not want to stay on the ward – 'I need some sleep'. Yet if mothers felt unable to sleep on the wards, how could the children? Children complained about poor standards of night nursing, noisy staff, and the babies calling for hours for their mothers. 'The night nurses go into their office for a chat, so they can't hear you if you shout', said an 11-year-old returning for her sixteenth spinal operation: 'I wish we had a call button like the adults have'. If parents are present, conditions tend to improve. Sixty-nine children aged 8–15 years said they wanted a parent to accompany them to the anaesthetic room,[31] but it was arranged for only 46.

Most young patients wanted their parents to stay somewhere in the hospital throughout their admission, but one hospital allowed parents of adolescents usually to stay only for five nights around each operation, which caused enormous distress. Fifteen-year-old Marie said, 'My mother stayed here in our caravan for five weeks. Otherwise I don't know how I'd have coped. I'd be devastated'. The caravan system was a good but limited way of increasing accommodation, but despite the need, parents' rooms were left vacant.

When parents can stay as a privilege, but not as a routine, they have greater difficulty in discussing matters with the staff, such as lack of accommodation, because raising it might be seen as a complaint. Sue threatened to go on hunger strike again if her mother left, and another mother said:

> Sue depends on her mother to carry her through. Her mother was crying all last night, she's terrified that they're going to send her away. If it was me I'd protest. I've been protesting about the way they treat my daughter. I'm not here to gain merit awards for myself. I'm here to do my best for her.

The seven wards we observed were markedly different in many respects. In some, parents could discuss problems on friendly, equal terms with the nurses, and many parents felt warmly supported. In others, staff criticized parents who tried to discuss problems, and parents were expected to take a subordinate, child-like position. A crucial factor in relations between families and professionals was the personality of the ward sister or manager. When children's priorities are respected, hospitals are humanely planned to ensure adequate access and accommodation for all the parents whose children wish them to stay.[32] However, hospitals are criticized for failing to meet basic standards.[33]

When immobilized after surgery or in body plasters, some usually confident independent adolescents became terrified; besides being in much discomfort, they were as helpless as babies, dependent on strangers for their every need. For example, nurses kept turning on radiators and shutting windows, but mothers kept altering these because their children felt miserably hot. Julie wanted to rub her neck but felt so weak that she asked her mother to turn back the sheet so that she could lift her arms from under it. She wanted to sip juice frequently. Jane was very embarrassed to be washed by male nurses, and felt that she would have fewer problems with her stitches and infection if her mother were allowed to nurse her. Tony longed to be turned more frequently to prevent pressure sores developing. They needed what could be called 'micro-nursing', tiny actions that were often too trivial to ask continually for the nurses' help but which changed misery into tolerable discomfort. Children's calls for help often went unheard, and they did not have working buzzers. Some adolescents who showed distress were called 'babies', told to 'buck out of it', or described as 'regressing', as if angry or tearful outbursts belong only to babyhood. The ward in which 'over-anxious mums' were most criticized had task-orientated nursing.[34] In other wards, nurses fully appreciated the parents' hard work, and where nurses were tolerant and supportive, children and parents expressed less anxiety in interviews, and more gratitude towards the nurses.

In many wards, individual child–parent relationships are increasingly respected. Primary nurses are each assigned to a few patients,[35] and come to know them well, working out with them how each child wishes the parents to be involved. Some hospitals lead the way in accepting each child's need both for parenting care and for independent privacy through skilful nursing and imaginative ward design. Young children's self-awareness and adolescents' partial dependence have important implications when discussing treatment options with them, and how it may be provided in sensitive, respectful ways.

## Schooling

In some of the wards we observed, children were primarily treated as school pupils instead of hospital patients.[36] Many children were grateful for the hospital teachers' help, for interesting lessons, and memorable activities, outings and visits by celebrities; school helped to pass the boring lonely hours, and to distract attention away from anxiety and pain. Teachers can be very supportive, and a few offered 'therapeutic teaching' while children were very unwell or distressed. 'The teacher may be the only person who has time to sit, and really listen', said one headteacher. Another hospital school headteacher organized multidisciplinary study days to encourage all the staff to understand children's experiences more deeply.

Other children, including intelligent academic ones, were bored and unhappy with routine lessons, saying they felt too unwell or distracted to work, and that similar demands were not made of adult patients.[37] In some wards, the teachers' stated aim was to provide 'normal activity in an abnormal environment', begging questions about the meaning of normality. After a surgeon had discussed whether to amputate the leg of a young girl with bone cancer, her parents were sent away and her maths lesson began. If children were seen mainly as pupils, their welfare as patients was affected. Nurses had far less contact with children, as did parents in the ward with the notice 'no visiting during school hours', a policy abandoned by almost every British hospital years ago and against government policy.[38] Some parents who would have stayed during the day were unable to visit after school; the hospital was very isolated and transport, as a social worker commented, was 'a nightmare'. Parents who were excluded from the wards missed meeting doctors, sharing information, giving nursing care and accompanying their child to the X-ray or plaster room. Alternatively, doctors spoke to parents but not to children having lessons, as we often observed. When play specialists were employed by the school, instead of as an independent play team, play was educational rather than therapeutic. There was less informal 'messy' play for younger children, fewer youth activities for older ones, and less interest in helping children to decorate the wards which could make even gloomy Victorian buildings look very attractive and welcoming. Because children's rights are officially better respected in the health service than in the education service,[39] child patients have a lower status in wards over-dominated by teachers. This affects how they are informed and involved in medical discussions. Children benefit when they assess their needs with their parents and with their teacher, nurse and play specialist and share in planning their care, as happens in some of the excellent wards in our study.

### Diet and digestion

Eating was frequently a serious problem. Surgery did not improve bowel and bladder function. Immobility increased the likelihood of constipation, which hospital diets of stodgy stews, pastries and puddings also seem designed to promote. Many children were unused to having two cooked meals a day: 'We have sandwiches and a salad for lunch, not these soggy meat things'. Some children lost weight, such as Julie who lost a stone between spinal fusions, which 'doesn't help her to build up her strength ready for her second operation', said her mother. In some wards, the food was served from large pans in dollops by nurses who filled in the 'individual choice menus' without consulting children. One area of informed choice could be to explain to every family how to reduce likely digestive problems, and to provide food in the imaginative ways adopted by some hospitals, with attractive menu cards and choice of portion size as in adult wards.

## Sharing choices

Hospitals epitomize the medical model of treating sickness rather than preserving health, when dieticians visit children on special diets but do not advise on menus served to all patients, or when psychologists treat very distressed surgical patients individually, but do not share in helping to change hospital routines which daily upset many children. However, many children's ward staff are promoting health through listening to children. Willingness to listen was illustrated by the medical journal which published a 14-year-old's view of having chemotherapy and how this 'nightmare' could be made more tolerable.[40] Choices arise at every stage of surgery, and when young patients are involved in taking them, fear and resistance are reduced, and the quality of care improves.

When children are 'provided with as much information as possible and their wishes ascertained and taken into account',[41] when they are able to exercise rights and choice, two conditions are necessary. One is that hospital professionals recognize when supposedly unalterable routines or professionals' decisions are actually choices which can be shared with children. An example is the surgical team who questioned each routine – children's theatre gowns, premeds, trolley-beds, parents in the anaesthetic room, and so on – to see how children's views could be accommodated. The other condition is that time is taken to discuss procedures and alternatives with each young patient. Choices are shared with children by professionals who know that this is possible and preferable.

## Notes

1 Department of Health (1991) *Welfare of Children and Young People in Hospital*, p. 6. London, HMSO.
2 *Code of Practice Pursuant to Section 118(4) of the Mental Health Act 1983* (1990) London, HMSO. Consent relates to all touching of the patient by all hospital staff (Section 15.3).
3 Cleave, M. (1992) Obituary of Dr Cicely Williams. *Independent*, 27 August, p. 15.
4 Dr Gene Bleck, Stanford Medical Center, California, personal communication.
5 As at St. Mary's Hospital, London.
6 Details of cleansing are in Chapter 2.
7 Professor Sharrod, Sheffield, personal communication.
8 Following the 1990 National Health Service and Community Care Act, responsibilities have been split between purchasers (such as health authorities) and providers (such as hospital trusts). One effect has been much more detailed accounting of all spending, another has been to draw up contracts for quality services, which

can be a vital means of raising standards when patients' needs are clearly understood and recorded in the contracts.

9 The young people were happier at home but some were still bored and lonely, and their mothers' personal and working lives were very disrupted unless children had adequate transport to go to school or a tuition unit and to go out socially.

10 Analysed by Goffman, E. (1968) *Asylums*. Harmondsworth, Penguin.

11 Oakley, A. and Rajan, L. (1991) Social class and social support: The same or different? *Sociology*, 25(1), 31–59.

12 Rubin, Z. (1980) *Children's Friendships*. Glasgow, Fontana.

13 Prout, A. (1986) 'Wet children and little actresses': Going sick in primary school. *Sociology of Health and Illness*, 8(2), 111–36.

14 Coopersmith, S. (1967) *The Antecedents of Self Esteem*. San Francisco, CA, W.H. Freeman.

15 Like Seligman's dogs who had unpredictable electric shocks, whatever they did. Seligman, M. (1975) *Helplessness: On Depression, Development and Death*. San Francisco, CA, W.H. Freeman.

16 Royal College of Surgeons of England, College of Anaesthetists (1990) *Report of the Working Party on Pain After Surgery*. London, RCS.

17 Eland, J. and Anderson, J. (1977) The experience of pain in children. In Jacox, A. (ed.), *Pain: A Source Book for Nurses and Other Health Professionals*. Boston, Little, Brown.

18 Lewis, N. (1978) The needle is like an animal. *Children Today*, January/February, pp. 18–21.

19 As Niki shows in Chapter 9.

20 Spufford, M. (1989) *Celebration*, p. 38. Glasgow, Collins.

21 Ibid., pp. 49–50.

22 Alderson, P. (1992) *Children and Pain: Family Information Leaflet*. London, Action for Sick Children.

23 Gureno, M. and Reisinger, C. (1991) Patient controlled analgesia for the young pediatric patient. *Pediatric Nursing*, 17(3), 251–4. Children using these methods need high levels of nursing and anaesthetist support, which are not available in many children's wards. Lloyd-Thomas, A., Howard, R. and other correspondents (1992) Solving the problems with PCA. *British Medical Journal*, 304: 1113, 1174–5.

24 Sokel, B., Lansdown, R. and Kent, A. (1990) The development of a hypnotherapy service for children. *Child: Care, Health and Development*, 16, 227–33.

25 Llewellen, N. (1992) *Research with Children and Pain*. London, CERES Open Meeting, May.

26 Nwokonkor, C. (1990) *Strategies for the Care of Patients with Sickle Cell Disease*. London, City and Hackney Health Authority.

27 These are reviewed in Chapter 5.

28 Discussed in Chapter 8.

29 Anna Forshaw, speaking at the Association of British Paediatric Nurses' Annual Conference, York, June 1991.

30 Montgomery, J. (1987) Confidentiality and the immature minor. *Family Law*, 101–6, draws attention to these important issues and discusses legal aspects of involving and excluding parents.

31 Some children replied 'no' they didn't want a parent to go with them to the

anaesthetic room seemingly because it was not allowed and they were talking about possibilities rather than personal preference.

32 Op. cit., note 1.

33 Audit Commission (1992) *Children First: A Study of Hospital-Based Services for Sick Children*. London, HMSO.

34 In this old-fashioned approach, each nurse carries out certain tasks for many patients; in primary or case-orientated nursing, each nurse cares almost fully for a few patients. Some parents convey high anxiety to their child. A positive nursing response is to support these parents and to try to relieve their anxiety, rather than to criticize or isolate them.

35 The benefits of primary nursing are detailed in Audit Commission (1992) *Making Time for Patients: A Handbook for Ward Sisters*. London, HMSO.

36 Schooling constructs differences between child and adult, by excluding children from everyday life, and implying that children must absorb a mass of formal knowledge before they can become adult. Yet the process of learning, selecting and forgetting countless ideas continues through life.

37 Hospital teachers are expected to reduce the most popular 'occupation' lessons (art, cooking) and provide more 'education' sessions so that academic achievement by children in hospital can compare well with that in all other schools. Lecture by Her Majesty's Inspector for Special Education, London Home and Hospital Teachers AGM, 27 March 1992. This policy ignores the pupils' status as patients.

38 Op. cit., note 1.

39 See Chapter 3.

40 Anon. (1990) Easing a childhood nightmare. *British Medical Journal*, 301, 244.

41 Op. cit., note 1.

# 11

# *RESPECTING CHILDREN'S CONSENT*

*If I'm not for myself, who will be for me?*
*If not this way, how? And if not now, when?*[1]

These are key questions for children's consent as an informed and committed decision. The young child as a unique 'me' who is 'for myself' is recognized by the concerned adults when they support decisions which are for, not against, the child. They respect the child's wishes and feelings,[2] as well as considering adult-defined interests. Then they can take the second question, 'if not this way, how?' and negotiate the best options. The benefits and harms of modern medical treatment form complex equations. Doctors assess clinical aspects; patients and relatives can best assess personal implications. The third question 'If not now, when?' raises vital questions about time. At what age will children be respected? When will time routinely be allocated to plan their treatment with them? When will misleading prejudices about their incompetence be questioned critically in the light of valid evidence? When will adults more willingly share power and responsibility with children?

Respect for adults' consent is recognized as a moral and legal[3] value which is too obvious and important to need justifying. Yet in addition, adults' consent is advocated as a means of increasing benefits and avoiding the harms of under- or over-treatment.[4] The main questions of the children's consent research project reported in this book are:

- How does children's consent differ from adults' consent?
- Can and should children's consent be respected as a good in itself?
- Is children's consent a means of increasing benefits and reducing harms for young patients having surgery?

This final chapter summarizes replies to these questions from earlier chapters.

## Talking with children

Originally, we wondered if it was worthwhile to interview surgical patients as young as 8 years. We met confident fluent interviewees and shy hesitant ones in each age group among the 120 young patients aged 8–15 years. Eight was chosen as the youngest age for research purposes, and not to imply that competence begins then; some interviewees discussed competence below 8 years. Certain young patients' mature responses as interviewees indicated their ability to understand and share in discussions with health professionals about their treatment. Most of them had previously had surgery, and time to discuss their current elective operation. They were not typical but they do show how well young patients can understand, given time and experience.

However, cases like Danny's (Chapter 1) show how complex, uncertain and disturbing information can be. The difficulty of knowing how to avoid brutal honesty arises with people in every age group. Danny's case illustrates a series of divisions: each leg was treated by a different doctor, hospital care was separated from home care, medical needs from personal needs, expectations were not borne out by experience, much information was not shared between staff and family, or between parents and child. A theme through all the chapters is the benefit to children when divisions are overcome, and the medical drive to partition and atomize is reversed; in Danny's mother's words, 'They treat one leg, but we've got to think about all of Danny'.

Surgery involves experiences and questions about which children have strong opinions. Informed and willing commitment is a vital part of therapy, especially when it is lengthy, if distress is to be reduced. Deferring non-urgent surgery until children understand and want treatment can prevent much distress for young children, contrary to the view of a consultant who thought that adult patients have 'more psychological problems'. Distress is also reduced when adults take children's preferences into account while deciding methods of administering treatment. Wanting treatment is linked to the patient's perception of the need for it, so that careful discussions about whether to treat, and when, and possible alternative courses are important. Children also want warning of definite or very likely harms, and continuing supportive discussion throughout treatment. However, warning of risks which are unlikely to be realized is more contentious. Our adult interviewees balanced the harm of introducing new anxieties against the benefits of preparing children for adverse events, and helping them to make informed choices. Some doctors and nurses added that discussing risks can alleviate children's unspoken fears, and can further respect and trust between adults and children. After initial shock, children who were given alarming information appeared to prefer to know; those who were unprepared for procedures or complications were upset and angry. Yet we interviewed parents who said that risks had not been discussed and some of these said they were satisfied that they were adequately informed. Relating reported satisfaction levels to the quality of services is notoriously difficult, and rigorous research attempts to discover whether everyone wishes to be informed about risks present insuperable practical and ethical problems. However, our interviews showed that clinicians who explained risks with great care appeared to increase the confidence of the parents and children we met. The important question appears to be not whether to give information, but how to give it, clearly, sensitively and at an acceptable pace.

There are obvious differences between babies and adults, but the more we examined supposed differences between children and adults, the less obvious these became. Apart from certain physical differences, and the tendency to discuss ideas less elaborately and abstractly, how do school-age children differ from adults? This is the crucial question in any discussion of children's consent. Many children exceed many adults in, for example, intelligence, ability, prudence, confidence, size, strength, and profound experience of certain aspects of life. Many children care for sick or disabled parents. Differences between adults and children lie mainly in social beliefs about childhood and behaviours affected by these beliefs, rather than in children's actual abilities.[5]

Recognizing similarities between children and adults includes an often disturbing relinquishing of deeply held but unjustified feelings about children's inadequacies and adults' rightful powers. These feelings tend to be propagated most passionately by adults who exercise power over children. Ironically, experts who advise society on children's abilities tend to be those who would have most to lose if children's abilities and choices were more fully respected. It is in the interests of many experts to reinforce myths about the inabilities of the 'normal' child. In doing so, they reveal their own, rather than children's, limitations. Amy and Tina (end of Chapter 3) showed how some children need to discuss unresolved questions, about normality, discrimination and quality of life, which affect their treatment decisions.

## Children's rights

Throughout history, children's interests have been identified with their fathers' rights, but over the past century many professions have encroached into the domain of decision making for children. When adults define children's needs for resources and protection, 'interests' is a more accurate term than 'rights'. The most basic human right, self-determination, began to be accorded to children when parents' rights were restated as responsibilities to promote the child's best interests. Consent or refusal, the act of exercising self-determination, is the key to all other rights. Many adults are loath to entrust this right to children because of old prejudices that minors cannot make informed, wise decisions. Low expectations are self-fulfilling, continually reinforcing beliefs in many adults and children that it is unwise and unkind to entrust children with major decisions. High expectations are also self-fulfilling, encouraging young children to develop mature competence.[6]

Children's human rights serve as an arena for power conflicts between parents, professionals and children. The concept of rights usefully emphasizes children's need for independence and some control over their integrity of body and mind, but the concept can understate children's dependence on adults' goodwill or whim. Rights are too starkly combative to encompass the love and trust between most of the children and parents we interviewed, who shared decisions or deferred to one another.[7] The rights movement justly challenges the tradition of the child as the parents' property, but can underestimate everyone's emotional need to 'belong' to significant others. Over-respect for each separate individual's rights can end in harming everyone, by blind self-interest which denies human inter-dependence. Moral conflicts between individualism and altruism, selfishness and self-sacrifice,[8] raise troubling questions about respecting children's individual and collective rights, and seeing the child as an individual or as a member of a family. Conflict is reduced when rights are combined with responsibilities and when children are recognized as capable of being rational, responsible moral agents. Over-protection can weaken children and make them more vulnerable by denying their own strengths.

Children's legal rights are split between two traditions. In the 1920s, minors under 21 were legal infants under the control of their fathers and ultimately of the courts. Yet many children also worked like adults and girls could marry at 12 years, so they shared certain adult rights. Today's lawyers confusingly invoke legal precedents from either the child–infant or the child–adult traditions, as shown in court disputes over children's rights to refuse or consent to medical treatment. Recent guidelines and laws stress the importance of listening to children and respecting their views. However, legal decisions are complicated by prejudices which judges share with the rest of society about children's inabilities, deep fears about allowing freedoms to young people, and the desire to protect them. 'It's such a big step for the adult to surrender power to the child'.[9]

## Research about children

Adult–child power relations also pervade research. A century of research about children has concentrated on observing and measuring them, employing 'hard' scientific methods used in animal research which takes no account of the research subject's viewpoint. Inevitably, therefore, children's views and specifically their consent are comparatively rare research topics; as a research practice, requesting children's consent tends to be seen as inconvenient or, with covert or emergency work, impossible. Elements of consent such as wisdom and competence are elusive, abstract concepts. They slip through the grid of 'hard' science which has tended to assume and so to reinforce beliefs about children's incompetence. Yet increasingly, qualitative or interpretive researchers are listening to children, respecting their understanding and wisdom, and aiming to treat them as informed and willing research partners. This approach is still unpopular with research funding bodies and scientific journals, and so far has had little influence on opinion leaders in research, law, education or medicine:

> The difficulties of interpreting information from patients should not detract from the aim of involving patients as fully as possible in their health care. Rather, this should act as an even greater incentive to research into communication between patients and health professionals.[10]

Some of the difficulties are created by many researchers' assumptions that only very formal methods and medicalized language count in 'real' research. Yet strict rules which are appropriate to a randomized trial exclude valuable data and lay people's understandings, and are inappropriate to research about communication. Over-formal methods ignore the reality that communication is a two-way process in which substance and methods are negotiated by both parties.

Drafts of this book have been criticized by traditional researchers as (a) piecemeal and anecdotal, (b) lacking clear standards on what children actually understand and whether they are correct, and (c) lacking guidance on how children should be informed. To respond to these criticisms: (a) From hundreds of interviews only a few examples can be selected for quotation. They have been used to illustrate the range of responses and to indicate the nature of children's experiences which tables of figures alone cannot do. (b) As the literature and interviews amply demonstrate, there are no agreed clear standards for assessing 'correct' understanding or competence. Detailed studies of particular conditions, patients and clinicians which compare later recall with transcripts of information-giving sessions can be useful, but such studies assume definitions of correctness and salience which may not be shared by either patients or clinicians. Doctors criticize lay people's inaccuracies, but medical language is also criticized for its sometimes brutal denial of its personal implications.[11] Medicine is too complex to be explained completely in a single discourse. Our study examined people's differing views on standards. (c) This book is not intended to prescribe how children *should* be informed, but to describe how the children and adults we met consider that children *are* being informed. Our exploratory study could be followed up in many ways.

Quantitative research aims at reduction, increasing scientists' and clinicians' ability to classify, predict, control and generalize about, for example, the course of disease. In contrast, qualitative research aims at expansion by demonstrating the variety, complexity and unpredictability of individuals. Qualitative findings complicate rather than simplify the work of health professionals, raise questions and problems rather than supply answers or short-cuts, and show children's widely varying abilities and interests. Most of all, children need time for discussion and careful listening.

## Children's competence

A powerful distorting pressure when assessing children's abilities is the tradition of the child negatively defined as not adult: not wise, informed or experienced, and so assumed to be foolish, ignorant and perverse. When children's capacity to be 'for myself' is denied, they are assumed to be 'against myself', self-destructive and in need of adult control. Narrow meanings of knowledge and maturity are used to justify withholding information from children and then to label them as ignorant and exclude them from sharing in decisions.

Yet competence to consent is not a fact, and it does not appear to develop evenly and gradually. Competence has more to do with qualities, experiences and perceptions. It is affected by the child's inner qualities (abilities, memories, confidence) and by outer influences (the nature and circumstances of the decision, its salience to the child's concerns, the adults' expectations and information, their support and respect for the child). Our interviewees' beliefs about the age of competence to consent ranged from early childhood to adulthood. On average, they thought that girls develop two years ahead of boys. Some 3- and 4-year-olds when very carefully informed were thought by adults caring for them to understand medical information 'as well as an average adult'. Exceptional 5- and 6-year-olds were thought to be able to make complex, wise decisions, whereas some adults are ignorant and foolish. If understanding and wisdom do not correlate with age, it is not necessarily logical or safe to enforce parents' decisions on unwilling children. Very few children in our orthopaedic study said they wanted their parents to be 'the main decider' about proposed treatment; most wanted their parents to be involved, but as mediators, supporters, interpreters and decision-sharers. The parents tended to have more confidence in their child's competence than the children had.[12] Most children wanted to make decisions with adults, and a few wanted adults to decide for them, suggesting that the often experienced young patients we interviewed made modest assessments of their own competence. The schools study indicates that inexperienced young patients are more likely to wish adults to decide for them.

Competence develops through relationships, which nourish yet restrict it. Respecting children by informing them honestly conflicts with the desire to protect them from anxiety. Tensions arise between what the child and parents want to do or feel they ought to do, as advised by a host of contradictory voices. Children and parents protect one another by hiding their own knowledge and distress. Loving interdependence and angry conflict between them complicate informed decision making, especially when decisions are urgent and shocking, very complex, serious or irrevocable. Adults' skill and motives vary when they give or withhold information. Though wanting to assert their own wishes, people fear the risks of failure, blame and guilt attendant on taking responsibility for decisions.

Most comments on child patients' consent also apply to adult patients. A range of complementary yet conflicting issues surround consent: information versus protection, choice or coercion, rights and interests, individualism or altruism, hopes and fears, knowledge but uncertainty, the wisdom to make a correct choice or the courage to stand by a best guess. These tensions act like the spokes of a wheel pressing on the hub of consent. The further it is examined, the more complex children's consent appears to be. General conclusions are too simplistic. Willing uncertainty is perhaps the best guide during dilemmas, when the adults and child concerned work together towards the least harmful decision.

## Risks and benefits of respecting children

Arrangements for proxy consent assume that adults are benign, but records of cruelty and neglect show that the reality can be very different.[13] Apart from fairly rare cases of parents fabricating the child's need for medical treatment,[14] in certain cases it is unclear whether surgery is for the benefit of the child, the parent or the surgeon. Parents can feel pressured into forcing children to undergo treatment for their present or future good. Surgeons may have difficulty in discovering the child's actual wishes.[15] The limitations of medical benevolence must be recognized if patients' consent as a means of self-protection is to be understood. Doctors are entrusted with the legal duties of ensuring that consent is informed and of assessing the child's competence. Hurried professionals who enforce procedures on resisting children, and who belittle children's views, mistreat them. They also set a highly influential example reinforcing the belief that adult might is right, a belief at the root of much mistreatment of children.

Recently, the courts have permitted doctors to enforce treatment,[16] without acknowledging that treatment allowed by judges and prescribed by doctors is often administered by junior doctors and nurses; decisions made through a remote hierarchy can legitimate treatment of resisting children, which would be criminal assault on resisting adults. If confrontation is vindicated at the highest level, the distressing choice between neglect or force, between under- or over-treatment, is resolved by opting for force. Yet there is often a middle way of reasoning and compromise. Growing understanding on all sides, as encouraged by the consent process and described by surgeons in previous chapters, can enable decisions to be made *with* children instead of *for* them.

During life-threatening emergencies and when patients are deranged this is impossible. Yet at times, claims that a case is one of emergency or insanity are contentious.[17] The threat to health, such as from anorexia, may misleadingly be redefined as an immediate threat to life. Some doctors oppose children's right to consent, from concern that adolescents with anorexia or diabetes will 'give in to their suicidal tendencies'. This response assumes that adult supervision can and must be vigilant enough to prevent such incidents. It also assumes that attacking their autonomy by treating adolescents as infants is the best way to control potential suicidal tendencies. Other professionals consider that unless the child's life is immediately threatened, this approach is harmful; respecting children and offering them choice and control can increase their self-esteem and their physical health.

Another concern is that respecting children's choices will cause them over-whelming anxiety and guilt. Yet choice primarily means respecting the child's wish to make, to share, or to delegate decisions. Children can also only accept medical proposals which doctors are willing to carry out, so that acceptance is always partly shared. The child alone may be responsible for refusal, but rejection of treatment can often be revoked if it is regretted. Worry about children's guilt implies that adults do not also feel guilt and regret decisions. The only way to become autonomous is to learn to be so through risking mistakes, which are seldom extremely serious and irrevocable. If they are, our interview and survey replies from over 1000 children suggested that children tend to be cautious about how much responsibility in decision making they can cope with. The alternative to the risk of guilt after choice, is the risk of frustration and resent-ment in reaction to coercion. How do children feel after unwanted amputation, or if denied an effective and greatly desired remedy for a defect, or if forced to have daily injections which eventually prove to be useless? Guilt can be a very serious problem at all ages, but the sense of being exploited can be a worse option. Both can be relieved by adults taking full account of children's wishes but sharing the conclusion with them. Even adults who would not make the same decision for themselves can give magnanimous support, in the spirit: 'You have to help them to make the best of it'. 'Whatever you choose will be valued . . . I'll do all I can to support you, and we'll go forward together'.[18]

Professionals who take time to decide with children set humane examples which accept the limits of adult wisdom. One surgeon said:

> *Surgeon*: I have changed a lot in my practice. I am much more hesitant about surgery than I used to be, particularly with idiopathic scoliosis. In the long term, they may be better left [without surgery and with a slight curve] but with complete flexibility. Rather than be straighter, though they're very rarely completely straight after surgery, but with a rigid spine, plus the risks and all the pain and disruption that is involved.
>
> *Int.*: What brought about this change in attitude and practice?
>
> *Surgeon*: Many things, years of experience, following up cases years later, the work of [named researchers], the schools screening programme [showing that minor curves left untreated do not develop seriously], the British Scoliosis Society conferences and papers. A lot of people are asking questions and urging caution.

Offering children medical choices can lead them into refusing vital benefits, or accepting serious risks. A consultant developing a painful and lengthy preventative treatment said, 'Yes, children can consent when they are seven. If the parents refuse and the child agrees, I would take the child's word and if necessary override the parents'. One suggested solution to ensure that the best decisions are made for children is to restore adult control and the 'fragile concept of protected childhood'.[19] In support of this approach, a psychologist said, 'Children's rights language is open to terrible abuse. Paedophiles use it to appear as if they are very liberal and respectful of children, when all they want is to trick and exploit them'.

Yet protection which increases adults' power while silencing and disarming children increases children's vulnerability. The preventable suffering of children in hospital has repeatedly been deplored.[20] One author concluded that adult patients are humiliated into imposed helplessness and their anxieties are trivialized by the emphasis on the purely medical. However, the effects are 'more obvious and more poignant in the case of children – and this experience has been most neglected in the research'.[21] Hospital care is being improved by the many professionals who attend to children's views. Yet listening to children also involves wider changes: in attitudes, policies and practices; in ways of planning and providing health services;[22] in professional training, and support such as in helping adults to cope with sharing children's distress. Change is also needed in many aspects of children's lives besides surgery. Parents, teachers, lawyers and other groups have to give away power before children can assert more control over their own lives. Just as the turning point for women's rights came with the recognition that they could be as rational as men, the turning point for children will come with the recognition that many children can be as rational as many adults. The present common underestimation of children's abilities and their exclusion from decision making reinforce learned incompetence.[23]

The case for excluding children from decision making breaks down once the following are recognized:

- the standard of informed consent for many adult patients, which children should minimally attain, is low;
- idealized standards of consent are unrealistic and discriminatory;
- much medical information is uncertain and contentious;
- competence cannot precisely be defined or assessed;
- adults, including doctors and parents, can make misguided decisions;
- excluding children can increase their fear and bewilderment;
- the anxiety and burden of decision making need not be carried by the child alone;
- young children can be wise and courageous;
- those with experience of severe illness or disability, especially, can contribute unique and essential knowledge during decision making.

## The cycle of consent

A decision is only as valid as the knowledge it is based on and knowledge about outcome has to be collected from the patients. Surgeons who carefully assess treatment taking account of their patients' views can make more informed decisions. Informed consent is a cycle when doctors inform new patients, using knowledge contributed by former patients. It is also cyclical in that surgeons who are willing to spend time discussing choices with patients before treatment are likely also to discuss after-effects with them. Patients' assessments can further be used when planning improvements in hospital care.

The consent cycle helps surgeons and patients to make informed decisions about the purpose and value of treatment as well as the process. Medical treatment is intended to prolong life and/or to improve its quality, by helping each patient to live a more fulfilling life, a topic on which patients are expert in their own case. Quality of life has been called 'the missing measurement in health care',[24] assessed through listening to patients,[25] a skill which doctors are not yet routinely helped to acquire with adult patients, still less with children. When we asked 62 of the young patients months after surgery about their recovery, they reported limited success for their three highest hopes concerning pain, mobility and sports. If clear improvement cannot be ensured, in order to avoid harms exceeding benefits, it is even more important to decide with children whether to embark on treatment and the best means of providing it:

> A sound, effective and ethical approach to chronic illness must lie in awareness of and attention to the experiences, values, priorities and expectations of patients and their families. [There is a need for professionals] increasingly to offer choices, not to make them.[26]

As a psychologist asked, 'In the end, how much misery do you put people through, and for what pay-off?' The answer partly depends on the patient's views. A policy adviser wrote of the National Health Service:

> Almost blind incrementalism has been the approach in the past. But if primacy is to be given to health gain – reducing premature death and improving quality of life – the pathway becomes clearer. Define the desirable future, the destination on the map, and mould the resources in support of its achievement. This will be the major strategic challenge for the 1990s.[27]

The map can refer to the national and also to each patient's desired destination.

## And if not now, when?

Researching with children has changed our views. We began with an idea that competence to consent to surgery might evolve at around 10–12 years. We did not expect to find the range of experience, ability, or of the desire to make, or share in making, or to delegate decisions in school-age children. Neither did we realize, at first, the importance of children's rights as a framework for analysing present practice and future progress. Respecting children's informed and willing consent is an important means of achieving the following:

- to respect children's ability and competence;
- to clarify relevant medical information through explaining it to children;
- to prevent coercion, fear, ignorance and the resentment of unwilling patients;
- to work with each child towards the best or least harmful decision;
- to reduce the incidence of unwanted or unnecessary treatment;
- to encourage informed and willing commitment to the chosen treatment as a vital part of therapy;
- to listen to and learn from children;
- to appreciate childhood as a valuable time in itself, not simply a prelude to adulthood;
- to encourage wider respect for children as members of society with rights and responsibilities, and so to address the root causes of their mistreatment.

Our study with 120 young patients, their parents and 70 health professionals suggests that competence develops, or at least is demonstrated, in response to experience and reasonably high expectations, rather than gradually over time through ages or stages. We hope that our findings will encourage adults to assume that school-age children can be competent – informed and wise – and then to require anyone who disagrees to demonstrate whether a particular child is incompetent. Children's competence to consent is continually changing in several ways: within each maturing child; in society's growing acceptance that a vital way to protect children is to help them to defend themselves and the adults they will become; in generally rising expectations and growing respect for children's rights and abilities. A surgeon said approvingly:

> Today's teenagers are very competent, particularly girls. An 11-year-old girl will have very strong views on what she wants, what she'll tolerate, and what she won't. Attitudes have changed and children are given more freedom, and encouraged much more, not just to listen and do as they're told, but to have strong views.

Professionals mentioned teenagers who were more informed and sensible than their parents, or who spoke English much more fluently. Commenting on social change, a sister said:

> We get really wild boys in here, completely beyond their parents' control, smoking, playing truant, their parents don't know where they are half the time. Yet doctors have to wait for mothers to come in to sign the consent forms. It's ludicrous to expect parents to sign on their behalf when they don't seem to influence anything else they do.

To end, here is an example of how having surgery can help children to mature. Before his operation, 13-year-old Nigel agreed with his mother that he would not be able to decide about proposed surgery until he was 18. A week after his operation, lying uncomfortably in a broomstick plaster, he said spontaneously:

> I think I'm changing from that idea that I have to be 18, for big things as well as little things. I've made sensible grown-up decisions before, and I can take care of myself. I see the others in here going through so much, so bravely. I think I can make difficult decisions and understand them now.

## Notes

1 Levi, P. (1986) *If Not Now, When?* London, Abacus. The Song of the Partisan. Primo Levi's novels celebrate autonomy as the energy which resists dehumanizing coercion.
2 As stated in the Children Act (1989).
3 The Department of Health endorses the patient's common law 'fundamental right to grant or withhold consent prior to examination or treatment': HC(90)22.
4 Beauchamp, T. and Childress, J. (1983) *Principles of Biomedical Ethics.* New York, Oxford University Press, combines analysis of consent as a good that does not need justifying and as a source of benefit.
5 Research is usually premised on a model of the child as dependent or parasite. This model, with children's economic and legal dependence, obscures interdependence between child and parent in emotional and practical aspects of living together which so far have been little researched. There are also questions of whether unrealized competence is latent, potential or non-existent, and when the desire to delegate personal decisions is an expression or a denial of personal autonomy, and what is the best response.
6 See Chapters 3–5, and reference to Ann Solberg's work.
7 Rowbotham, S. (1983) *Dreams and Dilemmas*, p. 353. London, Virago, discusses the same problem when asserting women's rights: 'How do we face conflict, dependence, domination between men and women without denying loving friendship and passionate desire? I am not sure how . . . But a culture shifts when people persevere'.
8 Such as the debate over whether children should take part in medical research, a practice vetoed by the deontologist Paul Ramsay (1979) *The Patient as Person.* New Haven, Yale University Press, but advocated by the utilitarian Richard McCormick (1981) *How Brave a New World?* Washington, DC, Georgetown University Press. Their ethics of justice is criticized as too extreme and needing to be complemented by the ethic of care, as in Bequaert Holmes, H. and Purdy, L. (1992) *Feminist Perspectives in Medical Ethics.* Buckingham, Open University Press/Indiana Press.
9 Hospital chaplain quoted at head of Chapter 9. The fear is complicated by fantasies about responsibility, and blame for the chaos which might follow liberal decisions. Menzies-Lyth, I. (1988) *Containing Anxiety in Institutions.* London, Free Association

Books, describes senior nurses' terror of delegating to juniors. The same anxiety exists between adults and children.

10 Sensky, T. (1992) Asking patients about their treatment. *British Medical Journal*, 305, 1109–10.

11 Frankenberg, R. (1993) Trust, culture, languages and time. In Alderson, P. (ed.), *Young People: Psychiatric Treatment and Consent*. London, Institute of Education.

12 Such as in the average ages of competence discussed in Chapter 9.

13 Newell, P. (1992) *One Scandal Too Many: The Case for Comprehensive Protection for Children in all Settings*. London, Gulbenkian Foundation, lists the unprecedented number of reported severe cases of abuse by parents and professionals since 1989.

14 Meadow, R. (1991) Neurological and developmental variants of Munchhausen syndrome by proxy. *Developmental Medicine and Child Neurology*, 33(3), 270–72.

15 The difficulty of ascertaining children's wishes, such as for cleft palate surgery, is described in Silverman, D. (1983) The clinical subject: adolescents in a cleft-palate clinic. *Sociology of Health and Illness*, 5(3): 253–74.

16 *In re* R., 1991; *in re* W., July 1992.

17 Ibid.

18 Mother and hospital chaplain quoted in Chapter 9.

19 McCall Smith, A. (1992) Review of Lyon, C. and de Cruz, P. (1990) *Child Abuse*. Bristol, Jordans. In *Journal of Medical Ethics*, 18, 164–5.

20 Robertson, J. (1958) *Young Children in Hospital*. London, Tavistock; Nobel, E. (1967) *Play and the Sick Child*. London, Faber; Bluebond Langner, M. (1978) *The Private Worlds of Dying Children*. Princeton, Princeton University Press; Hall, D. and Stacey, M. (1979) *Beyond Separation*. London, Routledge; Judd, D. (1989) *Give Sorrow Words*. London, Free Association Books.

21 Beuf, A. (1979) *Biting off the Bracelet*, p. 116. Philadelphia, University of Pennsylvania Press.

22 Williamson, C. (1992) *Whose Standards? Consumer and Professional Standards in Health Care*. Buckingham, Open University Press.

23 Bersoff, D. (1983) Children as participants in psycho-educational assessment. In Merton, G., Koocher, G. and Saks, M. (eds), *Children's Competence to Consent*, pp. 173–4. New York, Plenum Press.

24 Fallowfield, L. (1990) *The Quality of Life: The Missing Measurement in Health Care*. London, Souvenir Press. The reference is to psychosocial quality and not health economics QALYs.

25 Simes, R. (1986) Application of statistical decision theory to treatment choices: Implications for the design and analysis of clinical trials. *Statistical Medicine*, 5, 411–20.

26 Anderson, R. and Bury, M. (eds) (1988) *Living with Chronic Illness*, pp. 1–2. London, Unwin Hyman.

27 King's Fund Institute (1992) *Health Care in the UK*, p. 135. London, King's Fund.

# APPENDIX: NAMES AND AGES OF CHILDREN IN INTERVIEWS

(all the names have been changed)

| Name | Age | Page reference | Name | Age | Page reference |
|------|-----|----------------|------|-----|----------------|
| Alan | 8 | 98–9, 157 | Frank | 14 | 96 |
| Alison | 14 | 126–7, 135, 157–8 | Gemma | 11 | 43 |
| | | | George | 12 | 90–1 |
| Amy | 10 | 7, 25, 30, 36–9, 42, 84–5, 143, 152, 157, 158, 190 | Grant | 13 | 133 |
| | | | Heidi | 12 | 30, 94, 178 |
| | | | Helen | 14 | 81–2, 86, 91 |
| | | | Jane | 15 | 25, 30, 135–7, 178, 183 |
| Andy | 9 | 19–20, 164 | | | |
| Anita | 15 | 100–2, 118 | Jean | 8 | 1 |
| Annette | 14 | 119–21, 123 | Jim | 12 | 169 |
| Barry | 10 | 130–1 | John | 15 | 15, 25, 71, 176, 179 |
| Brenda | 9 | 100–1, 118 | | | |
| Bridget | 15 | 43, 84, 96 | Judy | 12 | 116, 126–7, 135 |
| Cliff | 15 | 132 | Julie | 11 | 83, 131, 163, 184 |
| Colin | 8 | 87 | | | |
| Danny | 10 | 1, 6–12, 25–6, 30, 189 | Katy | 10 | 179–80 |
| | | | Kazim | 15 | 164 |
| David | 10 | 71, 82, 86, 89, 116, 138 | Kerry | 12 | 70, 89, 123–4, 127, 129, 135, 167, 178, 179 |
| Efua | 9 | 19, 90–1 | | | |
| Elaine | 12 | 127 | | | |
| Elizabeth | 11 | 71, 84, 86 | Kevin | 11 | 135, 150–1 |
| Eric | 12 | 90–1, 138 | Krishna | 13 | 81, 159 |

# GLOSSARY OF MEDICAL TERMS

*achondroplasia*: one form of dwarfism
*acute*: short-term; as opposed to *chronic*: long-term
*anaesthesia*: loss of sensation
*anaesthetist*: doctor specializing in pain control and care of patients during
    surgery
*analgesia*: pain relief
*anorexia*: loss of appetite
*anterior horn cell damage*: damage to part of spinal cord causing weakness and
    wasting of muscle
*anti-emetics*: drugs which stop sickness and vomiting
*arthrogram*: X-ray film of joint
*atrophy*: wasting and weakness
*back conditions*:
    *congenital scoliosis*: unusual vertebral shape related to developmental abnor-
        mality, often mild
    *idiopathic scoliosis*: of unknown cause, usually affects adolescents
    *ball and socket*: hip or shoulder joint
    *kyphosis*: part of normal spinal shape but increase may cause deformity, for-
        ward bend in spine
    *lordosis*: part of normal spinal shape but increase may cause deformity,
        backward bend in spine
    *scoliosis*: sideways bend in spine, often with twist
*benign*: (good) not producing secondary cancers, not malignant (bad)
*biopsy*: sample of body tissue removed for microscopic examination
*calliper*: frame fitted to leg to aid walking
*cardiac catheterization*: passing a narrow tube into the heart for tests or treatment
*catheter*: narrow tube, also used to empty bladder

*cerebellum*: part of brain
*cerebrospinal fluid*: fluid in and around brain and spinal cord
*congenital*: born with
*cyst*: abnormal sac enclosing fluid or semi-solid matter
*cystic degeneration*: breaking down of tissue within a cyst
*cystic fibrosis*: severe genetic disease mainly affecting lungs and digestive organs
*doctors in order of experience are*: consultant, senior registrar, registrar, senior
    house officer
*drip*: thin tube inserted into the vein (IV) through which nutrition or medica-
    tion can flow
*Duchenne's*: one form of muscular dystrophy, affects boys
*elective*: planned, not urgent
*EMLA*: local anaesthetic cream
*epidural anaesthesia*: local pain relief into space around spinal cord
*femur*: thigh bone
*fibromas*: tumours
*fixator*: expanding metal rod used for limb lengthening (*see* Chapter 2)
*graft (bone)*: bone taken from one site and fitted to another site to strengthen it
*haemophilia*: inherited blood disorder causing uncontrolled bleeding
*haemorrhage*: bleeding
*Harrington rod*: metal rod inserted during surgery to straighten spine
*hydrocephalus*: rise in pressure of fluid in and around brain, can affect intelligence
    and movement, ranges from very mild to severe
*hypnotherapy*: skilful use of imagination to reduce pain or aid therapy
*IV cannula*: small plastic tube fixed into vein
*kyphosis*: *see* back conditions
*learning difficulties*: formerly called mental handicap
*log roll*: careful turning of patient after spinal surgery
*Milwaukee brace*: large body brace, now seldom used for treating scoliosis
*morbidity*: ill-health, injury
*mortality*: death
*muscular dystrophy*: genetic diseases which destroy muscle tissue, replacing it
    with fibrous tissue and fat, they range from mild to very severe
*naso-gastric tube*: feeding tube passed through nose and into stomach
*nerve block*: long-lasting pain-killing injection
*NFT*: neurofibromatosis, genetic disease of tumours developing in nerves and
    soft tissues, ranges from very mild to severe (*see* Chapter 1)
*orthopaedics*: correcting deformities of bone and muscle
*optic nerve*: eye nerve
*osteotomy*: surgical cutting of bone
*PCA*: patient-controlled analgesia, pain relief pump which patient can control
*perinatal*: around birth
*Perthes*: hip disease, mainly affecting young boys
*phlebotomist*: technician who collects blood samples

*premed*: sedative given before surgery

*prognosis*: predicted course of disease

*prosthesis*: artificial part replacing natural part of body

*pyrexia*: raised temperature

*radiographer*: X-ray technician

*scoliosis*: *see* back conditions

*SMA spinal muscular atrophy*: group of disorders affecting spinal cord, causing
    weakness and wasting of muscles

*spina bifida*: birth defect at base of spine, can affect lower limbs and continence,
    ranges from very mild to severe

*spinal cord*: cord of nerves inside spinal bones or vertebrae

*spinal fusion*: joining bones in the spine in order to strengthen and straighten it

*Stryker bed*: narrow orthopaedic bed which allows patient to be turned easily

*talipes*: club foot

*tendon*: cord which attaches muscle to bone

*tertiary care*: 'third level' or specialist care, GPs give primary and local hospitals
    give secondary care

*tibia*: shin bone

*traction*: steady drawing or pulling on the body to reduce or prevent deformity
  external or skin traction is fixed around body
  internal traction is fixed into bone, such as with leg lengthening or halo
    traction

*ureters*: natural tubes taking urine from kidney to bladder

*urethra*: natural tube for emptying bladder

*valgus*: turning outward

*ventilator*: machine used for people who cannot breathe independently

# INDEX

# EMOTIONAL AND PSYCHOLOGICAL ABUSE OF CHILDREN

## Kieran O'Hagan

Recent public inquiries, research and new legislation have all compelled child care professionals to widen their focus beyond the narrow parameters of the physical health of the child. Emotional and psychological health are now rightly regarded as crucial. This book aims to enable practitioners to articulate precisely what is meant by the terms 'emotional' and 'psychological' abuse; to be able to identify it, and to formulate effective strategies for dealing with it. The author identifies certain categories of parent and parental circumstances which are conducive to the emotional and psychological abuse of children. He makes clear however, that parents are not the only carers who abuse children in this way. He explores such abuse within a historical, global and cultural context, and examines recent inquiry reports which have exposed the emotional and psychological abuse of children within the child care and child protection systems. Numerous case histories are provided, and one is explored in detail within the context of new child care legislation.

## Contents

*Court out – Knowing or feeling – Definitions of emotional and psychological abuse – Global, cultural and historical contexts – Case histories – Parents – Observation, communication and assessment – The emotional and psychological abuse of Michelle – Implications for management and training – Bibliography – Index.*

176pp    0 335 09884 3 (Paperback)    0 335 09889 4 (Hardback)

# CHILD AND ADOLESCENT THERAPY: A HANDBOOK

## David A. Lane and Andrew Miller (eds)

Major changes are happening in child and adolescent therapy. The contexts in which the work is done, the range of problems tackled, and the models of intervention adopted are all in flux. This book is an overview of current developments. It presents diverse practice in multiple settings; it looks at the changing agenda for therapy, and the evaluation of interventions. It explores the challenges in play therapy, with non-speaking children, for the management of trauma, in child abuse, bullying and school phobia. In terms of settings, contributors cover the residential therapeutic community, the child guidance clinic, multidisciplinary approaches to support the school, and therapy in the community. In general, it reflects the excitement (and confusions) in current child and adolescent therapy, and is an important resource for trainee and prac-tising professionals in, for instance, social work, the health services, therapy and coun-selling, educational psychology and special educational needs.

### Contents
*Part I: 'The changing agenda – Child and adolescent therapy: a changing agenda – Evaluation of interventions with children and adolescents – Part II: Practice – An interactive approach to language and communication for non-speaking children – The barefoot play therapist: adapting skills for a time of need – Abuse of children – School phobia – Bullying – The management of trauma following disasters – Part III: Settings – The residential community as a therapeutic environment – The Child Guidance Clinic: problems and progress for the 1990s – School sup-port: towards a multi-disciplinary approach – Change in natural environments: community psychology as therapy – Index.*

### Contributors
Nigel Blagg, Maria Callias, Phil Christie, Danya Glaser, Peter Gray, Neil Hall, Roy Howarth, David A. Lane, Monica Lanyado, Andrew Miller, Elizabeth Newson, John Newson, Jim Noakes, Wendy Prevezer, Martin Scherer, Ruth M. Williams and William Yule.

272pp     0 335 09890 8 (Paperback)     0 335 09891 6 (Hardback)

## CHILDREN, TEENAGERS AND HEALTH: THE KEY DATA

**Caroline Woodroffe, Myer Glickman, Maggie Barker and Chris Power**

An invaluable source of information for anyone concerned with policies on child health.

Dr Sheila Adam, Director of Public Health,
North West Thames Regional Health Authority

What are the current patterns of health and illness among children and teenagers? What changes have taken place in recent years? What factors influence health? What are the health differences between parts of the UK, between sexes, ethnic groups, and social classes? This book uses a wide range of statistics from official and academic sources to answer these questions. Clear graphical presentation allows trends and comparisons to be seen at a glance.

This book is an essential reference for anyone concerned with child health, whether in the health and social services or the many areas of public policy which have an impact on health. The presentation makes the data easily accessible to non-specialists, enabling wider informed public debate on how best to improve the health of children and teenagers in the UK.

### Contents
*Introduction – Population and family – Mortality and morbidity – Socioeconomic environment – Physical environment – Cultural environment – Endpiece – Note on official data sources – Glossary – Index.*

208pp     0 335 19125 8 (Paperback)

# CHILD HEALTH MATTERS
## CARING FOR CHILDREN IN THE COMMUNITY

**Sally Wyke and Jenny Hewison (eds)**

The 1990s will be a time of considerable change in the organization and delivery of child health care services. On-going reforms of the National Health Service and the welfare state coupled with significant ethnic and social changes in British society mean that health care professionals are being forced to rapidly adjust their working practices. Such change cannot be achieved without information about the needs, characteristics and perceptions of service users or without up-to-date information about new developments and problems in community health care.

This book provides some of this information and presents it in a form accessible to those people in the front line of organizing and delivering child health care. It will therefore be an invaluable resource for health service managers, general practitioners, community paediatricians, community nurses and health visitors and will also be of interest to students of sociology and community medicine.

### Contents

*Introduction – Section 1: Resources for care – Women, child care and money – Section 2: Perspectives on health – Dealing with children's illness: mothers' dilemmas – Understanding the mother's viewpoint: the case of Pathan women in Britain – Ideologies of child care: mothers and health visitors – Section 3: Using health services – Children with cough: who consults the doctor? – Whether or not to consult a general practitioner: decision making by parents in a multi-ethnic inner-city area – 'Appropriate' use of child health services in East London: ethnic similarities and differences – Section 4: Available knowledge – The promotion of breastfeeding – Childhood asthma: stategies for primary and community health – Child sexual abuse and the trials of motherhood – Children with HIV infection: their care in the community – Index.*

### Contributors

Andy Clarke, Sarah Cunningham-Burley, Caroline Currer, Robert Drewett, Heather Fletcher, Jenny Hewison, Jenny Kitzinger, Una Maclean, Berry Mayall, Jacqueline Mok, Jennie Popay, Ian Russell, Elizabeth Watson, Sally Wyke.

176pp     0 335 09393 0 (Paperback)     0 335 09394 9 (Hardback)